Practical Site Reliability Engineering

Automate the process of designing, developing, and delivering highly reliable apps and services with SRE

Pethuru Raj Chelliah
Shreyash Naithani
Shailender Singh

BIRMINGHAM - MUMBAI

Practical Site Reliability Engineering

Copyright © 2018 Packt Publishing

All rights reserved. No part of this book may be reproduced, stored in a retrieval system, or transmitted in any form or by any means, without the prior written permission of the publisher, except in the case of brief quotations embedded in critical articles or reviews.

Every effort has been made in the preparation of this book to ensure the accuracy of the information presented. However, the information contained in this book is sold without warranty, either express or implied. Neither the authors, nor Packt Publishing or its dealers and distributors, will be held liable for any damages caused or alleged to have been caused directly or indirectly by this book.

Packt Publishing has endeavored to provide trademark information about all of the companies and products mentioned in this book by the appropriate use of capitals. However, Packt Publishing cannot guarantee the accuracy of this information.

Commissioning Editor: Gebin George
Acquisition Editor: Rohit Rajkumar
Content Development Editor: Priyanka Deshpande
Technical Editor: Rutuja Patade
Copy Editor: Safis Editing
Project Coordinator: Drashti Panchal
Proofreader: Safis Editing
Indexer: Mariammal Chettiyar
Graphics: Tom Scaria
Production Coordinator: Aparna Bhagat

First published: November 2018

Production reference: 1301118

Published by Packt Publishing Ltd.
Livery Place
35 Livery Street
Birmingham
B3 2PB, UK.

ISBN 978-1-78883-956-3

www.packtpub.com

I dedicate this book to my mother (Anna Mariyal)

– Pethuru Raj Chelliah

I would like to dedicate this book to my parents and brother.

– Shreyash Naithani

I dedicate this book to my parents!

– Shailender Singh

mapt.io

Mapt is an online digital library that gives you full access to over 5,000 books and videos, as well as industry leading tools to help you plan your personal development and advance your career. For more information, please visit our website.

Why subscribe?

- Spend less time learning and more time coding with practical eBooks and Videos from over 4,000 industry professionals

- Improve your learning with Skill Plans built especially for you

- Get a free eBook or video every month

- Mapt is fully searchable

- Copy and paste, print, and bookmark content

Packt.com

Did you know that Packt offers eBook versions of every book published, with PDF and ePub files available? You can upgrade to the eBook version at www.packt.com and as a print book customer, you are entitled to a discount on the eBook copy. Get in touch with us at customercare@packtpub.com for more details.

At www.packt.com, you can also read a collection of free technical articles, sign up for a range of free newsletters, and receive exclusive discounts and offers on Packt books and eBooks.

Contributors

About the authors

Pethuru Raj Chelliah (PhD) works as the chief architect at the Site Reliability Engineering Center of Excellence, Reliance Jio Infocomm Ltd. (RJIL), Bangalore. Previously, he worked as a cloud infrastructure architect at the IBM Global Cloud Center of Excellence, IBM India, Bangalore, for four years. He also had an extended stint as a TOGAF-certified enterprise architecture consultant in Wipro Consulting services division and as a lead architect in the corporate research division of Robert Bosch, Bangalore. He has more than 17 years of IT industry experience.

> *I sincerely acknowledge and appreciate the moral support provided by my managers, Mr. Anish Shah and Mr. Kiran Thomas, at Reliance Jio Infocomm. Ltd., and my esteemed colleagues, Mr. Senthil Arunachalam and Mrs. Vidya Hungud. I also recognize the enhanced tolerance level of my wife (Sweelin Reena) and my sons (Darren Samuel and Darresh Bernie). Above all, I give all the glory and honor to my Lord and Savior Jesus Christ for all the strength and knowledge granted to me.*

Shreyash Naithani is currently a site reliability engineer at Microsoft R&D. Prior to Microsoft, he worked with both start-ups and mid-level companies. He completed his PG Diploma from the Centre for Development of Advanced Computing, Bengaluru, India, and is a computer science graduate from Punjab Technical University, India. In a short span of time, he has had the opportunity to work as a DevOps engineer with Python/C#, and as a tools developer, site/service reliability engineer, and Unix system administrator. During his leisure time, he loves to travel and binge watch series.

> *I'd like to thank my parents, my brother, and my friends (Nipun Pathak and Sunil Baurai) for their help and support while the book was being written. A big thank you in particular to Meenakshi Gaur, for her tremendous help and support. This one's for you.*

Shailender Singh is a principal site reliability engineer and a solution architect with around 11 year's IT experience who holds two master's degrees in IT and computer application. He has worked as a C developer on the Linux platform. He had exposure to almost all infrastructure technologies from hybrid to cloud-hosted environments. In the past, he has worked with companies including Mckinsey, HP, HCL, Revionics and Avalara and these days he tends to use AWS, K8s, Terraform, Packer, Jenkins, Ansible, and OpenShift.

> *Writing a book is harder than I thought and more rewarding than I could have ever imagined. None of this would have been possible without my wife, Komal Rathore. She motivated and supported me to spend some time to write this book and asked me to share my experience with the IT industry.*

About the reviewers

Pankaj Thakur has a master's degree in computer applications from Dr. A.P.J. Abdul Kalam Technical University, formerly known as Uttar Pradesh Technical University (UPTU), one of the most reputable universities in India. With over 13 years experience and expertise in the field of IT, he has worked with numerous clients across the globe. Pankaj has a keen interest in cloud technologies, AI, machine learning, and automation. He has successfully completed several cloud migrations converting monolithic applications to microservice architectures. With his knowledge and experience, he believes readers are going to gain a lot from this book and that it will enhance their SRE skills.

Ashish Kumar has an engineering degree in IT from Himachal Pradesh University, Shimla. He has been working in the field of DevOps consultation, containerized-based applications, development, monitoring, performance engineering, and SRE practices. He has been a core team member of DevOps implementation and SRE practice implementation. He is passionate about identifying toil work and automating it using software practices. During his free time, he loves to go trekking, play outdoor games, and meditate.

Packt is searching for authors like you

If you're interested in becoming an author for Packt, please visit `aomuthors.packtpub.c`and apply today. We have worked with thousands of developers and tech professionals, just like you, to help them share their insight with the global tech community. You can make a general application, apply for a specific hot topic that we are recruiting an author for, or submit your own idea.

Table of Contents

Preface — 1

Chapter 1: Demystifying the Site Reliability Engineering Paradigm — 7
- Setting the context for practical SRE — 8
  - Characterizing the next-generation software systems — 8
  - Characterizing the next-generation hardware systems — 9
  - Moving toward hybrid IT and distributed computing — 9
  - Envisioning the digital era — 10
  - The cloud service paradigm — 12
    - The ubiquity of cloud platforms and infrastructures — 13
  - The growing software penetration and participation — 14
- Plunging into the SRE discipline — 16
  - The challenges ahead — 17
- The need for highly reliable platforms and infrastructures — 18
  - The need for reliable software — 19
    - The emergence of microservices architecture — 19
    - Docker enabled containerization — 21
    - Containerized microservices — 22
    - Kubernetes for container orchestration — 24
    - Resilient microservices and reliable applications — 28
- Reactive systems — 29
  - Reactive systems are highly reliable — 32
  - The elasticity of reactive systems — 32
- Highly reliable IT infrastructures — 33
  - The emergence of serverless computing — 35
- The vitality of the SRE domain — 36
  - The importance of SREs — 37
  - Toolsets that SREs typically use — 40
- Summary — 41

Chapter 2: Microservices Architecture and Containers — 43
- What are microservices? — 43
- Microservice design principles — 44
- Deploying microservices — 46
  - Container platform-based deployment tools — 46
  - Code as function deployment — 47
    - Programming language selection criteria in AWS Lambda — 48
  - Virtualization-based platform deployment — 48
- Practical examples of microservice deployment — 49
  - A container platform deployment example with Kubernetes — 49
  - Code as function deployment — 53

Example 1 – the Apex deployment tool	53
Example 2 – the Apex deployment tool	54
Example 3 – the Serverless deployment tool	55
Virtual platform-based deployment using Jenkins or TeamCity	57

Microservices using Spring Boot and the RESTful framework — 57
Jersey Framework — 59
Representational State Transfer (REST) — 60

Deploying the Spring Boot application	68
Monitoring the microservices	69
Application metrics	70
Platform metrics	73
System events	73
Tools to monitor microservices	73

Important facts about microservices — 75

Microservices in the current market	75
When to stop designing microservices	75
Can the microservice format be used to divide teams into small or micro teams?	76
Microservices versus SOA	76

Summary — 76

Chapter 3: Microservice Resiliency Patterns — 77
Briefing microservices and containers — 78

The containerization paradigm	79

IT reliability challenges and solution approaches — 81
The promising and potential approaches for resiliency and reliability — 85

MSA is the prominent way forward	85
Integrated platforms are the need of the hour for resiliency	88

Summary — 113

Chapter 4: DevOps as a Service — 115
What is DaaS? — 115

Selecting tools isn't easy	116
Types of services under DaaS	119
An example of one-click deployment and rollback	121
Configuring automated alerts	123
Centralized log management	124
Infrastructure security	125
Continuous process and infrastructure development	126
CI and CD	127
CI life cycle	129
CI tools	129
Installing Jenkins	130
Jenkins setup for GitHub	132
Setting up the Jenkins job	134
Installing Git	136
Starting the Jenkins job	137

CD	137
Collaboration with development and QA teams	138
The role of developers in DevOps	139
The role of QA teams in DevOps	139
QA practices	140
Summary	140
Chapter 5: Container Cluster and Orchestration Platforms	**143**
Resilient microservices	143
Application and volume containers	144
Clustering and managing containers	147
What are clusters?	149
Container orchestration and management	154
What is container orchestration?	155
Summary	165
Chapter 6: Architectural and Design Patterns	**167**
Architecture pattern	167
Design pattern	169
Design pattern for security	175
Design pattern for resiliency	176
Design pattern for scalability	177
Design pattern for performance	178
Design principles for availability	179
Design principles for reliability	180
Design patterns – circuit breaker	181
Advantages of circuit breakers	181
Closed state	183
Open state	184
Half-open state	184
Summary	186
Chapter 7: Reliability Implementation Techniques	**187**
Ballerina programming	188
A hello program example	189
A simple example with Twitter integration	190
Kubernetes deployment code	192
A circuit breaker code example	194
Ballerina data types	196
Control logic expression	197
The building blocks of Ballerina	199
Ballerina command cheat sheet	201
Reliability	202
Rust programming	202
Installing Rust	203
Concept of Rust programming	204
The ownership of variables in Rust	205

        Borrowing values in Rust   205
        Memory management in Rust   206
        Mutability in Rust   206
        Concurrency in Rust   207
        Error-handling in Rust   207
    The future of Rust programming   208
Summary   208

Chapter 8: Realizing Reliable Systems - the Best Practices   209
  Reliable IT systems – the emerging traits and tips   211
  MSA for reliable software   211
    The accelerated adoption of containers and orchestration platforms   212
        The emergence of containerized clouds   212
  Service mesh solutions   213
  Microservices design – best practices   213
    The relevance of event-driven microservices   214
    Why asynchronous communication?   214
    Why event-driven microservices?   216
  Asynchronous messaging patterns for event-driven microservices   218
  The role of EDA to produce reactive applications   223
    Command query responsibility segregation pattern   223
  Reliable IT infrastructures   227
    High availability   227
    Auto-scaling   230
  Infrastructure as code   231
  Summary   238

Chapter 9: Service Resiliency   239
  Delineating the containerization paradigm   239
    Why use containerization?   240
  Demystifying microservices architecture   242
  Decoding the growing role of Kubernetes for the container era   244
  Describing the service mesh concept   246
    Data plane versus control plane summary   252
  Why is service mesh paramount?   253
  Service mesh architectures   254
    Monitoring the service mesh   255
    Service mesh deployment models   257
  Summary   263

Chapter 10: Containers, Kubernetes, and Istio Monitoring   265
  Prometheus   266
    Prometheus architecture   267
    Setting up Prometheus   268
    Configuring alerts in Prometheus   271
  Grafana   273

Setting up Grafana	274
Configuring alerts in Grafana	278
Summary	283

Chapter 11: Post-Production Activities for Ensuring and Enhancing IT Reliability — 285
Modern IT infrastructure	286
Elaborating the modern data analytics methods	288
Monitoring clouds, clusters, and containers	290
The emergence of Kubernetes	290
Cloud infrastructure and application monitoring	293
The monitoring tool capabilities	295
The benefits	297
Prognostic, predictive, and prescriptive analytics	299
Machine-learning algorithms for infrastructure automation	301
Log analytics	302
Open source log analytics platforms	303
Cloud-based log analytics platforms	305
AI-enabled log analytics platforms	307
Loom	308
Enterprise-class log analytics platforms	309
The key capabilities of log analytics platforms	309
Centralized log-management tools	310
IT operational analytics	311
IT performance and scalability analytics	312
IT security analytics	314
The importance of root-cause analysis	314
OverOps enhances log-management	315
Summary	317
Further Readings	317

Chapter 12: Service Meshes and Container Orchestration Platforms — 319
About the digital transformation	320
Cloud-native and enabled applications for the digital era	321
Service mesh solutions	322
Linkerd	324
Istio	325
Visualizing an Istio service mesh	330
Microservice API Gateway	331
The benefits of an API Gateway for microservices-centric applications	333
Security features of API Gateways	335
API Gateway and service mesh in action	336
API management suite	337
Ensuring the reliability of containerized cloud environments	338
The journey toward containerized cloud environments	340

The growing solidity of the Kubernetes platform for containerized clouds — 341
Kubernetes architecture – how it works — 342
Installing the Kubernetes platform — 347
Installing the Kubernetes client — 351
Installing Istio on Kubernetes — 354
Trying the application — 358
Deploying services to Kubernetes — 358
Summary — 360

Other Books You May Enjoy — 361

Index — 365

Preface

Increasingly, enterprise-scale applications are being hosted and managed in software-defined cloud environments. As cloud technologies and tools are quickly maturing and stabilizing, cloud adoption as the one-stop IT solution for producing and running all kinds of business workloads is rapidly growing across the globe. However, there are a few crucial challenges in successfully running cloud centers (public, private, hybrid, and edge). The aspects of automation and orchestration are being lauded as the way forward to surmount the challenges that are brewing in operating clouds and for realizing the originally envisioned benefits of the cloud idea. The widely expressed concern associated with the cloud is reliability (resiliency and elasticity). The other noteworthy trend is the emergence of web-scale and mobile-enabled operational, transactional, and analytical applications. It is therefore essential to ensure the stability, fault tolerance, and high availability of data and process-intensive applications as far as possible. The reliability concern is being overwhelmingly tackled through the smart leveraging of pioneering technologies.

This book is articulating and accentuating how a suite of breakthrough technologies and tools blend well to ensure the highest degree of reliability, not only for professional and personal applications, but also for cloud infrastructures. Let's envisage and embrace reliable systems.

Who this book is for

Practical Site Reliability Engineering helps software developers, IT professionals, DevOps engineers, performance specialists, and system engineers understand how the emerging domain of **Site Reliability Engineering** (**SRE**) comes in handy in automating and accelerating the process of designing, developing, debugging, and deploying highly reliable applications and services.

What this book covers

Chapter 1, *Demystifying the Site Reliability Engineering Paradigm*, includes the new SRE domain and the need for SRE patterns, platforms, practices, programming models and processes, enabling frameworks, appropriate technologies, techniques, tools, and tips.

Chapter 2, *Microservices Architecture and Containers*, introduces concepts such as containerization, **microservice architecture** (**MSA**), and container management and clustering, which contribute to the realization of reliable applications and environments.

Preface

Chapter 3, *Microservice Resiliency Patterns*, covers DevOps under SRE since automation and DevOps play a big role in the SRE journey.

Chapter 4, *DevOps as a Service*, focuses on various microservice resiliency patterns that intrinsically and insightfully enable the design, development, debugging, delivery, and deployment of reliable systems.

Chapter 5, *Container Cluster and Orchestration Platforms*, provides a detailed explanation of the preceding technologies for ensuring the goals of SRE.

Chapter 6, *Architectural and Design Patterns*, explains how architecture and design are the ultimate building blocks during service or microservice development, giving you clarity and direction to implement any logic in the cloud era.

Chapter 7, *Reliability Implementation Techniques*, gives a guarantee that the future is bright and makes us optimistic that things are going to change in the cloud era.

Chapter 8, *Realizing Reliable Systems – the Best Practices*, includes the best practices arising from the expertise, experience, and education of site reliability engineers, DevOps people, and cloud engineers.

Chapter 9, *Service Resiliency*, explains all about the platforms for container enablement and orchestration purposes.

Chapter 10, *Containers, Kubernetes, and Istio Monitoring*, covers how we can monitor applications or services running on clusters, pods, and Kubernetes using Prometheus and Grafana.

Chapter 11, *Post-Production Activities for Ensuring and Enhancing IT Reliability*, look at the various activities to be performed in order to prevent any kind of disaster, so as to fully guarantee the SLAs agreed with customers, clients, and consumers.

Chapter 12, *Service Meshes and Container Orchestration Platforms*, conveys what and why the multi-cloud approach is gaining unprecedented market and mind shares.

To get the most out of this book

Readers have to have a basic knowledge of cloud infrastructure, Docker containers, MSA, and DevOps.

Download the example code files

You can download the example code files for this book from your account at `www.packt.com`. If you purchased this book elsewhere, you can visit `www.packt.com/support` and register to have the files emailed directly to you.

You can download the code files by following these steps:

1. Log in or register at `www.packt.com`.
2. Select the **SUPPORT** tab.
3. Click on **Code Downloads & Errata**.
4. Enter the name of the book in the **Search** box and follow the onscreen instructions.

Once the file is downloaded, please make sure that you unzip or extract the folder using the latest version of:

- WinRAR/7-Zip for Windows
- Zipeg/iZip/UnRarX for Mac
- 7-Zip/PeaZip for Linux

The code bundle for the book is also hosted on GitHub at `https://github.com/PacktPublishing/Practical-Site-Reliability-Engineering`. In case there's an update to the code, it will be updated on the existing GitHub repository.

We also have other code bundles from our rich catalog of books and videos available at `https://github.com/PacktPublishing/`. Check them out!

Download the color images

We also provide a PDF file that has color images of the screenshots/diagrams used in this book. You can download it here: `https://www.packtpub.com/sites/default/files/downloads/9781788839563_ColorImages.pdf`.

Conventions used

There are a number of text conventions used throughout this book.

`CodeInText`: Indicates code words in text, database table names, folder names, filenames, file extensions, pathnames, dummy URLs, user input, and Twitter handles. Here is an example: "Create a file using `vim` and run the `hello.bal` command:"

A block of code is set as follows:

```
fn main()
{
panic!("Something is wrong... Check for Errors");
}
```

When we wish to draw your attention to a particular part of a code block, the relevant lines or items are set in bold:

```
import ballerina/config;
import ballerina/io;
import wso2/twitter;
endpoint http:Listener listener {
port:9090
}
```

Any command-line input or output is written as follows:

```
$ apex deploy auth
$ apex deploy auth api
```

Bold: Indicates a new term, an important word, or words that you see on screen. For example, words in menus or dialog boxes appear in the text like this. Here is an example: "We can click on **Istio Mesh Dashboard** to see the global request volume and look at our success and failure rate."

Warnings or important notes appear like this.

Tips and tricks appear like this.

Get in touch

Feedback from our readers is always welcome.

General feedback: If you have questions about any aspect of this book, mention the book title in the subject of your message and email us at `customercare@packtpub.com`.

Errata: Although we have taken every care to ensure the accuracy of our content, mistakes do happen. If you have found a mistake in this book, we would be grateful if you would report this to us. Please visit `www.packt.com/submit-errata`, selecting your book, clicking on the Errata Submission Form link, and entering the details.

Piracy: If you come across any illegal copies of our works in any form on the internet, we would be grateful if you would provide us with the location address or website name. Please contact us at `copyright@packt.com` with a link to the material.

If you are interested in becoming an author: If there is a topic that you have expertise in, and you are interested in either writing or contributing to a book, please visit `authors.packtpub.com`.

Reviews

Please leave a review. Once you have read and used this book, why not leave a review on the site that you purchased it from? Potential readers can then see and use your unbiased opinion to make purchase decisions, we at Packt can understand what you think about our products, and our authors can see your feedback on their book. Thank you!

For more information about Packt, please visit `packt.com`.

Demystifying the Site Reliability Engineering Paradigm

To provide competitive and cognitive services to their venerable customers and clients, businesses across the globe are strategizing to leverage the distinct capabilities of IT systems. There is a widespread recognition that IT is the most crucial contributor and important ingredient for achieving the required business automation, augmentation, and acceleration. The unique advancements being harvested in the IT space directly enable the much-anticipated business productivity, agility, affordability, and adaptivity. In other words, businesses across the globe unwaveringly expect their business offerings, outputs, and operations to be robust, reliable, and versatile. This demand has a direct and decisive impact on IT, and hence IT professionals are striving hard and stretching further to put highly responsive, resilient, scalable, available, and secure systems in place to meet the varying needs and mandates of businesses. Thus, with the informed adoption of all kinds of noteworthy advancements being unearthed in the IT space, business houses and behemoths are to lustrously fulfil the elusive goal of customer satisfaction.

Recently, there has been a widespread insistence for IT reliability that, in turn, enables business dependability. There are refined processes, integrated platforms, enabling patterns, breakthrough products, best practices, optimized infrastructures, adaptive features, and architectures toward heightened IT reliability.

This chapter will explain the following topics:

- The origin
- The journey so far
- The fresh opportunities and possibilities
- The prospects and perspectives
- The impending challenges and concerns
- The future

Precisely speaking, the charter for any **Site Reliability Engineering** (**SRE**) team in any growing IT organization is how to create highly reliable applications, and the other is how to plan, provision, and put up highly dependable, scalable, available, performing, and secure infrastructures to host and run those applications.

Setting the context for practical SRE

It is appropriate to give some background information for this new engineering discipline to enhance readability. SRE is a quickly emerging and evolving field of study and research. The market and mind shares of the SRE field are consistently climbing. Businesses, having decisively understood the strategic significance of SRE, are keen to formulate and firm up a workable strategy.

Characterizing the next-generation software systems

Software applications are increasingly complicated yet sophisticated. Highly integrated systems are the new norm these days. Enterprise-grade applications ought to be seamlessly integrated with several third-party software components running in distributed and disparate systems. Increasingly, software applications are made out of a number of interactive, transformative, and disruptive services in an ad hoc manner on an as-needed basis. Multi-channel, multimedia, multi-modal, multi-device, and multi-tenant applications are becoming pervasive and persuasive. There are also enterprise, cloud, mobile, **Internet of Things** (**IoT**), blockchain, cognitive, and embedded applications hosted in virtual and containerized environments. Then, there are industry-specific and vertical applications (energy, retail, government, telecommunication, supply chain, utility, healthcare, banking, and insurance, automobiles, avionics, and robotics) being designed and delivered via cloud infrastructures.

There are software packages, homegrown software, turnkey solutions, scientific, and technical computing services, and customizable and configurable software applications to meet distinct business requirements. In short, there are operational, transactional, and analytical applications running on private, public, and hybrid clouds. With the exponential growth of connected devices, smart sensors, and actuators, fog gateways, smartphones, microcontrollers, and **single board computers** (**SBCs**), the software enabled data analytics and proximate moves to edge devices to accomplish real-time data capture, processing, decision-making, and action.

We are destined to move towards real-time analytics and applications. Thus, it is clear that software is purposefully penetrative, participative, and productive. Largely, it is quite a software-intensive world.

Characterizing the next-generation hardware systems

Similar to the quickly growing software engineering field, hardware engineering is also on the fast track. These days, there are clusters, grids, and clouds of IT infrastructures. There are powerful appliances, cloud-in-a-box options, hyper-converged infrastructures, and commodity servers for hosting IT platforms and business applications. The physical machines are touted as bare metal servers. The virtual versions of the physical machines are the virtual machines and containers. We are heading toward the era of hardware infrastructure programming. That is, closed, inflexible, and difficult to manage and maintain bare-metal servers are being partitioned into a number of virtual machines and containers that are highly flexible, open, easily manageable, and replaceable, not to mention quickly provisionable, independently deployable, and horizontally scalable. The infrastructure partitioning and provisioning gets sped up with scores of automated tools to enable the rapid delivery of software applications. The rewarding aspects of continuous integration, deployment, and delivery are being facilitated through a combination of containers, microservices, configuration management solutions, DevOps tools, and **Continuous Integration** (CI) platforms.

Moving toward hybrid IT and distributed computing

Worldwide institutions, individuals, and innovators are keenly embracing cloud technology with all its clarity and confidence. With the faster maturity and stability of cloud environments, there is a distinct growth in building and delivering cloud-native applications, and there are viable articulations and approaches to readily make cloud native software. Traditional and legacy software applications are being meticulously modernized and moved to cloud environments to reap the originally envisaged benefits of the cloud idea. Cloud software engineering is one hot area, drawing the attention of many software engineers across the globe. There are public, private, and hybrid clouds. Recently, we have heard more about edge/fog clouds. Still, there are traditional IT environments that are being considered in the hybrid world.

There are development teams all over the world working in multiple time zones. Due to the diversity and multiplicity of IT systems and business applications, distributed applications are being touted as the way forward. That is, the various components of any software application are being distributed across multiple locations for enabling redundancy enabled high availability. Fault-tolerance, less latency, independent software development, and no vendor lock-in are being given as the reason for the realm of distributed applications. Accordingly, software programming models are being adroitly tweaked so that they deliver optimal performance in the era of distributed and decentralized applications. Multiple development teams working in multiple time zones across the globe have become the new norm in this hybrid world of on-shore and off-shore development.

With the big-data era upon us, we need the most usable and uniquely distributed computing paradigm through the dynamic pool of commoditized servers and inexpensive computers. With the exponential growth of connected devices, the days of device clouds are not too far away. That is, distributed and decentralized devices are bound to be clubbed together in large numbers to form ad hoc and application-specific cloud environments for data capture, ingestion, pre-processing, and analytics. Thus, there is no doubt that the future belongs to distributed computing. The fully matured and stabilized centralized computing is unsustainable due to the need for web-scale applications. Also, the next-generation internet is the internet of digitized things, connected devices, and microservices.

Envisioning the digital era

There are a bunch of digitization and edge technologies bringing forth a number of business innovations and improvisations. As enterprises are embracing these technologies, the ensuring era is being touted as the digital transformation and intelligence era. This section helps in telling you about all that needs to be changed through the absorption of these pioneering and path-breaking technologies and tools.

The field of **information and communication technology** (**ICT**) is rapidly growing with the arrival of scores of pioneering technologies, and this trend is expediently and elegantly automating multiple business tasks. Then, the maturity and stability of orchestration technologies and tools is bound to club together multiple automated jobs and automate the aggregated ones. We will now discuss the latest trends and transitions happening in the ICT space.

Due to the heterogeneity and multiplicity of software technologies such as programming languages, development models, data formats, and protocols, software development and operational complexities are growing continuously. There are several breakthrough mechanisms to develop and run enterprise-grade software in an agile and adroit fashion. There came a number of complexity mitigation and rapid development techniques for producing production-grade software in a swift and smart manner. The leverage of "divide and conquer" and "the separation of crosscutting concerns" techniques is being consistently experimented with and developers are being encouraged to develop risk-free and futuristic software services. The potential concepts of abstraction, encapsulation, virtualization, and other compartmentalization methods are being invoked to reduce the software production pain. In addition, there are performance engineering and enhancement aspects that are getting the utmost consideration from software architects. Thus, software development processes, best practices, design patterns, evaluation metrics, key guidelines, integrated platforms, enabling frameworks, simplifying templates, and programming models are gaining immense significance in this software-defined world.

Thus, there are several breakthrough technologies for digital innovations, disruptions, and transformations. Primarily, the IoT paradigm generates a lot of multi-structured digital data and the famous **artificial intelligence** (**AI**) technologies, such as machine and deep learning, enables the extrication of actionable insights out of the digital data. Transitioning raw digital data into information, knowledge, and wisdom is the key differentiator for implementing digitally transformed and intelligent societies. Cloud IT is being positioned as the best-in-class IT environment for enabling and expediting the digital transformation.

With digitization and edge technologies, our everyday items become digitized to join in with mainstream computing. That is, we will be encountering trillions of digitized entities and elements in the years ahead. With the faster stability and maturity of the IoT, **cyber physical systems** (**CPS**), **ambient intelligence** (**AmI**), and pervasive computing technologies and tools, we are being bombarded with innumerable connected devices, instruments, machines, drones, robots, utilities, consumer electronics, wares, equipment, and appliances. Now, with the unprecedented interest and investment in AI (machine and deep learning, computer vision, and natural language processing), algorithms and approaches, and IoT device data (collaborations, coordination, correlation, and corroboration) are meticulously captured, cleansed, and crunched to extricate actionable insights/digital intelligence in time. There are several promising, potential, and proven digital technologies emerging and evolving quickly in synchronization, with a variety of data mining, processing, and analytics. These innovations and disruptions eventually lead to digital transformation. Thus, digitization and edge technologies in association with digital intelligence algorithms and tools lead to the realization and sustenance of digitally transformed environments (smarter hotels, homes, hospitals, and so on). We can easily anticipate and articulate digitally transformed countries, counties, and cities in the years to come with pioneering and groundbreaking digital technologies and tools.

The cloud service paradigm

The cloud era is setting in and settling steadily. The aiding processes, platforms, policies, procedures, practices, and patterns are being framed and firmed up by IT professionals and professors, to tend toward the cloud. The following sections give the necessary details for our esteemed readers.

The cloud applications, platforms, and infrastructures are gaining immense popularity these days. Cloud applications are of two primary types:

1. **Cloud-enabled**: The currently running massive and monolithic applications get modernized and migrated to cloud environments to reap the distinct benefits of the cloud paradigm
2. **Cloud-native**: This is all about designing, developing, debugging, delivering, and deploying applications directly on cloud environments by intrinsically leveraging the non-functional capabilities of cloud environments

The current and conventional applications that are hosted and running on various IT environments are being meticulously modernized and migrated to standardized and multifaceted cloud environments to reap all the originally expressed benefits of cloud paradigm. Besides enabling business-critical, legacy, and monolithic applications to be cloud-ready, there are endeavors for designing, developing, debugging, deploying, and delivering enterprise-class applications in cloud environments, harvesting all of the unique characteristics of cloud infrastructure and platforms. These applications natively absorb the various characteristics of cloud infrastructures and act adaptively. There is **microservices architecture** (**MSA**) for designing next-generation enterprise-class applications. MSA is being deftly leveraged to enable massive applications to be partitioned into a collection of decoupled, easily manageable, and fine-grained microservices.

With the decisive adoption of cloud technologies and tools, every component of enterprise IT is being readied to be delivered as a service. The cloud idea has really and rewardingly brought in a stream of innovations, disruptions, and transformations for the IT industry. The days of **IT as a Service** (**ITaaS**) will soon become a reality, due to a stream of noteworthy advancements and accomplishments in the cloud space.

Chapter 1

The ubiquity of cloud platforms and infrastructures

The other key aspect is to have reliable, available, scalable, and secure IT environments (cloud and non-cloud). We talked about producing versatile software packages and libraries. We also talked about setting up and sustaining appropriate IT infrastructures for successfully running various kinds of IT and business applications. Increasingly, the traditional data centers and server farms are being modernized through the smart application of cloud-enablement technologies and tools. The cloud idea establishes and enforces IT rationalization, the heightened utilization of IT resources, and optimization. There is a growing number of massive public cloud environments (AWS, Microsoft Azure, Google cloud, IBM cloud, and Oracle cloud) that are encompassing thousands of commodity and high-end server machines, storage appliance arrays, and networking components to accommodate and accomplish the varying IT needs of the whole world. Government organizations, business behemoths, various service providers, and institutions are empowering their own IT centers into private cloud environments. Then, on an as-needed basis, private clouds are beginning to match the various capabilities of public clouds to meet specific requirements. In short, cloud environments are being positioned as the one-stop IT solution for our professional, social, and personal IT requirements.

The cloud is becoming pervasive with the unique contributions of many players from the IT industry, worldwide academic institutions, and research labs. We have plenty of private, public, and hybrid cloud environments. The surging popularity of fog/edge computing leads to the formation of fog/edge device clouds, which are contributing immensely to produce people-centric and real-time applications. The fog or edge device computing is all about leveraging scores of connected and capable devices to form a kind of purpose-specific as well as agnostic device cloud to collect, cleanse and crunch sensor, actuator, device, machine, instrument, and equipment poly-structured and real-time data emanating from all sorts of physical, mechanical, and electrical systems on the ground. With the projected billions of connected devices, the future beckons and bats for device clusters and clouds. Definitely, the cloud movement has penetrated every industry and the IT phenomenon is redefined and resuscitated by the roaring success of the cloud. Soon, cloud applications, platforms, and infrastructures will be everywhere. IT is all set to become the fifth social utility. The pertinent and paramount challenge is how to bring forth deeper and decisive automation in the cloud IT space.

The need for deeply automated and adaptive cloud centers with clouds emerging as the most flexible, futuristic, and fabulous IT environments to host and run IT and business workloads, there is a rush for bringing as much automation as possible to speed up the process of cloud migration, software deployment and delivery, cloud monitoring, measurement and management, cloud integration and orchestration, cloud governance and security, and so on. There are several trends and transitions happening simultaneously in the IT space to realize these goals.

The growing software penetration and participation

Marc Andreessen famously penned the article *Why software is eating the world* several years ago. Today, we widely hear, read, and even sometimes experience buzzwords such as software-defined, compute, storage, and networking. Software is everywhere and gets embedded in everything. Software has, unquestionably, been the principal business automation and acceleration enabler. Nowadays, on its memorable and mesmerizing journey, software is penetrating into every tangible thing (physical, mechanical, and electrical) in our everyday environments to transform them into connected entities, digitized things, smart objects, and sentient materials. For example, every advanced car today has been sagaciously stuffed with millions of lines of code to be elegantly adaptive in its operations, outputs, and offerings.

Precisely speaking, the ensuing era sets the stage for having knowledge-filled, situation-aware, event-driven, service-oriented, cloud-hosted, process-optimized, and people-centric applications. These applications need to exhibit a few extra capabilities. That is, the next-generation software systems innately have to be reliable, rewarding, and reactive ones. Also, we need to arrive at competent processes, platforms, patterns, procedures, and practices for creating and sustaining high-quality systems. There are widely available **non-functional requirements (NFRs)**, **quality of service (QoS)**, and **quality of experience (QoE)** attributes, such as availability, scalability, modifiability, sustainability, security, portability, and simplicity. The challenge for every IT professional lies in producing software that unambiguously and intrinsically guarantees all the NFRs.

Agile application design: We have come across a number of agile software development methodologies. We read about extreme and pair programming, scrum, and so on. However, for the agile design of enterprise-grade applications, the stability of MSA is to activate and accelerate the application design.

Accelerated software programming: As we all know, enterprise-scale and customer-facing software applications are being developed speedily nowadays, with the faster maturity of potential agile programming methods, processes, platforms, and frameworks. There are other initiatives and inventions enabling speedier software development. There are component-based software assemblies, and service-oriented software engineering is steadily growing. There are scores of state-of-the-art tools consistently assisting component and service-based application-building phenomena. On the other hand, the software engineering aspect gets simplified and streamlined through the configuration, customization, and composition-centric application generation methods.

Automated software deployment through DevOps: There are multiple reasons for software programs to be running well in the developer's machine but not so well in other environments, including production environments. There are different editions, versions, and releases of software packages, platforms, programming languages, and frameworks. Coming to the running software is suites across different environments. There is a big disconnect between developers and operation teams due to constant friction between development and operating environments.

Further on, with agile programming techniques and tips, software applications get constructed quickly, but their integration, testing, building, delivery, and deployment aspects are not automated. Therefore, concepts such as DevOps, NoOps, and AIOps have gained immense prominence and dominance to bring in several automation enabling IT administrators. That is, these new arrivals have facilitated a seamless and spontaneous synchronization between software design, development, debugging, deployment, delivery and decommissioning processes, and people. The emergence of configuration management tools and cloud orchestration platforms enables IT infrastructure programming. That is, the term **Infrastructure as Code (IaC)** is facilitating the DevOps concept. That is, faster provisioning of infrastructure resources through configuration files, and the deployment of software on those infrastructure modules, is the core and central aspect of the flourishing concept of DevOps.

This is the prime reason why the concept of DevOps has started flourishing these days. This is quite a new idea that's gaining a lot of momentum within enterprise and cloud IT teams. Companies embrace this new cultural change with the leverage of multiple toolsets for **Continuous Integration (CI)**, **Continuous Delivery (CD)**, and **Continuous Deployment (CD)**. Precisely speaking, besides producing enterprise-grade software applications and platforms, realizing and sustaining virtualized/containerized infrastructures with the assistance of automated tools to ensure continuous and guaranteed delivery of software-enabled and IT-assisted business capabilities to mankind is the need of the hour.

Plunging into the SRE discipline

We have understood the requirements and the challenges. The following sections describe how the SRE field is used to bridge the gap between supply and demand. As explained previously, building software applications through configuration, customization, and composition (orchestration and choreography) is progressing quickly. Speedier programming of software applications using agile programming methods is another incredible aspect of software building. The various DevOps tools from product and tool vendors quietly ensures continuous software integration, delivery, and deployment.

The business landscape is continuously evolving, and consequently the IT domain has to respond precisely and perfectly to the changing equations and expectations of the business houses. Businesses have to be extremely agile, adaptive, and reliable in their operations, offerings, and outputs. Business automation, acceleration, and augmentation are being solely provided by the various noteworthy improvements and improvisations in the IT domain.

IT agility and reliability directly guarantees the business agility and reliability. As seen previously, the goal of IT agility (software design, development, and deployment) is getting fulfilled through newer techniques. Nowadays, IT experts are looking out for ways and means for significantly enhancing IT reliability goals. Typically, IT reliability equals IT elasticity and resiliency. Let's us refer to the following bullets:

- **IT elasticity**: When an IT system is suddenly under a heavy load, how does the IT system provision and use additional IT resources to take care of extra loads without affecting users? IT systems are supposed to be highly elastic to be right and relevant for the future of businesses. Furthermore, not only IT systems but also the business applications and the IT platforms (development, deployment, integration, orchestration, brokerage, and so on) have to be scalable. Thus, the combination of applications, platforms, and infrastructures have to contribute innately to be scalable (vertically, as well as horizontally).
- **IT resiliency**: When an IT system is under attack from internal as well as external sources, the system has to have the wherewithal to wriggle out of that situation to continuously deliver its obligations to its subscribers without any slowdown and breakdown. IT systems have to be highly fault-tolerant to be useful for mission-critical businesses. IT systems have to come back to their original situation automatically, even if they are made to deviate from their prescribed path. Thus, error prediction, identification, isolation, and other capabilities have to be embedded into IT systems. Security and safety issues also have to be dexterously detected and contained to come out unscathed.

Thus, when IT systems are resilient and elastic, they are termed reliable systems. When IT is reliable, then the IT-enabled businesses can be reliable in their deals, deeds, and decisions that, in turn, enthuse and enlighten their customers, employees, partners, and end users.

The challenges ahead

The following are some challenges you may come across:

- Bringing forth a bevy of complexity mitigation techniques. The formula is *heterogeneity + multiplicity = complexity*. IT (software and infrastructure) complexity is constantly improving.
- Producing software packages that are fully compliant to various NFRs and QoS/QoE attributes, such as scalability, availability, stability, reliability, extensibility, accessibility, simplicity, performance/throughput, and so on.
- Performing automated IT infrastructure provisioning, scheduling, configuration, monitoring, measurement, management, and governance.
- Providing VM and container placement, serverless computing/**Function as a Service** (**FaaS**), workload consolidation, energy efficiency, task and job scheduling, resource allocation and usage optimization, service composition for multi-container applications, horizontal scalability, and **Resource as a Service** (**RaaS**).
- Establishing IT automation, Integration, and orchestration for self-service, autonomous, and cognitive IT.
- Accomplishing log, operational, and performance/scalability analytics using AI (machine and deep learning). Algorithms for producing real-time, predictive, and prescriptive insights.
- Building technology sponsored solutions for enabling NoOps, ChatOps, and AIOps. The challenge is to bring forth viable and versatile solutions in the form of automated tools for fulfilling their unique requirements.
- Container clustering, orchestration, and management platform solutions for producing, deploying, and sustaining microservices-centric software applications.
- Bringing forth versatile software solutions such as standards-compliant service mesh solutions, API gateways, and management suites for ensuring service resiliency. With more microservices and their instances across containers (service run time), the operational complexity is on the rise.

- Building resilient and reliable software through pioneering programming techniques such as reactive programming and architectural styles such as **event-driven architecture** (**EDA**).

The idea is to clearly illustrate the serious differences between agile programming, DevOps, and the SRE movement. There are several crucial challenges ahead, as we have mentioned. And the role and responsibility of the SRE technologies, tools, and tips are going to be strategic and significant toward making IT reliable, robust, and rewarding.

The need for highly reliable platforms and infrastructures

We discussed about cloud-enabled and native applications and how they are hosted on underlying cloud infrastructures to accomplish service delivery. Applications are significantly functional. However, the non-functional requirements, such as application scalability, availability, security, reliability, performance/throughput, modifiability, and so on, are being used widely. That is, producing high-quality applications is a real challenge for IT professionals. There are design, development, testing, and deployment techniques, tips, and patterns to incorporate the various NFRs into cloud applications. There are best practices and key guidelines to come out with highly scalable, available, and reliable applications.

The second challenge is to setup and sustain highly competent and cognitive cloud infrastructures to exhibit reliable behavior. The combination of highly resilient, robust, and versatile applications and infrastructures leads to the implementation of highly dependable IT that meets the business productivity, affordability, and adaptivity.

Having understood the tactical and strategic significance and value, businesses are consciously embracing the pioneering cloud paradigm. That is, all kinds of traditional IT environments are becoming cloud-enabled to reap the originally expressed business, technical, and use benefits. However, the cloud formation alone is not going to solve every business and IT problem. Besides establishing purpose-specific and agnostic cloud centers, there are a lot more things to be done to attain the business agility and reliability. The cloud center operation processes need to be refined, integrated, and orchestrated to arrive at optimized and organized processes. Each of the cloud center operations needs to be precisely defined and automated in to fulfil the true meaning of IT agility. With agile and reliable cloud applications and environments, the business competency and value are bound to go up remarkably.

The need for reliable software

We know that the subject of software reliability is a crucial one for the continued success of software engineering in the ensuing digital era. However, it is not easy thing to do. Because of the rising complexity of software suites, ensuring high reliability turns out to be a tough and time-consuming affair. Experts, evangelists, and exponents have come out with a few interesting and inspiring ideas for accomplishing reliable software systems. Primarily, there are two principal approaches; these are as follows:

- Resilient microservices can lead to the realization of reliable software applications. Popular technologies include microservices, containers, Kubernetes, Terraform, API Gateway and Management Suite, Istio, and Spinnaker.
- Reactive systems (resilient, responsive, message-driven, and elastic)—this is based on the famous Reactive Manifesto. There are a few specific languages and platforms (`http://vertx.io/`, `http://reactivex.io/`, `https://www.lightbend.com/products/reactive-platform`, RxJava, play framework, and so on) for producing reactive systems. vAkka is a toolkit for building highly concurrent, distributed, and resilient message-driven applications for Java and Scala.

Here are the other aspects being considered for producing reliable software packages:

- Verification and validation of software reliability through various testing methods
- Software reliability prediction algorithms and approaches
- Static and dynamic code analysis methods
- Patterns, processes, platforms, and practices for building reliable software packages

Let's discuss these in detail.

The emergence of microservices architecture

Mission critical and versatile applications are to be built using the highly popular MSA pattern. Monolithic applications are being consciously dismantled using the MSA paradigm to be immensely right and relevant for their users and owners. Microservices are the new building block for constructing next-generation applications. Microservices are easily manageable, independently deployable, horizontally scalable, relatively simple services. Microservices are publicly discoverable, network accessible, interoperable, API-driven, composed, replaceable, and highly isolated.

The future software development is primarily finding appropriate microservices. Here are few advantages of the MSA style:

- **Scalability**: Any production-grade application typically can use three types of scaling. The x-$axis$ scaling is for horizontally scalability. That is, the application has to be cloned to guarantee high availability. The second type of scale is y-$axis$ scaling. This is for splitting the application into various application functionalities. With microservices architecture, applications (legacy, monolithic, and massive) are partitioned into a collection of easily manageable microservices. Each unit fulfils one responsibility. The third is the z-$axis$ scaling, which is for partitioning or sharding the data. The database plays a vital role in shaping up dynamic applications. With NoSQL databases, the concept of sharing came into prominence.
- **Availability**: Multiple instances of microservices are deployed in different containers (Docker) to guarantee high availability. Through this redundancy, the service and application availability is ensured. With multiple instances of services are being hosted and run through Docker containers, the load-balancing of service instances is utilized to ensure the high-availability of services. The widely used circuit breaker pattern is used to accomplish the much-needed fault-tolerance. That is, the redundancy of services through instances ensures high availability, whereas the circuit-breaker pattern guarantees the resiliency of services. Service registry, discovery, and configuration capabilities are to lead the development and discovery of newer services to bring forth additional business (vertical) and IT (horizontal) services. With services forming a dynamic and ad hoc service meshes, the days of service communication, collaboration, corroborations, and correlations are not too far away.
- **Continuous deployment**: Microservices are independently deployable, horizontally scalable, and self-defined. Microservices are decoupled/lightly coupled and cohesive fulfilling the elusive mandate of modularity. The dependency imposed issues get nullified by embracing this architectural style. This leads to the deployment of any service independent of one another for faster and more continuous deployment.
- **Loose coupling**: As indicated previously, microservices are autonomous and independent by innately providing the much-needed loose coupling. Every microservice has its own layered- architecture at the service level and its own database at the backend.
- **Polyglot microservices**: Microservices can be implemented through a variety of programming languages. As such, there is no technology lock-in. Any technology can be used to realize microservices. Similarly, there is no compulsion for using certain databases. Microservices work with any file system SQL databases, NoSQL and NewSQL databases, search engines, and so on.

- **Performance**: There are performance engineering and enhancement techniques and tips in the microservices arena. For example, high-blocking calls services are implemented in the single threaded technology stack, whereas high CPU usage services are implemented using multiple threads.

There are other benefits for business and IT teams by employing the fast-maturing and stabilizing microservices architecture. The tool ecosystem is on the climb, and hence implementing and involving microservices gets simplified and streamlined. Automated tools ease and speed up building and operationalizing microservices.

Docker enabled containerization

The Docker idea has shaken the software world. A bevy of hitherto-unknown advancements are being realized through containerization. The software portability requirement, which has been lingering for a long time, gets solved through the open source Docker platform. The real-time elasticity of Docker containers hosting a variety of microservices enabling the real-time scalability of business-critical software applications is being touted as the key factor and facet for the surging popularity of containerization. The intersection of microservices and Docker containers domains has brought in paradigm shifts for software developers, as well as for system administrators. The lightweight nature of Docker containers along with the standardized packaging format in association with the Docker platform goes a long way in stabilizing and speeding up software deployment.

The container is a way to package software along with configuration files, dependencies, and binaries required to enable the software on any operating environment. There are a number of crucial advantages; they are as follows:

- **Environment consistency**: Applications/processes/microservices running on containers behave consistently in different environments (development, testing, staging, replica, and production). This eliminates any kind of environmental inconsistencies and makes testing and debugging less cumbersome and less time-consuming.
- **Faster deployment**: A container is lightweight and starts and stops in a few seconds, as it is not required to boot any OS image. This eventually helps to achieve faster creation, deployment, and high availability.

- **Isolation**: Containers running on the same machine using the same resources are isolated from one another. When we start a container with the `docker run` command, the Docker platform does a few interesting things behind the scenes. That is, Docker creates a set of namespaces and control groups for the container. The namespaces and **control groups** (**cgroups**) are the kernel-level capabilities. The role of the namespaces feature is to provide the required isolation for the recently created container from other containers running in the host. Also, containers are clearly segregated from the Docker host. This separation does a lot of good for containers in the form of safety and security. Also, this unique separation ensures that any malware, virus, or any phishing attack on one container does not propagate to other running containers. In short, processes running within a container cannot see and affect processes running in another container or in the host system. Also, as we are moving toward a multi-container applications era, each container has to have its own network stack for container networking and communication. With this network separation, containers don't get any sort of privileged access to the sockets or interfaces of other containers in the same Docker host or across it. The network interface is the only way for containers to interact with one another as well as with the host. Furthermore, when we specify public ports for containers, the IP traffic is allowed between containers. They can ping one another, send and receive UDP packets, and establish TCP connections.
- **Portability**: Containers can run everywhere. They can run in our laptop, enterprise servers, and cloud servers. That is, the long-standing goal of write once and run everywhere is getting fulfilled through the containerization movement.

There are other important advantages of containerization. There are products and platforms that facilitate the cool convergence of containerization and virtualization to cater for emerging IT needs.

Containerized microservices

One paradigm shift in the IT space in the recent past is the emergence of containers for deftly hosting and running microservices. Because of the lightweight nature of containers, provisioning containers is done at lightning speed. Also, the horizontal scalability of microservices gets performed easily by their hosting environments (containers). Thus, this combination of microservices and containers brings a number of benefits for software development and IT operations. There can be hundreds of containers in a single physical machine.

The celebrated linkage helps to have multiple instances of microservices in a machine. With containers talking to one another across Docker hosts, multiple microservice instances can find one another to compose bigger and better composite services that are business and process-aware. Thus, all the advancements in the containerization space have a direct and indirect impacts on microservices engineering, management, governance, security, orchestration, and science.

The key technology drivers of containerized cloud environments are as follows:

- The faster maturity and stability of containers (application and data).
- New types of containers such as Kata Containers and HyperContainers.
- MSA emerging as the most optimized architectural style for enterprise-scale applications.
- There is a cool convergence between containers and microservices. Containers are the most optimized hosting and execution of runtime for microservices.
- Web/cloud, mobile, wearable and IoT applications, platforms, middleware, UI, operational, analytical, and transactional applications are modernized as cloud-enabled applications, and the greenfield applications are built as cloud-native applications.
- The surging popularity of Kubernetes as the container clustering, orchestration, and management platform solution leads to the realization of containerized clouds.
- The emergence of API gateways simplifies and streamlines the access and usage of microservices collectively.
- The faster maturity and stability of service mesh solutions ensures the resiliency of microservices and the reliability of cloud-hosted applications.

The challenges of containerized cloud environments are as follows:

- Moving from monoliths to microservices is not an easy transition.
- There may be thousands of microservices and their instances (redundancy) in a cloud environment.
- For crafting an application, the data and control flows ought to pass through different and distributed microservices spread across multiple cloud centers.
- The best practice says that there is a one to one mapping between microservice instances and containers. That is, separate containers are being allocated for separate microservice instances.
- Due to the resulting dense environments, the operational and management complexities of containerized clouds are bound to escalate.

- Tracking and tracing service request messages and events among microservices turn out to be a complex affair.
- Troubleshooting and doing root cause analyses in microservices environments become a tough assignment.
- Container life cycle management functionalities have to be automated.
- Client-to-microservice (north-to-south traffic) communication remains a challenge.
- Service-to-service (east-to-west traffic) communication has to be made resilient and robust.

Kubernetes for container orchestration

A MSA requires the creating and clubbing together of several fine-grained and easily manageable services that are lightweight, independently deployable, horizontally scalable, extremely portable, and so on. Containers provides an ideal hosting and run time environment for the accelerated building, packaging, shipping, deployment, and delivery of microservices. Other benefits include workload isolation and automated life-cycle management. With a greater number of containers (microservices and their instances) being stuffed into every physical machine, the operational and management complexities of containerized cloud environments are on the higher side. Also, the number of multi-container applications is increasing quickly. Thus, we need a standardized orchestration platform along with container cluster management capability. Kubernetes is the popular container cluster manager, and it consists of several architectural components, including pods, labels, replication controllers, and services. Let's take a look at them:

- As mentioned elsewhere, there are several important ingredients in the Kubernetes architecture. Pods are the most visible, viable, and ephemeral units that comprise one or more tightly coupled containers. That means containers within a pod sail and sink together. There is no possibility of monitoring, measuring, and managing individual containers within a pod. In other words, pods are the base unit of operation for Kubernetes. Kubernetes does not operate at the level of containers. There can be multiple pods in a single server node and data sharing easily happens in between pods. Kubernetes automatically provision and allocate pods for various services. Each pod has its own IP address and shares the localhost and volumes. Based on the faults and failures, additional pods can be quickly provisioned and scheduled to ensure the continuity of services. Similarly, under heightened loads, Kubernetes adds additional resources in the form of pods to ensure system and service performance. Depending on the traffic, resources can be added and removed to fulfil the goal of elasticity.

- Labels are typically the metadata that is attached to objects, including pods.
- Replication controllers, as articulated previously, have the capability to create new pods leveraging a pod template. That is, as per the configuration, Kubernetes is able to run the sufficient number of pods at any point in time. Replication controllers accomplish this unique demand by continuously polling the container cluster. If there is any pod going down, this controller software immediately jumps into action to incorporate an additional pod to ensure that the specified number of pods with a given set of labels are running within the container cluster.
- Services is another capability that embedded into Kubernetes architecture. This functionality and facility offers a low-overhead way to route all kinds of service requests to a set of pods to accomplish the requests. Labels is the way forward for selecting the most appropriate pods. Services provide methods to externalize legacy components, such as databases, with a cluster. They also provide stable endpoints as clusters shrink and grow and become configured and reconfigured across new nodes within the cluster manager. Their job is to remove the pain of keeping track of application components that exist within a cluster instance.

The fast proliferation of application and data containers in producing composite services is facilitated through the leveraging of Kubernetes, and it fastening the era of containerization. Both traditional and modern IT environments are embracing this compartmentalization technology to surmount some of the crucial challenges and concerns of the virtualization technology.

API Gateways and management suite: This is another platform for bringing in reliable client and service interactions. The various features and functionalities of API tools include the following:

- It acts as a router. It is the only entry point to our collection of microservices. This way, microservices are not needed to be public anymore but are behind an internal network. An API Gateway is responsible for making requests against a service or another one (service discovery).
- It acts as a data aggregator. API Gateway fetches data from several services and aggregates it to return a single rich response. Depending on the API consumer, data representation may change according to the needs, and here is where **backend for frontend** (BFF) comes into play.
- It is a protocol abstraction layer. The API Gateway can be exposed as a REST API or a GraphQL or whatever, no matter what protocol or technology is being used internally to communicate with the microservices.

- Error management is centralized. When a service is not available, is getting too slow, and so on, the API Gateway can provide data from the cache, default responses or make smart decisions to avoid bottlenecks or fatal errors propagation. This keeps the circuit closed (circuit breaker) and makes the system more resilient and reliable.
- The granularity of APIs provided by microservices is often different than what a client needs. Microservices typically provide fine-grained APIs, which means that clients need to interact with multiple services. The API Gateway can combine these multiple fine-grained services into a single combined API that clients can use, thereby simplifying the client application and improving performance.
- Network performance is different for different types of clients. The API Gateway can define device-specific APIs that reduce the number of calls required to be made over slower WAN or mobile networks. The API Gateway being a server-side application makes it more efficient to make multiple calls to backend services over LAN.
- The number of service instances and their locations (host and port) changes dynamically. The API Gateway can incorporate these backend changes without requiring frontend client applications by determining backend service locations.
- Different clients may need different levels of security. For example, external applications may need a higher level of security to access the same APIs that internal applications may access without the additional security layer.

Service mesh solutions for microservice resiliency: Distributed computing is the way forward for running web-scale applications and big-data analytics. By the horizontal scalability and individual life cycle of management of various application modules (microservices) of customer-facing applications, the aspect of distributed deployment of IT resources (highly programmable and configurable bare metal servers, virtual machines, and containers) is being insisted. That is, the goal of the centralized management of distributed deployment of IT resources and applications has to be fulfilled. Such kinds of monitoring, measurement, and management is required for ensuring proactive, preemptive, and prompt failure anticipation and correction of all sorts of participating and contributing constituents. In other words, accomplishing the resiliency target is given much importance with the era of distributed computing. Policy establishment and enforcement is a proven way for bringing in a few specific automations. There are programming language-specific frameworks to add additional code and configuration into application code for implementing highly available and fault-tolerant applications.

It is therefore paramount to have a programming-agnostic resiliency and fault-tolerance framework in the microservices world. Service mesh is the appropriate way forward for creating and sustaining resilient microservices. Istio, an industry-strength open source framework, provides an easy way to create this service mesh. The following diagram conveys the difference between the traditional **ESB** tool-based and service-oriented application integration and the lightweight and elastic microservices-based application interactions:

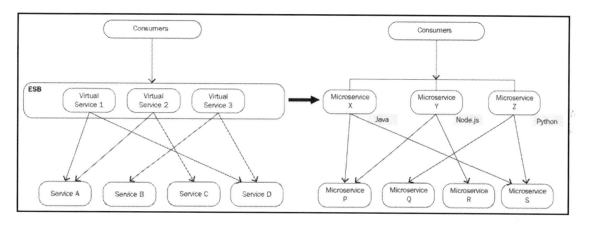

A service mesh is a software solution for establishing a mesh out of all kinds of participating and contributing services. This mesh software enables the setting up and sustaining of inter-service communication. The service mesh is a kind of infrastructure solution. Consider the following:

- A given microservice does not directly communicate with the other microservices.
- Instead, all service-to-service communications take place on a service mesh software solution, which is a kind of sidecar proxy. Sidecar is a famous software integration pattern.
- Service mesh provides the built-in support for some of the critical network functions such as microservice resiliency and discovery.

That is, the core and common network services are being identified, abstracted, and delivered through the service mesh solution. This enables service developers to focus on business capabilities alone. That is, business-specific features are with services, whereas all the horizontal (technical, network communication, security, enrichment, intermediation, routing, and filtering) services are being implemented in the service mesh software. For instance, today, the circuit-breaking pattern is being implemented and inscribed in the service code. Now, this pattern is being accomplished through a service mesh solution.

The service mesh software works across multiple languages. That is, services can be coded using any programming and script languages. Also, there are several text and binary data transmission protocols. Microservices, to talk to other microservices, have to interact with the service mesh for initiating service communication. This service-to-service mesh communication can happen over all the standard protocols, such as **HTTP1.x/2.x**, **gRPC**, and so on. We can write microservices using any technology, and they still work with the service mesh. The following diagram illustrates the contributions of the service mesh in making microservices resilient:

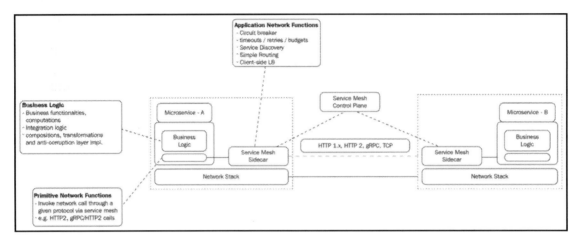

Finally, when resilient services get composed, we can produce reliable applications. Thus, the resiliency of all participating microservices leads to applications that are highly dependable.

Resilient microservices and reliable applications

Progressively, the world is connected and software-enabled. We often hear, read, and experience software-defined computing, storing, and networking capabilities. Physical, mechanical, electrical, and electronics systems in our everyday environments are being meticulously stuffed with software to be adroit, aware, adaptive, and articulate in their actions and reactions. Software is destined to play a strategic and significant role for producing and sustaining digitally impacted and transformed societies, one stand-out trait of new-generation software-enabled systems are responsive all the time through one or other ways. That is, they have to come out with a correct response. If the system is not responding, then another system has to respond correctly and quickly. That is, if a system is failing, an alternative system has to respond.

This is typically called **system resiliency**. If the system is extremely stressful due to heavy user and data loads, then additional systems have to be provisioned to respond to user's requests without any slowdown and breakdown. That is, auto-scaling is an important property for today's software systems to be right and relevant for businesses and users. This is generally called **system elasticity**. To make systems resilient and elastic, producing message-driven systems is the key decision. Message-driven systems are called **reactive systems**. Let's digress a bit here and explain the concepts behind system resiliency and elasticity.

A scalable application can scale automatically and accordingly to continuously function. Suddenly, there can be a greater number of users accessing the application. Still, the application has to continuously transact and can gracefully handle traffic peaks and dips. By adding and removing virtual machines and containers only when needed, scalable applications do their assigned tasks without any slowdown or breakdown. By dynamically provisioning additional resources, the utilization rate of scalable applications is optimal. Scalable applications support on-demand computing. There can be many users demanding the services of the application, or there can be more data getting pushed into the application. Containers and virtual machines are the primary resource and runtime environment for application components.

Reactive systems

We have seen how reliable systems are being realized through the service mesh concept. This is another approach for bringing forth reliable software systems. A reactive system is a new concept based on the widely circulated reactive manifesto. There are reactive programming models and techniques to build viable reactive systems. As described previously, any software system is comprised of multiple modules. Also, multiple components and applications need to interact with each other reliably to accomplish certain complex business functionality. In a reactive system, the individual systems are intelligent. However, the key differentiator is the interaction between the individual parts. That is, the ability to operate individually yet act in concert to achieve the intended outcome clearly differentiates reactive systems from others. A reactive system architecture allows multiple individual applications to co-exist and coalesce as a single unit and react to its surroundings adaptively. This means that they are able to scale up or down based on user and data loads, load balance, and act intelligently to be extremely sensitive and royally responsive.

It is possible to write an application in a reactive style using the proven reactive programming processes, patterns, and platforms. However, for working together to achieve evolving business needs quickly, it needs a lot more. In short, it is not that easy making a system reactive. Reactive systems are generally designed and built according to the tenets of the highly popular Reactive Manifesto. This manifesto document clearly prescribes and promotes the architecture that is responsive, resilient, elastic, and message driven. Increasingly, microservices and message-based service interactions become the widely used standard for having flexible, elastic, resilient, and loosely coupled systems. These characteristics, without an iota of doubt, are the central and core concepts of reactive systems.

Reactive programming is a subset of asynchronous programming. This is an emerging paradigm where the availability of new information (events and messages) drives the processing logic forward. Traditionally, some action gets activated and accomplished using threads of execution based on control and data flows.

This unique programming style intrinsically supports decomposing the problem into multiple discrete steps, and each step can be executed in an asynchronous and non-blocking fashion. Then, those steps can be composed to produce a composite workflow possibly unbounded in its inputs or outputs. Asynchronous processing means the processing of incoming messages or events happen sometime in the future. The event creators and message senders need not wait for the processing and the execution to get done to proceed with their responsibilities. This is generally called non-blocking execution. The threads of execution need not compete for a shared resource to get things done immediately. If the resource is not available immediately, then the threads need not wait for the unavailable resource and instead continue with other tasks at hand, using their respective resources. The point is that they can do their work without any stoppage while waiting for appropriate resources for a particular task at a particular point in time. In other words, they do not prevent the thread of execution from performing other work until the current work is done. They can perform other useful work while the resource is being occupied.

In the future, software applications have to be sensitive and responsive. The futuristic and people-centric applications, therefore, have to be capable of receiving events to be adaptive. Event capturing, storing, and processing are becoming important for enterprise, embedded, and cloud applications. Reactive programming is emerging as an important concept for producing event-driven software applications. There are simple as well as complex events. Events are primarily being streamed continuously, and hence the event-processing feature is known as streaming analytics these days. There are several streaming analytics platforms, such as Spark Streams, Kafka Streams, Apache Flink, Storm, and so on, for extricating actionable insights out of streams.

In the increasingly event-driven world, EDAs and programming models acquire more market and mind shares. And thus reactive programming is a grandiose initiative to provide a standard solution for asynchronous stream processing with non-blocking back pressure. The key benefits of reactive programming include the increased utilization of computing resources on multi-core and multi-processor hardware. There are several competent event-driven programming libraries, middleware solutions, enabling frameworks, and architectures to carefully capture, cleanse, and crunch millions of events per second. The popular libraries for facilitating event-driven programming include Akka Streams, Reactor, RxJava, and Vert.x.

Reactive programming versus reactive systems: There is a huge difference between reactive programming and reactive systems. As indicated previously, reactive programming is primarily event-driven. Reactive systems, on the other hand, are message-driven and focus on creating resilient and elastic software systems. Messages are the prime form of communication and collaboration. Distributed systems coordinate by sending, receiving, and processing messages. Messages are inherently directed, whereas events are not. Messages have a clear direction and destination. Events are facts for others to observe and act upon with confidence and clarity. Messaging is typically asynchronous with the sender and the reader is decoupled. In a message-driven system, addressable recipients wait for messages to arrive. In an event-driven system, consumers are integrated with sources of events and event stores.

In a reactive system, especially one that uses reactive programming, both events and messages will be present. Messages are a great tool for communication, whereas events are the best bet for unambiguously representing facts. Messages ought to be transmitted across the network and form the basis for communication in distributed systems. Messaging is being used to bridge event-driven systems across the network. Event-driven programming is therefore a simple model in a distributed computing environment. That is not the case with messaging in distributed computing environments. Messaging has to do a lot of things because there are several constraints and challenges in distributed computing. That is, messaging has to tackle things such as partial failures, failure detection, dropped/duplicated/reordered messages, eventual consistency, and managing multiple concurrent realities. These differences in semantics and applicability have intense implications in the application design, including things such as resilience, elasticity, mobility, location transparency, and management complexities of distributed systems.

Reactive systems are highly reliable

Reactive systems fully comply with the reactive manifesto (resilient, responsive, elastic, and message-driven), which was contemplated and released by a group of IT product vendors. A variety of architectural design and decision principles are being formulated and firmed up for building most modernized and cognitive systems that are innately capable of fulfilling todays complicated yet sophisticated requirements. Messages are the most optimal unit of information exchange for reactive systems to function and facilitate. These messages create a kind of temporal boundary between application components. Messages enable application components to be decoupled in time (this allows for concurrency) and in space (this allows for distribution and mobility). This decoupling capability facilitates the much-needed isolation among various application services. Such a decoupling ultimately ensures the much-needed resiliency and elasticity, which are the most sought-after needs for producing reliable systems.

Resilience is about the capability of responsiveness even under failure and is an inherent functional property of the system. Resilience is beyond fault-tolerance, which is all about graceful degradation. It is all about fully recovering from any failure. It is empowering systems to self-diagnose and self-heal. This property requires component isolation and containment of failures to avoid failures spreading to neighboring components. If errors and failure are allowed to cascade into other components, then the whole system is bound to fail.

So, the key to designing, developing, and deploying resilient and self-healing systems is to allow any type of failure to be proactively found and contained, encoded as messages, and sent to supervisor components. These can be monitored, measured, and managed from a safe distance. Here, being message-driven is the greatest enabler. Moving away from tightly coupled systems to loosely and lightly coupled systems is the way forward. With less dependency, the affected component can be singled out, and the spread of errors can be nipped in the bud.

The elasticity of reactive systems

Elasticity is about the capability of responsiveness under a load. Systems can be used by many users suddenly, or a lot of data can be pumped by hundreds of thousands of sensors and devices into the system. To tackle this unplanned rush of users and data, systems have to automatically scale up or out by adding additional resources (bare metal servers, virtual machines, and containers). The cloud environments are innately enabled to be auto-scaling based on varying resource needs. This capability makes systems to use their expensive resources in an optimized manner. When resource utilization goes up, the capital and operational costs of systems comes down sharply.

Systems need to be adaptive enough to perform auto-scaling, replication of state, and behavior, load-balancing, fail-over, and upgrades without any manual intervention, instruction, and interpretation. In short, designing, developing, and deploying reactive systems through messaging is the need of the hour.

Highly reliable IT infrastructures

So far in this chapter, we have concentrated on the application side to ensure IT reliability. But there is a crucial role to play by the underlying IT infrastructures. We have clusters, grids, and clouds to achieve high availability and scalability at the infrastructures level. Clouds are being touted as the best-in-class IT infrastructure for digital innovation, disruption, and transformation. For simplifying, streamlining, and speeding up the cloud setup and sustenance, there came a number of enabling tools for automating the repetitive and routine cloud scheduling, software deployment, cloud administration, and management. Automation and orchestration are being pronounced as the way forward for the ensuing cloud era. Most of the manual activities in running cloud centers are being precisely defined and automated through scripts and other methods. With the number of systems, databases, and middleware, network and storage professionals manning cloud environments has come down drastically. The **total cost of ownership** (TCO) of cloud IT is declining, whereas the **return on investment** (RoI) is increasing. The cost benefits of the cloud-enablement of conventional IT environments is greatly noticeable. Cloud computing is typically proclaimed as the marriage between mainframe and modern computing and is famous for attaining high performance while giving cost advantages. The customer-facing applications with varying loads are extremely fit for public cloud environments. Multi-cloud strategies are being worked out by worldwide enterprises to embrace this unique technology without any vendor lock-in.

However, for attaining the much-needed reliability, there are miles to traverse. Automated tools, policies, and other knowledge bases, AI-inspired log and operational analytics, acquiring the capability of preventive, predictive, and prescriptive maintenance through machine and deep learning algorithms and models, scores of reusable resiliency patterns, and preemptive monitoring, are the way forward.

A resilient application is typically highly available, even in the midst of failures and faults. If there is any internal or external attack on a single application component/microservice, the application still functions and delivers its assigned functionality without any delay or stoppage. The failure can be identified and contained within the component so that the other components of the application aren't affected. Typically, multiple instances of the application components are being run in different and distributed containers or VMs so that one component loss does not matter much to the application. Also, application state and behavior information gets stored in separate systems. Any resilient application has to be designed and developed accordingly to survive in any kind of situation. Not only applications but also the underlying IT or cloud infrastructure modules have to be chosen and configured intelligently to support the unique resilient goals of software applications. The first and foremost thing is to fully leverage the distributed computing model. The deployment topology and architecture have to purposefully use the various resiliency design, integration, deployment, and patterns. Plus, the following tips and techniques ought to be employed as per the infrastructure scientists, experts, architects, and specialists:

- Use the various network and security solutions, such as firewalls, load balancers, and **application delivery controllers** (**ADCs**). **Network access control systems** (**NACLs**) also contribute to security. These help out in intelligently investigating every request message to filter out any ambiguous and malevolent message at the source. Furthermore, load balancers continuously probe and monitor servers and distribute traffic to servers that are not fully loaded. Also, they can choose the best server to handle certain requests.
- Employ multiple servers at different and distributed cloud centers. That is, disaster recovery capability needs to be part of any IT solution.
- Attach a robust and resilient storage solution for data recovery and stateful applications.
- Utilize software infrastructure solutions, such as API gateways and management suites, service mesh solutions, additional abstraction layers, to ensure the systems resiliency.
- Leveraging the aspects of compartmentalization (virtualization and containerization) have to be incorporated to arrive at virtualized and containerized cloud environments, which intrinsically support the much-needed flexibility, extensibility, elasticity, infrastructure operations automation, distinct maneuverability, and versatility. The software-defined environments are more conducive and constructive for application and infrastructure resiliency.
- Focus on log, operational, performance, and scalability analytics to proactive and preemptively monitor, measure, and manage various infrastructure components (software, as well as hardware).

Thus, reliable software applications and infrastructure combine well in rolling out reliable systems that, in turn, guarantee reliable business operations.

In summary, we can say the following:

- *Reliability = resiliency + elasticity*
- Automation and orchestration are the key requirements for a reliable IT infrastructure
- IT reliability fulfilment—resiliency is to survive under attacks, failures, and faults, whereas elasticity is to auto-scale (vertical and horizontal scalability) under a load
- IT infrastructure operational, log, and performance/scalability analytics through AI-inspired analytics platforms
- Patterns, processes, platforms, and practices for having reliable IT Infrastructure
- System and application monitoring are also significant

The emergence of serverless computing

Serverless computing allows for the building and running of applications and services without thinking about server machines, storage appliances, and arrays and networking solutions. Serverless applications don't require developers to provision, scale, and manage any IT resources to handle serverless applications. It is possible to build a serverless application for nearly any type of applications or backend services. The scalability aspect of serverless applications is being taken care of by cloud service and resource providers. Any spike in load is being closely monitored and acted upon quickly. The developer doesn't need to worry about the infrastructure portions. That is, developers just focus on the business logic and the IT capability being delegated to the cloud teams. This hugely reduced overhead empowers designers and developers to reclaim the time and energy wasted on the IT infrastructure plumbing part. Developers typically can focus on other important requirements, such as resiliency and reliability.

The surging popularity of containers comes in handy when automating the relevant aspects to have scores of serverless applications. That is, a function is developed and deployed quickly without worrying about the provisioning, scheduling, configuration, monitoring, and management. Therefore, the new buzzword, FaaS, is gaining a lot of momentum these days. We are moving toward NoOps. That is, most of the cloud operations get automated through a host of technology solutions and tools, and this transition comes in handy for institutions, individuals, and innovators to deploy and deliver their software applications quickly.

On the cost front, users have to pay for the used capacity. Through the automated and dynamic provisioning of resources, the resource utilization goes up significantly. Also, the cost efficiency is fully realized and passed on to the cloud users and subscribers.

Precisely speaking, serverless computing is another and additional abstraction toward automated computing and analytics.

The vitality of the SRE domain

As discussed previously, the software engineering field is going through a number of disruptions and transformations to cope with the growth being achieved in hardware engineering. There are agile, aspect, agent, composition, service-oriented, polyglot, and adaptive programming styles. At the time of writing this book, building reactive and cognitive applications by leveraging competent development frameworks is being stepped up. On the infrastructure side, we have powerful cloud environments as the one-stop IT solution for hosting and running business workloads. Still, there are a number of crucial challenges in achieving the much-wanted cloud operations with less intervention, interpretation, and involvement from human administrators. Already, there are several tasks getting automated via breakthrough algorithms and tools. Still, there are gaps to be filled with technologically powerful solutions. These well-known and widely used tasks include dynamic and automated capacity planning and management, cloud infrastructure provisioning and resource allocation, software deployment and configuration, patching, infrastructure and software monitoring, measurement and management, and so on. Furthermore, these days, software packages are being frequently updated, patched, and released to a production environment to meet emerging and evolving demands of clients, customers, and consumers. Also, the number of application components (microservices) is growing rapidly. In short, the true IT agility has to be ensured through a whole bunch of automated tools. The operational team with the undivided support of SREs has to envision and safeguard highly optimized and organized IT infrastructures to successfully and sagaciously host and run next-generation software applications. Precisely speaking, the brewing challenge is to automate and orchestrate cloud operations. The cloud has to be self-servicing, self-configuring, self-healing, self-diagnosing, self-defending, and self-governing to be autonomic clouds.

The new and emerging SRE domain is being prescribed as the viable way forward. A new breed of software engineers, who have a special liking of system engineering, are being touted as the best fit to be categorized as SREs. These specially skilled engineers are going to train software developers and system administrators to astutely realize highly competent and dependable software solutions, scripts, and automated tools to speedily setup and sustain highly dependable, dynamic, responsive, and programmable IT infrastructures. An SRE team literally cares about anything that makes complex software systems work in production in a risk-free and continuous manner. In short, a site reliability engineer is a hybrid software and system engineer. Due to the ubiquity and usability of cloud centers for meeting the world's IT needs, the word *site* represents cloud environments.

Site Reliability Engineers usually care about infrastructure orchestration, automated software deployment, proper monitoring and alerting, scalability and capacity estimation, release procedures, disaster preparedness, fail-over and fail-back capabilities, **performance engineering and enhancement** (PE2), garbage collector tuning, release automation, capacity uplifts, and so on. They will usually also take an interest in good test coverage. SREs are software engineers who specialize in reliability. SREs are expected to apply the proven and promising principles of computer science and engineering to the design and development of enterprise-class, modular, web-scale, and software applications.

The importance of SREs

An SRE is responsible for ensuring the systems availability, performance-monitoring, and incident response of the cloud IT platforms and services. SREs must make sure that all software applications entering production environments fully comply with a set of important requirements, such as diagrams, network topology illustrations, service dependency details, monitoring and logging plans, backups, and so on. A software application may fully comply with all of the functional requirements, but there are other sources for disruption and interruption. There may be hardware degradation, networking problems, high usage of resources, or slow responses from applications, and services could happen at any time. SREs always need to be extremely sensitive and responsive. The SREs effectiveness may be measured as a function of **mean time to recover** (**MTTR**) and **mean time to failure** (**MTTF**). In other words, the availability of system functions in the midst of failures and faults has to be guaranteed. Similarly, when the system load varies sharply, the system has to have the inherent potential to do scale up and out.

Software developers typically develop the business functionality of the application and do the necessary unit tests for the functionality they created from scratch or composed out of different, distributed, and decentralized services. But they don't always focus on creating and incorporating the code for achieving scalability, availability, reliability, and so on. System administrators, on the other hand, do everything to design, build, and maintain an organization's IT infrastructure (computing, storage, networking, and security). System administrators do try to achieve these QoS attributes through infrastructure sizing and by provisioning additional infrastructural modules (**bare metal** (**BM**) servers, **virtual machines** (**VM**) servers, and containers) to authoritatively tackle any sudden rush of users and bigger payloads. As described previously, the central goal of DevOps is to build a healthy and working relationship between the operations and the development teams. Any gaps and other friction between developers and operators ought to be identified and eliminated at the earliest by SREs so as to run any application on any machine or cluster without many twists and tweaks. The most critical challenges are how to ensure NFRs/QoS attributes.

SREs solve a very basic yet important problem that administrators and DevOps professionals do not. The infrastructures resiliency and elasticity to safeguard application scalability and reliability has to be ensured. The business continuity and productivity through minute monitoring of business applications and IT services along with other delights for customers, has to be guaranteed. The meeting of the identified NFRs through infrastructure optimization alone is neither viable nor sustainable. NFRs have to be rather realized by skillfully etching in all the relevant code snippets and segments in the application source code itself. In short, the source code for any application has to be made aware of and is capable of easily absorbing the capacity and capability of the underlying infrastructure. That is, we are destined toward the era of infrastructure-aware applications, and, on the other side, we are heading toward application-aware infrastructures.

This is where SREs pitch in. These specially empowered professionals, with all the education, experience, and expertise, are to assist both developers and system administrators to develop, deploy, and deliver highly reliable software systems via software-defined cloud environments. SREs spend half of their time with developers and the other half with operation team to ensure much-needed reliability. SREs set clear and mathematically modeled **service-level agreements** (**SLAs**) that set thresholds for the stability and reliability of software applications.

SREs have many skills:

- They have a deep knowledge of complex software systems
- They are experts in data structures
- They are excellent at designing and analyzing computer algorithms

- They have a broad understanding of emerging technologies, tools, and techniques
- They are passionate when it comes to coding, debugging, and problem-solving
- They have strong analytical skills and intuition
- They learn quickly from mistakes and eliminate them in the subsequent assignments
- They are team players, willing to share the knowledge they have gained and gathered
- They like the adrenaline rush of fast-paced work
- They are good at reading technical books, blogs, and publications
- They produce and publish technology papers, patents, and best practices

Furthermore, SREs learn and position themselves to be a **single point of contact** (**SPOC**) in the following areas:

- They have a good understanding of code design, analysis, debugging, and optimization.
- They have a wide understanding about various IT systems, ranging from applications to appliances (servers, storage, network components (switches, routers, firewalls, load balancers, intrusion detection and prevention systems, and so on)).
- They are competent in emerging technologies:
    - Software-defined clouds for highly optimized and organized IT infrastructures
    - Data analytics for extracting actionable insights in time.
    - IoT for people-centric application design and delivery
    - Containerization-sponsored DevOps
    - FaaS for simplified IT operations
    - Enterprise mobility
    - Blockchain for IoT data and device security
    - AI (machine and deep-learning algorithms) for predictive and prescriptive insights
    - Cognitive computing for realizing smarter applications
    - Digital twin for performance increment, failure detection, product productivity, and resilient infrastructures

- Conversant with a variety of automated tools
- Familiar with reliability engineering concept
- Well-versed with the key terms and buzzwords such as scalability, availability, maneuverability, extensibility, and dependability
- Good at IT systems operations, application performance management, cyber security attacks and solution approaches
- Insights-driven IT operations, administration, maintenance, and enhancement

Toolsets that SREs typically use

In the case of SREs, ensuring the stability and the highest uptime of software applications are the top priorities. However, they should have the ability to take the responsibility and code their own way out of hazards, hurdles, and hitches. They cannot add to the to-do lists of the development teams. SREs are typically software engineers with a passion for system, network, storage, and security administration. They have to have the unique strength of development and operations, and they are highly comfortable with a bevy of script languages, automation tools, and other software solutions to speedily automate the various aspects of IT operations, monitoring, and management, especially application performance management, IT infrastructure orchestration, automation, and optimization. Though automation is the key competency of SREs, SREs ought to educate themselves and gain experience to gain expertise in the following technologies and tools:

- Object-oriented, functional, and script languages
- Digital technologies (cloud, mobility, IoT, data analytics, and security)
- Server, storage, network, and security technologies
- System, database, middleware, and platform administration
- Compartmentalization (virtualization and containerization) paradigms, DevOps tools
- The MSA pattern
- Design, integration, performance, scalability, and resiliency patterns
- Cluster, grid, utility, and cloud computing models
- Troubleshooting software and hardware systems
- Dynamic capacity planning, task and resource scheduling, workload optimization, VM and container placement, distributed computing, and serverless computing

- AI-enabled operational, performance, security, and log analytics platforms
- Cloud orchestration, governance, and brokerage tools
- Automated software testing and deployment models
- OpenStack and other cloud infrastructure management platforms
- Data center optimization and transformation

Summary

With IT being recognized as the greatest automation technology, there is a heightened awareness and keenness by business executives in leveraging the delightful developments and advancements in the IT space to steer their organizations in the right direction and destination. With the greater penetration and participation of IT applications, platforms, and infrastructures, every small, medium, and large corporation has to have competent IT environments. The challenge now is to ensure highly resilient, elastic, available, and secure IT that has a positive vibe on business operations. Thus, the fresh concept of SRE got started and is being meticulously sustained through a host of collaborative endeavors and execution. SRE is definitely a new enterprise-wide and strategically sound initiative that is being used by various industry verticals across the globe so that they have highly reliable IT that benefits their customers.

In the next chapter, we will be learning about emerging concepts such as containerization, the microservices architecture, container management, and clustering.

Microservices Architecture and Containers

Microservices are changing the mentality of people who design software. In this chapter, we are going to cover various definitions, principles, deployment techniques, tools, and techniques related to microservices. We are also going to show deployments using tools and technologies that are widely available in the cloud era. We will be covering how to deploy Serverless containers, and we will also mention existing virtualization technology. We will then provide some examples regarding how to develop microservices using the Spring Framework.

In this chapter, we will learn about the following topics:

- Introducing microservices
- Microservices design principles
- Different options for deploying microservices
- Microservices using the Spring Boot framework and the RESTful framework
- Monitoring microservices
- Important information about microservices

What are microservices?

Microservices are a software development style that has recently been developed to set up practices intended to increase the efficiency and speed of developing and managing software solutions so that they can be scaled easily. This set of practices is technology agnostic, which means that there is not one single programming language or technology to build microservices. In fact, you can build microservices with any programming language. It's more about applying a certain number of architectural patterns and principles to your program.

Microservice design principles

There are several different microservices design principles available. Different terms are likely to be used in different places. In this book, we will refer to the microservices design principles as follows:

- **High cohesion among services**: A microservice should have one single focus and the sole responsibility for that action. It should not change as a result of other related services. Services should be easily rewritable so that we can achieve scalability, reliability, and flexibility. It should handle a single business function and domain-specific functionality.

- **Autonomous service**: A service should independently handle its work without the help of any other services. It should not be tightly integrated with any other service; it should remain loosely coupled in nature. By autonomous, we mean that a microservice should not change because of the external components with which it interacts. Autonomous services honor contracts and interfaces. They should be stateless, independently changeable, independently deployable, backwards compatible, and they should support concurrent development.

- **Business domain-centric service**: Each individual service should perform or represent a single business function. This could be a calculation of sales, tax, income tax, or any other function related to a specific area. Each service should bound or define its scope. Business-centric code can help to provide more cohesion and make services more responsive to handle any changes in the domain or business logic requirements.

- **Resilience:** Resilience is a standard these days when providing a service to a customer. Failure to provide resilience may result in another endpoint not providing a response to your microservices. Designing your service in micro-format helps to overcome failure. Our service should register itself during startup and de-register itself upon failure. This should be part of a dynamic discovery service, such as the auto-creation of a queue or the auto-removal of the queue in a message queue. There could be a number of problems or exceptions that a network-based service could encounter. It should be able to handle delays and the unavailability of another service.

- **Observable service or functionality**: Observability is another important design principle while working on distributed microservices. When a complex interconnected service breaks, it can take hours or days to isolate issues. We should design our services in such a way that we can check the health of any service by either showing its status on a health page or by sending it to a central logging service such as Splunk, Logstash, syslogd, Logentries, Datadog, or Sumo Logic. Observability is required to support reliable, scalable, and cost-effective services and metrics to scale up, metrics to scale down, and metrics to alert the team. This kind of monitoring and logging needs to be located at a central place. In a containerized environment, auto deployment should be able to auto-detect when a deployment fails so that it can be rolled back quickly to an older running version. Observability can be related to CPU usage, memory usage, network input/output metrics, disk metrics, the number of connections to a service, and so on. All these metrics are easily available and measurable through tools such as Check_MK, Nagios, New Relic, AppDynamics, StatsD, and Graphana. Observability not only helps in terms of providing a technical solution but also so that we can identify business decision-making, like the sales of a specific service or the returns for a specific product.
- **Automation**: Microservices also create challenges for an operation team with regard to deployment, verifying functionality, and performing various types of testing. There is now a wide range of automation tools available on market that can easily be integrated to achieve automated deployment, verification, testing, failure, and rollbacks. Some of the famous tools are Jenkins; Teamcity; Bamboo; Git workflow plugins; GitLab CI/CD; UI test tools, such as Selenium, PhantomJS, Nightwatch, BrowserStack; and many more. One important point here is that while Docker changed the container market when it was developed, it was hard to implement in a production environment, where a complete stack is required to maintain it as a production-level service. There wasn't much clarity with regard to monitoring or deployment. After that, Google released Borg in the form of Kubernetes and changed the container market again by providing easy deployment and rollback options with easy service and routing functionalities that were perfect for production-grade deployments.

Deploying microservices

Let's start to think practically about microservice deployment. We are going to look at the latest container technologies and orchestrator tools that are dominating the microservice market. First, we will list the availability of tools and options and then we will look at an example to show you how things can be deployed in the microservice model.

Microservices can be deployed on the following platforms:

- **Container platforms**: These include technologies such as Docker, rkt, AWS ECS, and AWS EKS.
- **Code as a function:** We can deploy bare functions written in supported programming languages on AWS Lambda-like platforms. These platforms will run that configured code and store the result on an S3-like bucket or a supported database on a cloud vendor platform. Alternatively, the code might trigger a further configured action. It can be called through AWS API Gateways, a similar service available on Microsoft Azure, or over **Google's Cloud Platform** (**GCP**).
- **Virtual platforms**: These include virtual machines such as VMware, vSphere VM, Xen VM, and KVM-based VMs.

There are different tools available for deployment in each category in these platforms. We will take a look at these in the following sections.

Container platform-based deployment tools

There are multiple orchestration or deployment tools available in the market, both in the open source world and in the enterprise world. The industry has rapidly changed over the past few years, moving away from enterprise products and adapting open source solutions instead. While enterprise products have great features that are well tested, their cost is one of the biggest factors driving the trend toward open source tools. We are going to focus more on recent trends and open source tools, as these can be downloaded easily on your local setup.

Currently, in the container domain, the major players are Docker and rkt. rkt is the default container option in the CoreOS container operating system, while Docker can be used with all operating systems.

The three most common tools that are trending in the container platform deployment or orchestration market are the following:

- Kubernetes
- Red Hat's OpenShift (it uses Kubernetes)
- CI/CD-based tools such as Jenkins, TeamCity, and GoCD

Code as function deployment

This domain, otherwise known as **Function as a Service** (**FaaS**) is very immature at the moment. Often, people working in this domain don't even know when new tools are launched by new vendors. However, the tools that do exist are capable of performing the expected work. Some of the tools that we can use for AWS Lambda deployments are the following:

- **Serverless**: This allows deployment engineers to build and deploy Lambda-like functions. More details can be found at the following website: `https://serverless.com/`.
- **Apex**: Apex is used to deploy, manage, and build Amazon Lambda functions. Non-supported languages in AWS Lambda can be supported using the Apex-like Go language, using Node.js shim injections in the build. More details can be found at the following website: `http://apex.run/`.
- **Chalice**: Chalice is a micro framework for writing Serverless apps in Python. It allows you to create and deploy applications that use AWS Lambda quickly. It provides the following features:
    - A command-line tool for creating, deploying, and managing your app.
    - A decorator-based API for integrating with Amazon API Gateway, Amazon S3, Amazon SNS, Amazon SQS, and other AWS services.
    - Automatic IAM policy generation. More details can be found on the following website: `https://github.com/aws/chalice`.
- **Claudia.js**: This tool easily deploys Node.js projects to Amazon Lambda.
- **AWS Serverless Application Model (SAM)**: This is the Amazon way of deploying Serverless code and applications. Amazon has released it under the Apache 2.0 license for partners and Amazon customers.
- **Serverless express**: Mainly for Node.js.
- **Traditional Bash scripts**: CI/CD tools such as **Jenkins**, **TeamCity**, or other similar tools, with the integration of previously mentioned tools or especially with bash-based scripting languages.

Programming language selection criteria in AWS Lambda

When dealing with lambda-like functions, we should consider the launch speed of the language. For example, C# and Java are slower, while Node.js and Python are faster. Keep this information in mind when designing your service, as heavy Java or C# code will create a delay in your service response, whereas Node.js and Python will be faster.

Virtualization-based platform deployment

Virtual environments may be losing momentum in the microservice domain after the entrance of Docker and Rocket entrance in the market, but many companies are still invested in them. Virtual machines keep all the microservice design principles intact, so fundamentally, we can't remove them from the microservice platform list. The tools for deployment include the following:

- **Traditional scripts** (such as Windows PowerShell or Linux Bash): These are very handy, but I wouldn't recommend them, as easier options are available. For example, we can use the Serverless tool for FaaS deployment or Ansible for any package or code deployment on VMs, Kubernetes, or OpenShift. Learning those tools is likely to be more helpful.
- **Traditional Makefiles**: People are using it in inventive way, and they are deploying using it. These are often thought of as dominating the build world, but they can be easily used in the deployment world as well.
- **Capistrano**: This is an open source tool used to run scripts on many servers at the same time.
- **CI/CD**: This is based on traditional tools, such as Jenkins or TeamCity.

There are also a variety of enterprise products available, which are often built for monolithic or SOA-based applications. Vendors are extending their functionalities so that they support container platforms as well:

- HP HPSA (previously known as Opsware)
- BMC

Practical examples of microservice deployment

In this section, we're going to look at some relevant examples using the latest technologies. This will give you an easy reference guide to consult when implementing your own deployment strategy.

A container platform deployment example with Kubernetes

In the following Kubernetes YAML configuration, we will define various Kubernetes keywords related to deployment. One important variable is *container: image*. Here, we are referring to an existing Docker container image that Kubernetes will use to create a container under pod deployment. This container image should already be customized to suit your requirements. The `kubectl` command will read this configuration and start your container as appropriate. It will start three replica pods with the same container image and it will use the `matchLables` value to replace the specific container inside the three newly created pods. The keyword *replica* indicates that a specific value has been used to create pods with the same container image.

There are three different kinds of replicas:

- `kind`: Kind defines the type of work `kubectl` will be doing on the given configuration. Currently, we are using `Deployment`.
- `metadata`: This will assign a name to the deployment and label your POD with the given name under `app`.
- `spec`: This stands for specification, where you configure the number of replicas, the selector name for pod replacement, and so on.

Create a deployment controller file with the following content. This can then be provided to the `kubectl` command as a parameter during the create or apply steps.

The file name is as follows: `/my-hello-packt-application-deployment.yaml`. Refer to the following code:

```
#vim my-packt-application-deployment.yaml

apiVersion: apps/v1
kind: Deployment
metadata:
```

Microservices Architecture and Containers

```
      name: my-hello-packt-application-deployment
      labels:
        app: my-hello—packt-application
  spec:
    replicas: 3
    selector:
      matchLabels:
        app: my-hello-packt-application
    template:
      metadata:
        labels:
          app: my-hello-packt-application
      spec:
        containers:
        - name: my-hello-packt-application
          image: repository-hub.packthub.example.com/my-hello-packt-application:1.1
          ports:
          - containerPort: 8080
```

In this example code, we have carried out the following steps:

1. We have created a deployment named `my-hello-packt-application-deployment`, indicated by the `.metadata.name` field
2. This deployment creates three replicated pods, which is shown in the replicas field
3. The selector field is used by the deployment module to identify which pod to manage
4. The template field contains the following sub fields:
    - The pods are labeled `app: my-hello-packt-application-deployment` using the labels field
    - The pod template's specification, or the `.template.spec` field, indicates that the pods run on one container, `my-hello-packt-application`, which runs the NGINX Docker hub image Version 1.7.9
    - We have created one container and named it `my-hello-packt-application-deployment` using the name field
    - We have run the `my-hello-packt-deployment` image Version 1.1
    - We have opened port `8080` so that the container can send and accept traffic

Chapter 2

Let's take a look at the following steps that show how to create or deploy services using the previously mentioned configuration file:

1. To create this deployment, run the following command:

   ```
   kubectl create -f my-hello-packt-application-deployment.yaml
   ```
   OR
   ```
   kubectl apply -f my-hello-packt-application-deployment.yaml
   ```

   It would be useful to read more about imperative or declarative object configuration on the Kubernetes website, as both commands are accepted by the `kubectl` command to deploy new contents on the cluster. Refer to this link for more details: `https://kubernetes.io/docs/concepts/overview/object-management-kubectl/declarative-config/`.

2. We can append the `--record` to this command to record the current command in the annotations of the created or updated resource. This is useful for future reviews, such as investigating which commands were executed in each deployment revision.

3. Next, run `kubectl` to get the deployments. The results will look as follows:

4. When you check your deployments in your Kubernetes cluster, the following fields are shown:
   - `NAME`: The deployment name
   - `DESIRED`: The desired number of replicas of our application
   - `CURRENT`: The number of replicas currently running
   - `UP-TO-DATE`: The number of replicas that have been updated to get the desired state
   - `AVAILABLE`: The number of replicas of the application are available to our users
   - `AGE`: The amount of time that the application has been running

5. To see the `rollout status deployment`, run the following `kubectl` command:

    ```
    kubectl rollout status deployment/my-hello-packt-application-deployment
    ```

    This command will show the `rollout status` of the `kubectl apply` command. It will also show you the number of desired pods. In the following screenshot, you will notice that it has created three replica sets, which are all up to date, with the corresponding provided `YAML` file:

Then, run the following command a few seconds later:

```
kubectl get deployments
```

In the following output, we can see that the deployment created three replicas:

7. To see the **ReplicaSet (rs)** created by the deployment, run the following command:

    ```
    kubectl get rs
    ```

    The ReplicaSet is always shown or formatted as follows:

    ```
    [DEPLOYMENT-NAME]-[POD-TEMPLATE-HASH-VALUE].
    ```

8. Hash values are auto-generated during deployment. The following screenshot shows the dynamically generated value. Run the following command to get the auto-generated label for the `pods`:

    ```
    kubectl get pods --show-labels
    ```

The following output is returned:

```
NAME                                                      READY   STATUS    RESTARTS   AGE   LABELS
my-hello-packt-application-deployment-2035384211-7ci7o    1/1     Running   0          18s   app=my-hello-packt-application,pod-template-hash=203
my-hello-packt-application-deployment-2035384211-kssei    1/1     Running   0          18s   app=my-hello-packt-application,pod-template-hash=203
my-hello-packt-application-deployment-2035384211-qqmn     1/1     Running   0          18s   app=my-hello-packt-application,pod-template-hash=203
```

Code as function deployment

In this section, we're going to show you some examples of FaaS like solutions. We will look at two examples of the Apex tool and one example of the Serverless tool.

Example 1 – the Apex deployment tool

Apex projects are made up of a `project.json` configuration file and might have one or more AWS Lambda functions defined in the `functions` directory. An example file structure looks as follows:

```
-project.json
-functions
├── bar
│   ├── function.json
│   └── index.js
└── foo
    ├── function.json
    └── index.js
```

The `project.json` file defines the project-level configuration that applies to all functions and defines the dependencies. In this simple example, we can use the following command:

```
{ "name": "packt-example", "description": "Example Packt project"}
```

Each function uses a `function.json` configuration file to define function-specific properties, such as the runtime, the amount of memory allocated, and the timeout. This file is completely optional, as you can specify defaults in your `project.json` file. The following code snippet shows an example of the properties in the form of a key value pair. We use these properties to define a function:

```
{
    "name": "packt-bar",
```

```
            "description": "Packt Node.js example function",
            "runtime": "nodejs4.3",
            "memory": 128,
            "timeout": 5,
            "role": "arn:aws:iam::293503197324:role/lambda"
    }
```

The directory structure for your project would look as follows:

```
-project.json
-functions
├── packt-bar
│   └── index.js
└── foo
    └── index.js
```

In Node.js, the source code for the functions themselves look as follows:

```
console.log('start packt-bar')exports.handle = function(e, ctx) {
ctx.succeed({ hello: e.name })}
```

Apex operates at the project level, but many commands allow you to specify specific functions. For example, you can deploy the entire project with a single command:

```
$ apex deploy
```

Alternatively, we can white list functions to deploy:

```
$ apex deploy foo packt-bar
```

We can invoke or call a function using the following method. Here, we are passing a name to the pipe, and `apex` invokes our function. The output is shown as `"hello": "Tobi"`:

```
$ echo '{ "name": "Tobi" }' | apex invoke packt-bar

Output:
{
    "hello": "Tobi"
}
```

Example 2 – the Apex deployment tool

In this second example, we will demonstrate how to deploy all functions, specific functions, and function deployment, using wild card sign where it will include all matching functions from the mentioned directory.

Deploy all functions in the current directory:

```
$ apex deploy
```

Deploy all functions in the directory `~/dev/myapp`:

```
$ apex deploy -C ~/dev/myapp
```

Deploy specific functions:

```
$ apex deploy auth
$ apex deploy auth api
```

Deploy all functions that have a name starting with `auth`:

```
$ apex deploy auth*
```

Deploy all functions ending with `_reporter`:

```
$ apex deploy *_reporter
```

Deploy from an existing `zip` file:

```
$ apex build auth > /tmp/auth.zip
$ apex deploy auth --zip /tmp/auth.zip
```

Example 3 – the Serverless deployment tool

Serverless is widely used by enterprises working in this domain. We have provided examples of both Apex and Serverless for your reference. Make sure Serverless is installed, and then install the Serverless command-line. We can then call it using Serverless or using the alias name of the `sls` command.

> Check for the Serverless configuration file at: https://github.com/serverless/serverless/tree/master/lib/plugins/create/templates/aws-python.

There are two important files that you have to configure while working with the Serverless command:

- `serverless.yml`: This contains details about how to deploy the `serverless` function. This file is used by the `sls/serverless` command.
- `handler.py`: This file contains the actual function code. Your function will be defined here.

The `sls` command can be used as a shortcut for `serverless` as shown here:

```
$ sls
```

The following steps demonstrate how to create and deploy a service using the Serverless tool:

1. **Create a service**: This command is used to create a service template so that we can write our functionality. With the `sls create` command, we can specify `aws-python`, among other available templates. In this example, we are going to use `aws-python` with the `--template` or shorthand `-t` flag. The `--path` or shorthand `-p` is used to update the path where the template service file will be created:

   ```
   # sls create --template aws-python --path my-service
   ```

2. **Deploy the function**: The following code will deploy the function to AWS Lambda based on the configuration that you created in the `serverless.yml` file:

   ```
   # sls deploy
   ```

3. **Invoke the deployed function**: The `sls invoke` command is used run the function. The `--` function or the shorthand `-f` can be used to mention the function name:

   ```
   # sls invoke -f hello
   ```

In your Terminal window, you should see the following response from AWS Lambda:

```
{
    "status Code": 200,
    "body": "{\"message\":\"Go Serverless v1.0! Your function executed successfully!\",\"input\":{}}"
}
```

Congratulations! You have now deployed and run your first `Hello World` function!

Virtual platform-based deployment using Jenkins or TeamCity

If we have a cloud-based Instance such as AWS EC2 or a virtual machine such as VMware VM or Window's Hyper-V server, we can use Jenkins as a deployment tool instead of others such as GoCD or TeamCity. We can use Jenkins in many different ways, for both normal jobs and for complex pipeline-based deployment jobs.

Jenkins jobs can either be configured manually or we can use a Jenkins's **descriptive scripting language (DSL)** language that is one of the modified groovy forms, and normally you will find it in form of `Jenkinsfile` in your project. The following steps give a brief overview of how to create a new Jenkins job for deployment:

1. Configure Jenkins jobs using Jenkin's DSL or using pure groovy language, and call the following script from your `Jenkinsfile`.
2. Write your deployment steps using a traditional scripting language such as Bash or Python.
3. The previous two steps will do your most of the work for deployment, and your script steps will define what exactly you would like to achieve in your Jenkins job.
4. Finally, run your Jenkins deployment jobs.

We aren't showing these steps with screenshots, as there are many examples that can easily be searched for on the internet. We have a Jenkins-based deployment example in `Chapter 4`, *DevOps as a Service*, so that you can refer to how to configure and deploy using Jenkins.

Microservices using Spring Boot and the RESTful framework

The code bases of different companies often grow exponentially and increase in complexity. In a monolithic process, we have multiple independent development teams. These teams are not actually that independent at all; they simultaneously work on the same code bases and change the same sections of code. It is tough for new developers to contribute to the business, and the development process is slow. Because of this, we have seen a gradual shift toward microservices.

The following diagram shows the microservice container, the business logic image container, the data access layer container, and, in total, a working model of a microservice-based distributed model:

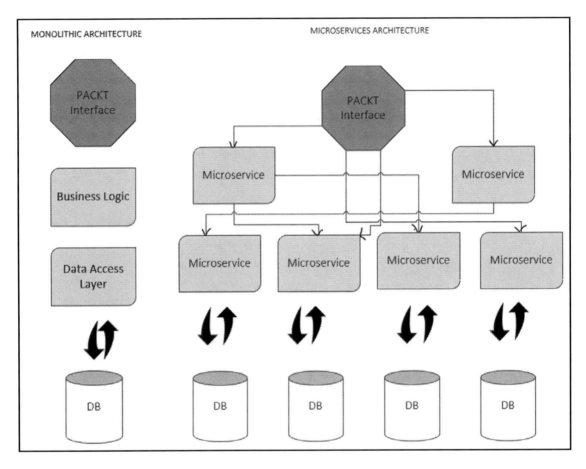

The Spring Framework is an enterprise Java framework that lets us write enterprise Java applications. Spring Boot is the way in which we can bootstrap, or quickly start, a simple Spring application. We can also build more complex applications quickly using Spring Boot. It allows us to create a production-ready application easily.

Let's think about what Spring Boot actually is. Spring is something we are already familiar with, that is, a framework to create enterprise Java applications. It is a huge framework and has a lot of different functionalities. Boot is something that enables you to bootstrap a Spring Framework. The official definition found at https://spring.io/ states: *Spring Boot makes it easy to create stand-alone, production-grade spring-based applications that you can run.*

Let's talk about primary characteristics of Spring Boot:

- **Convention over configuration:** Spring Boot has certain default configurations that can be used in applications. If necessary, we can change these according to our requirements, but these default configurations make building applications with Spring Boot much faster. There is often no configuration necessary. Let's look at an example: if we had 100 different things to do to configure something, we can often use the default configuration for 80% of those tasks.
- **Stand-alone:** Typically, when you build Spring applications, you are building a war file or a web application that you are going to deploy over Tomcat or any container or application server. With Spring Boot, however, what you get are stand-alone applications that you can run directly. You don't need to use any application servers or containers for deployments.
- **Production ready:** We don't need to do anything else to make microservices ready for production.

Jersey Framework

Jersey is an open source framework developed by Oracle. It is the official reference implementation of JAX-RS API, which is very similar to Apache CFX. On the server side, Jersey provides a servlet implementation that scans through the predefined classes we define to identified the restful resources. In the `web.xml` file, which is the deployment file for web applications, we can configure either the restful servlet or the jersey servlet.

Jersey provides the implementation of the client library, which is fully compliant with the JAX-RS API. It also provides several tools for security such as authorization or bean validation. Furthermore, it allows us to integrate testing for container deployments. The current version of Jersey is 2.27. You can learn more about Jersey by going to its official website at `http://jersey.java.net`.

For Spring integration, we have to add the `jersey-spring4` dependency, as follows:

```
<dependency>
<groupId>org.glassfish.jersey.ext</groupId>
<artifactId>jersey-spring4</artifactId>
<version>2.26</version>
</dependency>
```

Let's take a look at a basic example of how to implement the Jersey framework:

```
public class SimpleTest extends JerseyTest
{
    @Path("hello")
    public static class HelloResource
{
    @GET

public String getHello()
{
return "Hello World!";
  }
}
@Override
protected Application configure()
{
return new ResourceConfig(HelloResource.class);
  }
@Test
public void test()
{
Response response = target("hello").request().get();
String hello = response.readEntity(String.class);
assertEquals("Hello World!", hello);
response.close();
}
}
```

The web request from `projectURL/hello/` will match `Hello World!`, via `@Path("/hello")`.

Representational State Transfer (REST)

This is used for the purpose of data communication across web APIs. The REST API works pretty much in the same way as a website: you make a call from the client to the server and get a HTTP response back. REST uses HTTP methods to interact with the client and the server. REST allows a variety of data formats such as JSON or XML. It is generally faster and uses less bandwidth. It is also easy to integrate with other applications.

Commonly used HTTP methods in REST APIs include the following:

- `GET`: This is used for retrieving a data through APIs. It is a read-only method. It is safe to use duplicate `GET` methods.
- `PUT`: This is used to change or update a data using APIs. It is a write method, and we can use duplicate `PUT` methods.
- `POST`: This is used to create or insert data. It is a write method.
- `DELETE`: This is used to remove a particular piece of data.

Any web service that uses a REST architecture is called a RESTful API or a REST API.

Let's take an example of a Packt Publishing application developed with a microservices architecture. In this example, each microservice is focused on single business capability. `PacktBookBase`, `PacktAuthorBase`, `PacktReaderBase`, and `PacktBookBase` each have their instance (server) and communicate with one another. In the startup of Spring Boot, we need to add the following dependencies:

```
<parent>
<groupId>org.springframework.boot</groupId>
<artifactId>spring-boot-starter-
parent</artifactId><version>1.2.0.RELEASE</version>
</parent>
<dependencies>
<dependency>
<groupId>org.springframework.boot</groupId>
<artifactId>spring-boot-starter-web</artifactId>
</dependency>
<dependency>
<groupId>org.springframework.boot</groupId>
<artifactId>spring-boot-starter-jersey</artifactId>
</dependency>
</dependencies>
```

To enable the discovery client, we should add the preceding annotation to the `PacktPubApplication` class. This will make the service discoverable by the client.

The `PacktPubApplication` class will look as follows:

```
package com.example.demo;
import org.springframework.boot.SpringApplication;
import org.springframework.boot.autoconfigure.SpringBootApplication;
@EnableDiscoveryClient
@SpringBootApplication

public class PacktPubApplication
```

```
{
  public static void main(String[] args)
  {
     SpringApplication.run(PacktPubApplication.class, args);
  }
}
```

The preceding class will be the same for both the `PacktAuthorBase` and the `PacktReaderBase` projects since `PacktBookBase` consumes these services.

The class to use in the `PacktAuthorBase` project is as follows. This will be our REST service to search the authors:

```
package com.example.demo;
import javax.inject.Named;
import org.glassfish.jersey.server.ResourceConfig;
import org.springframework.context.annotation.Bean;
import org.springframework.context.annotation.Configuration;
import org.springframework.web.client.RestTemplate;

@Configuration

public class PacktPubApplication
{
 @Named
 static class JerseyConfig extends ResourceConfig
 {
   public JerseyConfig()
   {
     this.packages("com.example.demo");
   }
 }
 @Bean
 public RestTemplate restTemplate()
 {
   RestTemplate restTemplate = new RestTemplate();
   return restTemplate;
 }
}
```

Let's create our first service, `PackAuthorBase`, which basically gives us all the details about the author, along with their email IDs. Later, we call this `PackAutherBase` service through our mail service, `PackBookBase`. Let's see what it looks like:

```
package com.example.demo;
import java.util.ArrayList;
import java.util.List;
import javax.inject.Named;
import javax.ws.rs.GET;
import javax.ws.rs.Path;
import javax.ws.rs.Produces;
import javax.ws.rs.QueryParam;
import javax.ws.rs.core.MediaType;
@Named
@Path("/")

public class PacktAuthorBase
{
   private static List<Author> clients = new ArrayList<Author>();
static
{
    Author Author1 = new Author();
    Author1.setId(1);
    Author1.setName("PackAuthor 1");
    Author1.setEmail("Author1@hotmail.com");
    Author Author2 = new Author();
    Author2.setId(2);
    Author2.setName("PackAuthor 2");
    Author2.setEmail("Author2@hotmail.com");
    clients.add(Author1);
    clients.add(Author2);
}
@GET
@Produces(MediaType.APPLICATION_JSON)

public List<Author> getClientes()
{
    return clients;
}

@GET
@Path("Author")
@Produces(MediaType.APPLICATION_JSON)

public Author getCliente(@QueryParam("id") long id)
{
```

```java
            Author cli = null;
            for (Author a : clients)
              {
                  if (a.getId() == id)
                  cli = a;
              }
              return cli;
        }
    }
```

Now, let's create a new class called the `Reader` class, which will help the reader to search for books through their `id`, `sku`, or `description`. The reader class will look as follows:

```java
package com.example.demo;

public class Reader
{
    private long id;
    private String sku;
    private String description;

public long getId()
{
    return id;
}
public void setId(long id)
{
    this.id = id;
}
public String getSku()
{
    return sku;
}
public void setSku(String sku)
{
    this.sku = sku;
}
public String getDescription()
{
    return description;
}
public void setDescription(String description)
  {
    this.description = description;
  }
}
```

Chapter 2

Let's create one more service, `PacktReaderBase`, which will have all the readers' data, along with their ID, sku, and description. Here, we import a few predefined namespaces such as `core.MediaType` to get a list of media types, `QueryParams` (to integrate the URI query parameter into our method), the arraylist, and other namespaces:

```
package com.example.demo;
import java.util.ArrayList;
import java.util.List;
import javax.inject.Named;
import javax.ws.rs.GET;
import javax.ws.rs.Path;
import javax.ws.rs.Produces;
import javax.ws.rs.QueryParam;
import javax.ws.rs.core.MediaType;
@Named
@Path("/")
public class PacktReaderBase
{
private static List<Reader> Readers = new ArrayList<Reader>();
static
  {
     Reader reader1 = new Reader();
     reader1.setId(1);
     reader1.setSku("packpub1");
     reader1.setDescription("Reader1");
     Reader reader2 = new Reader();
     reader2.setId(2);
     reader2.setSku("packpub2");
     reader2.setDescription("Reader2");
     Readers.add(reader1);
     Readers.add(reader2);
}
@GET
@Readers(MediaType.APPLICATION_JSON)

public List<Reader> getProdutos()
  {
     return Readers;
  }
@GET
@Path(Reader)
@Readers(MediaType.APPLICATION_JSON)

public Reader getProduto(@QueryParam("id") long id)
{
    Reader prod = null;
    for (Reader r : re)
```

[65]

```
    {
        if (r.getId() == id)
            prod = r;
    }
  return prod;
 }
}
```

Let's create our main class that will consume all the other services called `PacktBookBase` as follows:

```
package com.example.demo;
import java.util.Date;
import javax.inject.Inject;
import javax.inject.Named;
import javax.ws.rs.GET;
import javax.ws.rs.Path;
import javax.ws.rs.Produces;
import javax.ws.rs.QueryParam;
import javax.ws.rs.core.MediaType;
import org.springframework.web.client.RestTemplate;
@Named
@Path("/")

public class PacktBookBase
{
    private static long id = 1;
    @Inject
    private RestTemplate restTemplate;
@GET
@Path("book")
@Produces(MediaType.APPLICATION_JSON)

public book submitbook(@QueryParam("idAuthor") long idAuthor,
@QueryParam("idProduct") long idProduct,
@QueryParam("amount") long amount)
{
    book book = new book();
    Author Author = restTemplate.getForObject
       ("http://localhost:9001/Author?id={id}", Author.class,idAuthor);
    Reader reader = restTemplate.getForObject
       ("http://localhost:9002/reader?id={id}", Reader.class,idProduct);
    book.setAuthor(Author);
    book.setReader(Reader);
    book.setId(id);
    book.setAmount(amount);
    book.setbookDate(new Date());
    id++;
```

Chapter 2

```
        return book;
    }
}
```

We have now completed the coding part, so let's try to run this application and test it. First, we need to start our REST services. Start the `PacktAuthorBase` service on port 9001, the `PacktReaderBase` in 9002, and the `PacktBookBase` on port 9003. We need to verify the following ports and see whether they are running:

- Dserver.port=9001
- Dserver.port=9002

After restarting the services, open the browser or Postman to test our code. We can test the `PacktAuthorBase` service by going through the following link:

http://localhost:9001/

This will return the response in JSON format, as follows:

```
[{"id":1,"name":"PackAuthor 1","email":"Author1@hotmail.com"},{"id":2,"name":"PackAuthor 2","email":"Author2@hotmail.com"}}]
```

As you can see, the response consists of all the registered authors as per our code base. It shows that the `PacktAuthorBase` service is working properly. We can also test this service by another method, where we can only return one particular author's details, as follows:

http://localhost:9001/Author?id=2

This returns a JSON with the author's data:

```
{
"id":2,
"name":"PackAuthor 2",
"email":"Author2@hotmail.com"
}
```

Similarly, to test whether the `PacktReaderBase` service is functioning properly, call the following URL:

http://localhost:9002/

Microservices Architecture and Containers

This produces the following result in JSON:

```
[{"id":1,"item":"packpub1","Description":"Reader1"},{"id":2,"item":"packpub
2","Description":"Reader2"}}]
```

Let's test the functionality of our final service: `PacktBookBase`. We will make an API call to get the author whose ID is **2**, the product with an ID of **1**, and the amount of **4**:

```
http://localhost:9003/book?idAuthor=2&idProduct=3&amount=4
```

We produce the following JSON, which represents the header of a book:

```
{"id":1,"amount":4,"bookDate":1419530726399,"Author":{"id":2,"name":"PackAu
thor
2","email":"Author2@hotmail.com"},"reader":{"id":1,"sku":"packpub1","Descri
ption":"Reader1"}
```

With a simple but powerful implementation, Spring Boot is a good option to implement a microservices architecture.

Deploying the Spring Boot application

To deploy the Spring Boot application, you need to have knowledge of MVN and Tomcat servlets. MVN will be used for building the Web Application Resource or the **Web Application Archive (WAR)** file, and Apache Tomcat is our application server. Let's see how we can install the Spring Boot application in the application servers:

```
# Download Tomcat 9.0.13 latest version using below commands:

PacktPub$ curl -O
http://www-us.apache.org/dist/tomcat/tomcat-9/v9.0.13/bin/apache-tomcat-9.0
.13.tar.gz
 % Total % Received % Xferd Average Speed Time Time Time Current
 Dload Upload Total Spent Left Speed
100 9112k 100 9112k 0 0 799k 0 0:00:11 0:00:11 --:--:-- 1348k

# Extract it and provide sufficient permissions.

$ tar -xvzf apache-tomcat-9.0.13.tar.gz

# Maven clean and package everything into a WAR file.

$ mvn clean package

# Copy WAR created by MVN to Tomcat/webapp, we are renaming WAR to
 springbootcode.war
```

```
$ cp target/PacktPub-spring-boot-example.war apache-
tomcat-9.0.13/webapps/springbootcode.war

# Start Tomcat like below

$ ./apache-tomcat-9.0.13/bin/startup.sh
Using CATALINA_BASE: /Users/springbootcode/projects/PacktPub-spring-boot-
example/apache-tomcat-9.0.13
Using CATALINA_HOME: /Users/springbootcode/projects/PacktPub-spring-boot-
example/apache-tomcat-9.0.13
Using CATALINA_TMPDIR: /Users/springbootcode/projects/PacktPub-spring-boot-
example/apache-tomcat-9.0.13/temp
Using JRE_HOME:
/Library/Java/JavaVirtualMachines/jdk1.8.0_74.jdk/Contents/Home
Using CLASSPATH: /Users/springbootcode/projects/PacktPub-spring-boot-
example/apache-tomcat-9.0.13/bin/bootstrap.jar:
/Users/springbootcode/projects/PacktPub-spring-boot-example/apache-
tomcat-9.0.13/bin/tomcat-juli.jar
Tomcat started.
```

Monitoring the microservices

Monitoring is always a crucial part of managing any application. When we talk about how we can monitor microservices, however, there are several unique challenges to consider. In a monolithic architecture, we have one common build or library for all the services deployed in a couple of application servers that may have had dependencies across other libraries. In this section, we'll focus on the changes required to monitor an application in production more efficiently.

We can monitor, maintain, and operate containers using Kubernetes. We need to enable application insights to see what's running inside the container. Here, we can set the alerts on the performance of the service, rather than the performance of the container. As we are using the cloud, we need to set up our infrastructure according to our project requirements. We need to monitor our APIs, although in microservices it is easy to detect and diagnose the unhealthy nodes quicker than in monolithic systems. Every microservice may interact with other services or a backend database, so we need to enable monitoring for all loose points that could lead to application failure. We need to set up monitoring that can detect problems early. If we can implement self-healing in certain common scenarios, we can improve the uptime of an application. There are a few common metrics that we need to measure, which we'll look at in the following sections.

Application metrics

Application-level metrics enable IT teams or developers to investigate and diagnose application issues. Depending on what we know about our application, we can set up some critical metrics for monitoring. A few important application-level metrics are listed here:

- **Average application response time**: This refers to the performance of our application. In other words, it is the amount of time taken by website to return a HTTP/HTML/request to an end user. These metrics will give us a sense of the performance from the end user's side. There are many tools by which we can monitor the application response time. SolarWinds is an example of a tool that can identify the root-cause of response time issues and improve slow server and application performance:

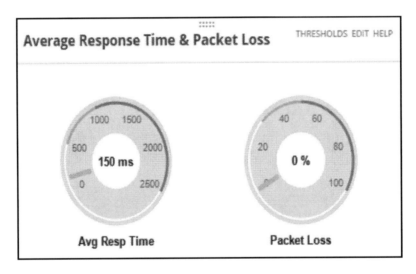

The following screenshot gives an example of the top ten application response times:

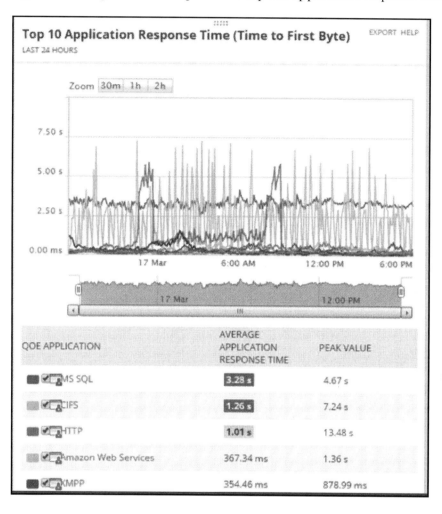

- **Peak response time**: The peak response time metric enables IT teams to identify slow elements within the application. It help to improve the overall application performance. For example, one particular element might take 10 seconds to load, while the average response time is much less than that.
- **Error rate**: This metric enables companies and IT teams to understand when the application will fail. It is expressed as a rate of error per unit. The error rate is a calculation of how many requests failed compared to the total requests.
- **Concurrent users**: This refers to the number of people using the resources within a predefined period of time. Each web server has a limit on the maximum number of concurrent users. It may correlate with the average response time because if the concurrent users increase on a web server, this will increase the average response time as well. Moreover, with an increase in concurrent users, a system will need more resources, such as bandwidth, memory or CPU cycles, depending on the hardware of the server and the type of requests that are being served.
- **Requests per second** (**RPS**): This indicates how many requests (such as web pages, images, video, audio files, or resources from databases) are being sent to the backend server every second. The average RPS rate may differ from company to company depending on how much the high load is per application. For example, content such as images or HTML (static content) is served by a web server such as Apache or NGINX. Content that needs to query the database, however, will require more resources, as it needs to connect to the web server and the backend database as well.
- **Throughput**: This is the amount of data, information, requests, and packets that pass through a system. It is a measure of how much bandwidth is required to handle concurrent users and requests. A higher throughput value is a good thing for an application, as it indicates that an application can handle an increasing number of concurrent users.

Platform metrics

This will give you insights into an applications' infrastructure, such as what the average execution time for the top databases queries was, or the top DTU/CPU consuming queries, or resource consumption by application, or average response time for each service endpoint, or each services success/failure ratio. We should set up some alerts on these metrics with high priority, as this could directly impact the user experience. We need to catch these issues/outage before customer by proactive approach. For example, we can set up some automation that will auto-scale our system resource during peak hours. This monitoring will help us understand the platform's performance.

System events

As we are aware, external forces try to compromise systems all the time. Every IT team knows that there is a strong correlation between new code changes, or new release deployments, and system errors. To investigate these issues, we need to have a log of the deployments with respect to the system and applications. We need to have correct time-series data to find out the actual root-cause of the system or deployment failure. We should record these using logs for investigative purposes.

Tools to monitor microservices

One of the best tools for monitoring microservices is AppDynamics. This allows us to monitor application performance and infrastructure and gives us code-level visibility. It is supported for all major technologies (including Java, .NET, PHP, Node.js, and NOSQL) and can be installed either on premise or as a SaaS solution. The benefits of AppDynamics are that we can view the server health and the chart application topology. This helps us find and fix performance issues by drilling down to code-level detail. It is easy to track important server metrics and trend performance and ensures that end users are not impacted by fixing bottlenecks.

Microservices Architecture and Containers

Using **APPDYNAMICS**, we can view the servers health and other metrics. It will help to find and fix performance slowness by drilling down to the code. Each application is installed with an agent. This agent works in the backend of the application and collects all the necessary dumps or metrics and forwards these to the master server. The master server presents these reports in a web browser. We can also set up alerts on these collected metrics and generate reports:

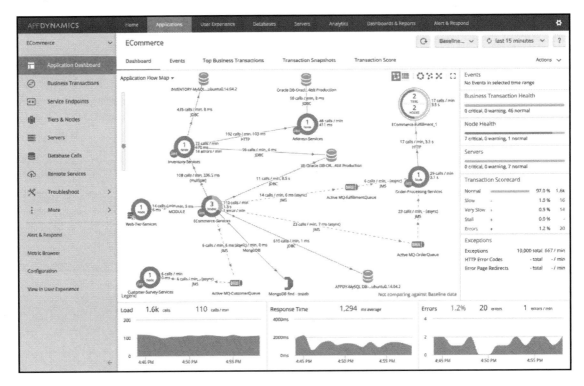

APPDYNAMICS-Application Dashboard

A couple of other tools that can be used to monitor microservices are **JFR** (free) and **Dynatrace**.

In the following section, we are going to cover some of the most frequently asked questions about microservices and what they are like.

Important facts about microservices

Let's take a look at the following facts, which can give us a clearer picture of microservices.

Microservices in the current market

There are multiple reasons why, at this moment, people are starting to focus more on microservices architecture than monolithic architecture and even **service-oriented architecture** (**SOA**). This is because microservices have the following advantages:

- The ability to respond to change quickly
- Domain-driven design
- The availability of automated test tools
- The availability of release and deployment tools
- The availability of on-demand hosting technology
- The availability of on-line cloud services
- The ability to embrace new technology
- Reliability
- The availability of asynchronous communication technology
- The availability of simpler server-side and client-side technology

When to stop designing microservices

Designing microservices can often feel more like an art than a science. There is lots of general advice available in the domain, but at times this can be too abstract. Let's quickly list some important points:

- Microservices should not share their databases with another microservice.
- They should be limited to a number of database tables.
- We need to make sure we have either built our microservices as stateful or stateless. Alternatively, we can convert stateful microservices to stateless ones by having common databases or filesystems such as shared RDS, AWS, EFS, or NFS-like systems.
- We should consider all the required inputs for the microservice before writing the microservice code and running the application.
- The output should be a single source of truth.

Can the microservice format be used to divide teams into small or micro teams?

This might be a bit off topic, but it can be a fun way to get to know the technology a bit further. Let's think about the recent "two pizzas rule" introduced by Jeff Bezos, the CEO of Amazon, which indicates the maximum number of people that should be present in a meeting. You can refer to the following link to understand more about the two pizzas rule: `https://www.businessinsider.in/The-two-pizza-rule-is-Amazon-CEO-Jeff-Bezos-secret-to-productive-meetings/articleshow/59026121.cms`. This showcases that the concept of microservices is also applicable in a workplace environment to help keep a team be more focused.

Over the last 15 years, code bases have expanded rapidly and increased in complexity due to newer technology and distributed environments such as message queues, asynchronous calls, containers, and so on. Many organizations choose to move to a microservices-based architecture, which makes it easier to replace and upgrade any components without having any impact on the customer.

Microservices versus SOA

Microservices and SOA are very similar architectures, and we might wonder why microservices were developed when SOA was already present. A useful explanation that clearly differentiates between SOA and microservices can be found at the following link: `https://www.bmc.com/blogs/microservices-vs-soa-whats-difference/`.

Summary

In this chapter, we have tried to cover almost everything to do with microservices, including how to design and implement them. We can design microservices according to our product specification, and we can pick different design principles, deployment technologies, languages, and techniques for our own products. We have looked at various examples using the Spring RESTful framework. Be confident and consult the guidelines mentioned in this chapter; these will make your application easy to manage, scale, and automate.

In the next `Chapter 3`, *Microservice Resiliency Patterns*, we will learn about its various approaches, best practices, optimization techniques, patterns, and algorithms, which have been recommended by **subject matter experts** (**SMEs**).

3
Microservice Resiliency Patterns

It is an overwhelmingly recognized fact that businesses across the globe can easily attain the elusive goal of reliability by putting highly reliable IT systems in place, as IT is the most direct and greatest business-enabler. However, producing reliable IT systems is beset with a number of challenges and concerns, since IT complexity is consistently on the rise due to the heightened heterogeneity and the growing multiplicity of various information technologies and tools. There have been various approaches, best practices, optimization techniques, patterns, and algorithms recommended by **subject matter experts** (**SMEs**) and accomplished architects for consistently moderating IT complexity and for producing reliable IT systems in plenty. Resiliency and elasticity are the top two ingredients for having reliable systems. In other words, business workloads and IT services have to be elegantly resilient and elastic to be reliable in their operations, offerings, and outputs. **Microservices architecture** (**MSA**) is being touted as the best way for producing mission-critical, enterprise-grade, production-ready, process-aware, event-driven, service-oriented, and people-centric applications. Furthermore, there are a bevy of innovations and improvements in the MSA space to build and deploy applications that are ingrained with availability, reliability, scalability, performance/throughput, security, simplicity, flexibility, and sustainability capabilities. In this chapter, we will focus on various microservice resiliency patterns that intrinsically and insightfully enable the design, development, debugging, delivery, and deployment of reliable systems.

In this chapter, we will cover the following topics:

- The beneficial convergence of microservices and containers
- The IT reliability challenges and solution approaches
- Microservices design, development, deployment, and operations patterns
- Microservice resiliency patterns

- Highly available microservice patterns
- Microservice API Gateway design patterns
- Patterns for application decomposition into microservices

Briefing microservices and containers

Microservices are API-enabled, self-contained, loosely coupled, and fine-grained services. MSA represents a high-level architectural style for composing microservices-centric enterprise-grade applications. MSA is a direct and distinct off-shoot of the **service oriented architecture (SOA)** paradigm to surmount the various SOA drawbacks. Luminaries and pundits, based on their vast experiences with service-oriented enterprise, embedded, and cloud applications, have brought in this new paradigm, which is rapidly sweeping the whole IT industry. MSA brings forth a number of unique business technologies and user benefits. Business systems are greatly empowered to be flexible and extensible through the incorporation of the various MSA characteristics. MSA are typically business-centric to realize next-generation business applications in a configurable, customizable, and composable manner. MSA ultimately provides the relevant capability for the swift and risk-free realization of highly reliable enterprise-class applications. Generally, a microservices-based application isolates the various business functionalities into a collection of smaller and easily manageable services. Precisely speaking, microservices are independently deployable, horizontally scalable, interoperable, composable, publicly discoverable, network-accessible, and portable. Furthermore, with the steady maturity and stability of the DevOps concept and culture in worldwide enterprises, the MSA is bound to fulfil the long-standing goals of agile application design, development, and deployment in production environments.

Microservices make complex and large-scale application design, development, and deployment easier and faster. Essentially, MSA is a proven process of developing software applications as a suite of small and independent services in which each service runs a unique application functionality in an isolated process, and communicates through a well-defined and lightweight mechanism (REST APIs). Microservices team up with one another to fulfil quickly evolving business needs. MSA is the most appropriate architectural pattern for producing next-generation mobile, enterprise, embedded, connected, and cloud applications. Microservices can be business-specific as well as agnostic to succulently cater for varying demands. There are several open source and commercial-grade frameworks, toolsets, programming languages, and accelerators to design and build microservices.

There are a few service composition (orchestration and choreography) platforms to rapidly compose process-centric and business-aware microservices. There are API Gateway and management solutions to enable correct communication between disparate and distributed microservices, and there are several powerful DevOps tools to enable the continuous integration, delivery, and deployment of microservice based applications. At the end, the cool convergence between containers and microservices is to open a number of fresh opportunities and possibilities.

A key aspect of MSA is that each microservice can have its own life cycle. Different teams situated at geographically distributed locations can independently design, develop, deploy, and manage their respective microservices. The only constraint is that they have to maintain the API compatibility to support backward and forward compatibility. Each microservice is typically owned and operated by a team of architects, designers, developers, and deployers. This autonomy and agility, when combined with continuous integration, delivery, and deployment tools, enable new and refurbished applications to be deployed very frequently (that is, several times per day). Microservices are self-contained and hence autonomous. Due to the decoupling nature, the failure of one microservice does not impact the other microservices.

The containerization paradigm

A container is typically dependent on the host's operating system/kernel to deftly get and use various compute, network, and storage resources of the host machine in an optimal manner. Containers innately use the resource isolation features of the Linux kernel, such as kernel namespaces. This namespace mechanism isolates an application's view of the operating environment, including process trees, network, user IDs, and mounted file systems. The other vital feature being directly provided by kernel is cgroups, which provides the resource limiting capability. The main resources include the CPU/cores, memory, block I/O, and network. The third feature is none other than the union-capable file system, such as AUFS and others. These together allow independent and isolated containers to run on a Linux machine. This OS virtualization phenomenon comes in handy when removing the overhead of starting and maintaining **virtual machines** (**VMs**). The sharing of OS functionalities through containerization brings forth a number of strategically sound benefits, such as enhanced resource utilization, real-time and horizontal elasticity of containerized IT infrastructures, dynamic composition of containerized microservices, and container allocation for tasks and applications.

The key differentiators of containers compared to VMs are the aspects of application packaging, reproduction, portability (containers encompassing applications can be built in an automated fashion, packaged using a standardized format, shipped across, and run anywhere), and simplicity. Containers are highly optimized and blessed with fewer footprints. An application container carries everything to run that application on any platform, and hence containers are self-defined and contained. Provisioning containers happen speedily because of the lightweight nature of containers. For achieving real-time and horizontal scalability, containers are being positioned as the best-in-class solution. Furthermore, containers are immutable infrastructures; they inherently support repeatability and guarantee better resource utilization of physical/**bare metal** (**BM**) servers. Finally, the containerization paradigm goes hand-in-hand with the quickly emerging and evolving DevOps concept. With the arrival of a number of DevOps tools, continuous integration, delivery, and deployment of containerized applications and services is being fulfilled in an automated manner. Containers come in handy when automating the core tasks of DevOps. Containers intrinsically enable better coordination and integration with the components of software engineering. Containers foster scalability, resilience, and faster deployments, and hence emerge as an important entity for embracing highly distributed application architectures. Containers are typically used in constantly changing application environments, with new or updated code being introduced or incorporated on a regular basis.

A resilient application keeps processing data and doing transactions, even when one or more components of the application fails or slows down due to various reasons and causes. Errors and any kind of deviations have to be identified proactively and preemptively to isolate and container them before making any irreparable damages to the system. That is, faults are contained within that affected component so that other components are not getting affected. Error propagation to other functional components of the system has to be stopped instantaneously, thereby one error in one part of the system does not bring down the whole system. The management and control system has to plunge into appropriate action to repair the component, or kill it to regenerate a fresh instance of that component. A system that has not been designed with resiliency in mind is bound to fail. That is, not only the underlying IT infrastructures but also the applications have to be sagaciously designed, developed, and deployed to attain the elusive goal of reliability. For the forthcoming IoT and AI-enabled digital transformation and intelligence era, reliable IT infrastructures and platforms, along with resilient business applications are the most important ingredient to attain the intended and envisaged success. Let's digress a bit and discuss why this is so.

IT reliability challenges and solution approaches

A resilient application keeps processing data and doing transactions, even when one or more components of the application fail due to an internal or external reason. That is, when a software system is under attack, the system has to find a way out to survive or to come back to the original state quickly. Therefore, it is imperative that every complicated and mission-critical system has to be designed, developed, and deployed using the most applicable resiliency properties. In other words, a system that is not designed with resiliency as the core feature is bound to fail at some point. For the forthcoming IoT, blockchain, and AI-enabled digital transformation and intelligence era, resilient IT infrastructures, platforms, and software applications are the most important ingredients to attain the intended and envisaged success. Let's digress a bit and discuss why this is so.

Highly distributed environments pose new challenges—centralized computing paves the way for decentralized and distributed computing to stock and analyze big data and for accomplishing large scale processing needs. Single servers make way for clustered, grid, and cloud servers. Even appliances and **Hyper-Converged Infrastructures** (HCI) are clubbed together to solve big-data capture, storage, and processing. But distributed computing poses several challenges. Primarily, the enigmatic dependences create a lot of problems. The dependency on third-party and other external services creates havoc. There is no 100 percent guarantee that all non co-located servers and services are functioning all the time and are responsive. We have to be mindful of the fact that each and every integration point possesses and poses one or more risks. They may fail at some point, and we have to be technologically prepared for any unexpected and unwanted failure. The lesson here is that we cannot put too much faith in an external source. Every call to third-party services or a backend database is liable to break at some point. If we fail to protect ourselves from these breaches and nuisances, our systems may ultimately become invalid and useless at some point in time. We may not be able to guarantee the **service level agreement** (SLA) and **operational level agreement** (OLA) qualities agreed with service consumers and clients.

The performance bottlenecks may come to the surface as too many disparate and distributed systems start to interact with one another to fulfil business goals. The fulfilment of various **non-functional requirements (NFRs)**/the **Quality of Service (QoS)** attributes remain the core challenges and concerns in distributed environments. Preventing cascading failures, that is, completely avoiding failure in any complicated yet sophisticated system especially IT systems is next to impossible. Therefore, we have to deftly design and empower them to be inherently able to cope with any failures and fissions and to automatically surmount them. The very key to ensure resiliency is that we need to design in such a way that a failure does not precipitate and propagate to other components and layers of the system to bring down the whole system. Any mischievous thing in a component has to be proactively and preemptively captured and contained to keep other components to do their tasks continuously. Generally speaking, there are two prominent and dominant failures: an external resource might respond with an error immediately, or it might respond slowly. Receiving an error straightaway is always preferred instead of receiving a slow response. Therefore, it is recommended to explicitly specify a time-out while calling an external resource. This enables that you get the reply quickly. If not, the request binds and strangulates the execution threads. If a time-out is not indicated, in a worst-case scenario, all the threads are blocked, resulting in disaster. The point is that any failure in one part of the system should not cascade to other parts to bring down the entire system. Employ circuit breakers—this is an important resiliency pattern. In the normal closed state, the circuit breaker executes operations as usual, and calls will be forwarded to the external resources. When a call fails to get the proper response, the circuit breaker makes a note of the failure. If the number of failures exceeds a certain limit, then the circuit breaker automatically trips and opens the circuit. That is, thereafter, no call is allowed. Calls are bound to fail immediately, without any attempt to execute the real and requested operation. After a while, the circuit breaker switches into a half-open state, wherein the next call is allowed to execute the operation. Depending on the outcome of that call, the circuit breaker either switches to the closed or to the open state again.

The following diagram illustrates everything in a vivid manner:

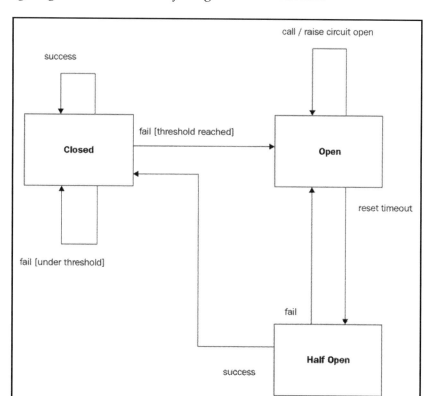

Hystrix is an open source framework that was developed by the company Netflix. This provides an implementation of the famous circuit breaker pattern. This framework helps in building resilient services. The key advantages of the circuit breaker pattern are as follows:

- Fail fast and rapid recovery
- Prevent cascading failure
- Fall-back and gracefully degrade when possible

Microservice Resiliency Patterns

The Hystrix library provides the following features:

- Implements the circuit breaker pattern
- Provides near real-time monitoring via the Hystrix stream and the Hystrix dashboard
- Generates monitoring events that can be published to external systems such as Graphite

As services are being built and released by different teams, it is not prudent to expect each service to have the same performance and reliability capabilities. Due to the dependency on other downstream services, the performance and reliability of any calling service may vary considerably. A front-facing service may be held hostage if one or more of its serving services is unable to meet their SLAs. This, in turn, would definitely impact the SLA of the calling service. This drawback finally results in a bad experience for service users. This situation is pictorially represented here:

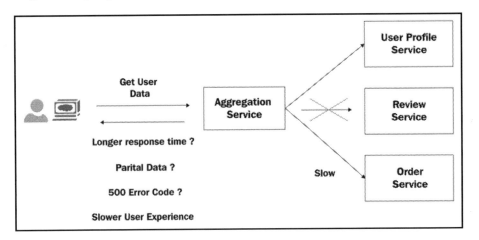

The key parameters affecting the SLAs of MSA are given as follows:

1. **Connection timeouts**: This happens when the client is unable to connect to a service within a given time frame. This may be caused due to a slow or unresponsive service.
2. **Read timeouts**: This is when the client is unable to read the results from the service within a given time frame. The service may be doing a lot of computation or using some inefficient ways to prepare data to be returned.

3. **Exceptions:** These are being caused due to the following reasons:
    - The client sends bad data to the requested service
    - The service is down, or there is an issue with the service
    - The client faces some issues while parsing the response
    - There may be some changes enacted on the service, and the client is unaware of them

Thus, implementing resilient microservices and subsequently realizing reliable software applications is beset with a number of issues. Therefore, there is an insistence on enabling patterns, easy to understand and use best practices, integrated platforms, evaluation metrics, and viable solution approaches.

The promising and potential approaches for resiliency and reliability

Resiliency patterns are good to a certain extent in providing the required resiliency. In this section, we will be focusing on the various aspects of establishing and enforcing the mandated resiliency.

MSA is the prominent way forward

With the faster proliferation of mobile, wearable, portable, nomadic, wireless, and various other I/O devices, the users are demanding ubiquitous access to various applications, services, data sources, and content. For realizing sophisticated applications, not only the pervasive access but also the easy and quick leverage of data and services is essential. That means software applications and services ought to be made available all the time. Even if there is an attack on one or more services, the system has to continuously function by tolerating all kinds of faults, failures, and mishaps. If the application is under a heavy load, then the system has to scale up or out accordingly to respond without any slowdown and breakdown. That is, system resilience and responsiveness have to be ensured through pioneering technological solutions and resiliency patterns. For this to happen innately, businesses increasingly need to move out from static, error-prone, closed, inflexible, and centralized architectures in favor of flexible, open, dynamic, distributed, and elastic systems. MSA is the way forward to realize resilient, robust, and versatile applications. Thus, MSA is one such prominent and dominant approach for realizing resilient and elastic systems.

Microservice Resiliency Patterns

Microservices layered architecture: With MSA, a single software application/functionality is achieved through a dynamic and adroit combination of multiple microservices and their purposeful interactions. Hence, the communication, coordination, collaboration, corroboration, and correlation among all the participating and contributing services is vital for a successful realization of microservices-based and multi-container applications. In the SOA era, an **enterprise service bus (ESB)**, which is a combination of several proven patterns, is adept at integrating disparate applications through the exposition of service-oriented interfaces. With the faster acceptance and adoption of MSA, the interconnectivity, enrichment, orchestration, integration, brokerage, governance, security, and intermediation capabilities of ESB get dispersed across microservices.

Therefore, some level of logical organization of the microservices-based on their granularity and responsibilities/capabilities is paramount when it comes to the implementation of various microservices. The following architecture through layering is being touted as the most competent one for the ensuing microservices era. Let's dig deeper and describe the key layers of the architecture in detail:

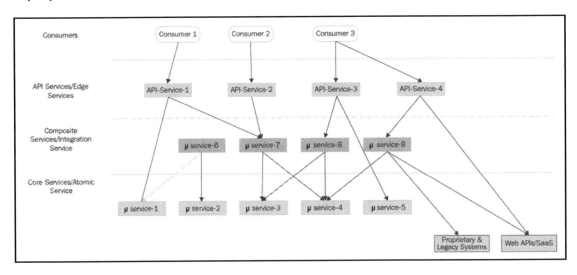

Atomic microservices: At the bottom layer, we have a dynamic pool of fine-grained and self-contained services, and these do not have any external service dependencies. These are easily findable, publicly accessible, assessable, portable, interoperable, and composable. These services mostly comprise of the business logic. The networking and communication logic details are not being incorporated in these basic and core services.

Composite microservices: Atomic microservices often cannot be used straightaway, as they are not directly implementing a business functionality. Atomic services typically follow the single purpose principle. Hence, for fulfilling a specific business functionality, multiple atomic microservices need to be identified, assessed for their unique capability, and composed. Therefore, this middle layer in the **reference architecture** (**RA**) comprises of such composite services, which are coarse-grained. Some of these composite services often contribute to integration, message enrichment, intermediation, security-enablement, transformation, orchestration, and choreography services. Also, as the resiliency aspect gains mainstream importance, the intermediary and integration services act as resiliency-enablement services. In the SOA world, ESB is the prominent and dominant middleware for enabling application integration. Now, the distinct functionalities of ESB product are being realized through the smart combination of several atomic services. There are several patterns of integration, resiliency, scalability, and availability. These composite services implement these special patterns to automate several techniques and solutions.

API services: Some services are ordained as API or edge services. These are designated as special kinds of composite services. These are part of the growing microservices ecosystem as API life cycle management services. They have routing capabilities. These take care of API versioning, security, and throttling. They apply monetization and create API compositions. Microservice architecture brings in a lot of flexibility and simplicity with application development and deployment, but it introduces a new complexity. That is, due to their dense nature, service communication and collaboration have to be adroitly controlled. Also, handling transactions in this architecture is also a complex affair. This architecture leads to the era of the service web. The futuristic web will consist of several types of services and each service finds, binds, and talks to one or more of the other services to bring forth bigger and better things.

A microservices architecture is depicted in the following diagram:

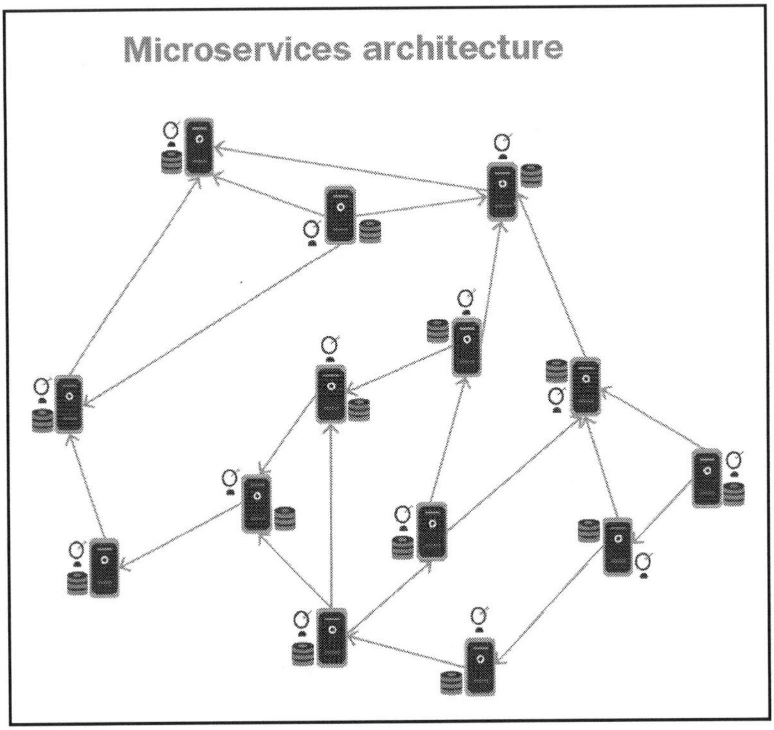

Microservices architecture

The MSA pattern is the powerful solution for producing and running enterprise-grade applications, and the architecture is being stuffed with everything that is needed to produce resiliency, responsive, message-driven, and elastic microservices. Microservices is the most powerful building block for constructing fine-grained and highly reusable services.

Integrated platforms are the need of the hour for resiliency

This is the second contributing element to fulfilling the elusive resiliency. When monolithic and massive applications are partitioned via the microservice architecture pattern, the number of microservices is definitely on the higher side for every software application. When we have microservices in a large number, the software complexity is bound to increase. The complexity mitigation techniques are given prime importance. The only possible way to manage rising complexity is to embark on platform-assisted and augmented automation.

There are a bunch of resiliency patterns such as timeout, bulkhead, and circuit breaker. It is hard to make an application resilient, responsive, self-healing, stable, and anti-fragile by leveraging microservices alone. We need competent platforms as well. To arrive at a truly resilient and adaptive application architecture, we need isolation, external monitoring, measurement and management, and autonomous decision-making capabilities fulfilled at service and platform levels. These principal requirements can be met through path-breaking and insightful platforms.

The issues with the bulkhead pattern: The bulkhead pattern is not about thread pools alone. The core concept of this pattern is to isolate the various elements of an application into pools so that if one element fails to take off, then the other elements do not get affected. There are multiple levels at which the famous bulkhead pattern can be applied, as illustrated in the following diagram. We have written about the open source Hystrix framework earlier. Thread pools with Hystrix are the starting point:

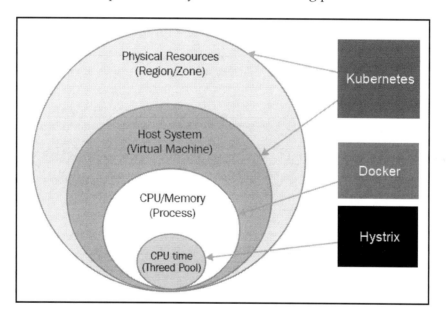

Hystrix extensively uses thread pools to ensure that the CPU time dedicated to an application process is better distributed among and used by the different threads of the application. This will prevent a CPU-intensive failure from going beyond a thread pool. Further on, this arrangement enables that other parts of the service still get some that CPU time to continue with their assignment. But there are other types of application failures, and they could not be attended through thread pools. The well-known failures include memory leaks in the application, some sort of infinite loop, and a fork bomb. These failures cannot be accommodated through thread pools.

The issues with the circuit breaker pattern: We have written about this resiliency pattern in detail. This pattern is very famous because it has the important characteristics and capability for auto-recovery and self-healing. But a circuit breaker can only protect and recover from failures related to service communications and interactions. To completely recover from other kinds of the failures (memory leaks, infinite loops, and fork bombs), we need some other means of performing failure detection, containment, and self-healing.

Isolation is the key: For surmounting these kinds of unique and catastrophic failures, the best way forward mooted by experts is to bring isolation. There are services and their instances spread across multiple bare metal servers, VMs, and containers. The service and resource isolation are what we want to achieve the resiliency goals. The approach here is we ought to guarantee the much-needed isolation of different microservices and their instances through containers. This isolation comes in handy when isolating and containing all kinds of anticipated and unanticipated errors and faults. The next step is to protect VMs and container hosts. In a cloud environment, VMs are dynamic. If something happens to a VM, all the service instances running on the VM also vanish. This means that the same service instance has to be replicated across multiple VMs within the same bare-metal server and across multiple bare-metal servers. This arrangement sharply enhances the service's availability and auditability. Next in line are the ways and means of arresting hardware failures. If a BM server goes down, then all the VMs and containers running on it are bound to collapse together. Herein, the aspect of data and disaster recovery surfaces, and this is done through distributed yet networked cloud centers.

External monitoring and autonomous decision making capabilities: Apart from the isolation facility, we need to have a few more proven mechanisms in place to precisely monitor, measure, and manage external systems. In the increasingly connected and distributed environment, dependencies can cause irreparable losses. Thus, the precise monitoring of all external services continuously come in handy in establishing and ensuring the much-needed resiliency. The real-time operational, performance, and log details of the external and third-party services enable requesting services to take appropriate decisions in time. We know that microservices are self-contained to be autonomous in their functions, and yet there is a need for empowering microservices to take their own decisions in time. This is regarded as one of the key points for making resilient microservices.

The integrated platform approach: Competent platforms are the need of the hour for arresting failures and guaranteeing resiliency by leveraging the competencies such as service isolation, consistent monitoring of external services and resources, and empowering autonomous decision-making. For containerized clouds, a container orchestrator, such as Google's Kubernetes, can spread the service instances on multiple nodes using an anti-affinity feature. Even further, the widely insisted anti-affinity requirement can spread service instances across hardware racks, availability zones, and regions. This setup is designed to sharply reduce a wider variety of failures.

The health check is another important requirement. Every hardware and software system has to be continuously checked for its health. Any unhealthy system can damage the SLAs. The health check feature is, therefore, being incorporated in popular management platforms. For example, the Kubernetes platform, which has the "liveness and readiness probes" minutely monitors and detects failures in the services and restarts them if there is a need for it. This is a powerful feature, as it allows scores of polyglot and containerized services to be proactively monitored in a unified way. If there is a need, they can be recovered in a uniform manner. Restarting a service is a way out for service recovery only, but Kubernetes has the innate capability to do auto-scaling to strengthen and guarantee the service availability. Health checks, service restart, and auto-scaling can deal with individual service failures. But if the whole node or even the server rack fails, then the Kubernetes schedule kicks in immediately and places the services on a functioning host that has the capacity and capability to run the services comfortably.

The other important need is to have system software that can self-heal from any kinds of failures. The point to be noted here is that we need more than what a circuit breaker does. That is the reason there is an insistence on integrated and insightful platforms toward fulfilling resiliency needs. A bevy of tools and engines in Kubernetes facilitate container management and orchestration. The resource isolation, health check, killing, and starting containers on an as-needed basis, the optimal placement of containers in hosts, auto-scaling functionalities and facilities, and so on, are also provided by the Kubernetes platform to simplify and streamline the ideals of resiliency. These platform-supported capabilities do help in achieving application resiliency, self-healing, and, most importantly, antifragility.

In a similar fashion, the responsibility of implementing other relevant patterns such as timeouts, retries, and circuit breaking is being shifted from the application on to the platform. However, there are certain features that are not yet part of the Kubernetes platform. Having considered the importance of incorporating these features, product companies came out with a new solution type called a *service mesh*. This is a software framework for facilitating the resiliency aspect. There are a couple of service mesh implementations. The prominent ones include Istio and Linkerd. Typical service mesh solutions bring on additional capabilities in enhancing the resiliency of microservices.

Istio, the most popular service mesh solution, is emerging as an open source platform facilitating the integration of microservices, the traffic management across microservices, the enforcement of policies, the aggregation of telemetry data, and so on. Istio has two planes: the control and data planes. The control plane is the master and management plane. It ensures policies and their changes. The control plane provides an additional abstraction layer over the underlying container clustering and orchestration management platform such as Kubernetes and others. Istio is primarily made out of the following components:

- **Envoy**: This is the data plane for Istio. This leverages the proven deployment model. That is, it can be deployed as a sidecar proxy per microservice/pod/node to elegantly handle ingress/egress traffic between services in the Kubernetes cluster. The proxy is able to manage the traffic from a service to external services. The proxies eventually helps to form a secure and reliable service mesh. This provides a dazzling array of new features/functions, such as service discovery, routing at layer 7, circuit breaking, policy establishment, and enforcement and telemetry recording/reporting functions.
- **Mixer**: This is the policy management solution. This is the central component that is used by the proxies and microservices to enforce appropriate policies such as authorization, rate limits, quotas, authentication, request tracing, and telemetry collection.
- **Pilot**: This is an important component fully responsible for configuring the proxies at runtime.
- **CA**: This is a centralized and core module that's exclusively responsible for certificate issuance and rotation.
- **Node agent**: This is a per-node component that's responsible for certificate issuance and rotation.
- **Broker**: This is a budding component stringently implementing the **open service broker (OSB)** API for Istio-based services. OSB is emerging as the broker solution standard in the cloud arena.

A service mesh solution can be deployed in two different patterns—per-host proxy deployment and sidecar proxy deployment. Through a separate chapter, we will pinpoint the various unique properties of Istio in fulfilling the resiliency goals. The service mesh solutions will shift all the network related concerns from layer 7 to layer 4/layer 5. Additional capabilities are being steadily envisioned and embedded in service mesh platforms.

In short, along with resiliency patterns, there is an important role and responsibility for integrated and advanced platforms toward producing, hosting, and delivering resilient microservices. Platforms are being stuffed with newer capabilities consistently and are being positioned as the viable and venerable approach for achieving resiliency.

The resiliency patterns for microservices: As described previously, there are several approaches and articulations for achieving resiliency. We have discussed how the MSA paradigm and orchestration platforms contribute to the realization of resilient services, which turn out to be the most important ingredient for constructing reliable applications. In this section, we will discuss the key resiliency patterns. There are some special patterns being unearthed and articulated for resiliency, and application architects have to employ them in a smart fashion toward offering resiliency.

Client resiliency patterns: These are primarily focused on protecting service clients calling remote microservices. There can be multiple service consumers, depending on the client, to get the services of one or more remote resources. The remote resource can be a third-party service or a database. When the remote resource is falling or throwing errors or an event is performing poorly, there should not be any impact on the client. That is, the client should not crash because something has gone wrong with the remote resource. The goal of these patterns is to allow the service client to fail fast so that it should not consume valuable resources such as database connections and thread pools eternally. These patterns also prevent any fault of the remote service from spreading to other client's consumers. There are four client resiliency patterns:

- Client-side load balancing
- Circuit breakers
- Fall-backs
- Bulkheads

Microservice Resiliency Patterns

These patterns are stringently implemented in the service client calling any remote resource.

Client-side load balancing: Empowers the client to have the load balancing capability and to have a deep look at the remote service and its various instances. The load balancer collects the physical locations of the remote service and its instances. The client then caches the physical location of those service instances. The service discovery agent or mechanism aids the client in getting all this useful information about the target service. Whenever a service consumer needs to call that remote service instance, the client-side load balancer returns a location from the pool of service locations. The load balancer can detect whether a service instance throws errors or behaves poorly, and if so the client-side load balancer can remove that service instance from the pool and prevent any future service calls to that failed service instance.

Circuit breaker: The circuit breaker pattern is a client resiliency pattern. With a circuit breaker in place, when a remote service is called, the circuit breaker monitors the call. If a call takes too long to fetch the response, then the circuit breaker intercedes and terminates the call to save the various resources. Furthermore, the circuit breaker pattern meticulously monitors all requests to any remote resource, and if a sufficient number of calls fails to get any response, then the circuit breaker prevents future calls to the failing remote resource.

Fall-back processing: The fall-back pattern is always used for sustaining availability. When a remote service call fails to evoke any response, typically, an exception happens. But with this pattern, the service consumer searches for and executes an alternative code path, and tries to carry out the already initiated action through some other sources. The request usually involves looking for data from another data source to complete the transaction. Otherwise, the user's request may be queued for processing at a later point in time.

Bulkheads: With the famous bulkhead design, a ship is generally partitioned into multiple completely isolated and watertight compartments called bulkheads. The idea behind this approach is that a bulkhead keeps the water confined to the area of the ship where a puncture or a problem has occurred. This setup prevents the water filling up the entire ship and saves the ship from sinking. The same concept can be applied to a service interacting with multiple remote resources to accomplish a process. The calls to different remote sources can be achieved through different thread pools. That is, there is a separate thread pool for each remote service. This sharply reduces the risk that a problem with one slow remote resource call brings down the entire application. The thread pools act as the bulkheads for the service. If one service responds slowly, then the thread pool for that type of service call becomes saturated and stops processing requests. Service calls to other services won't be affected because they are assigned to other thread pools. The following diagram clearly describes the role of all four client resiliency patterns:

Chapter 3

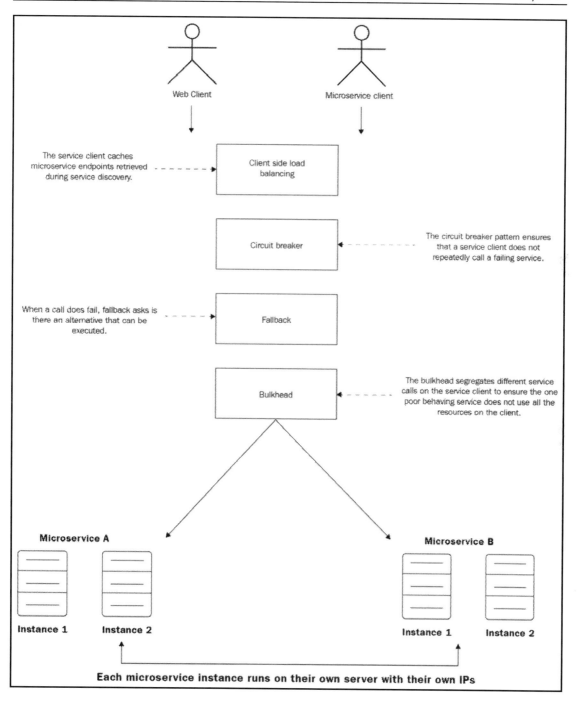

Operations patterns for microservices: The microservices model hugely simplifies and streamlines the process of modifying and deploying a constituent service in an application. But the MSA style also complicates the overall application deployment while increasing the effort of managing and maintaining a big set of services compared to the traditional application deployment. Therefore, to lessen the operational complexity of microservices, there came a few operations patterns, which were originally unearthed and popularized for conventional application management.

Service registry pattern: Microservices need to be registered in a central place to be readily and rewardingly found and bound. Microservices undergo changes frequently to absorb any technical, business, and location changes. This pattern is for avoiding hard-coding microservice endpoints so that if there is a change, requesting services still can find and use the appropriate microservice dynamically. Thus, a service registry is essential for microservices-centric applications to function without any blunder.

Correlation ID and log aggregator patterns: These patterns achieve better isolation, which simplifies debugging and deploying microservices. The correlation ID pattern enables the trace getting propagated through all the participating and contributing microservices, which are typically polyglot in nature. The log aggregator pattern complements the correlation ID pattern. This pattern allows all kinds of logs created by and captured from different microservices to be aggregated into a single and searchable entity. The trace details, along with the log insights, facilitate efficient and understandable debugging of microservices.

Circuit breaker pattern: We have already discussed this pattern. The following diagram clearly illustrates how this pattern helps to avoid the wastage of execution threads and connection pools:

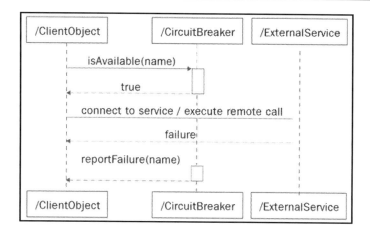

Handshaking pattern: This enables a partial state on the simple breaker that states on and off, and adds throttling to a deployed application. We can introduce throttling by asking a component whether it has the bandwidth to do more. A component that is too busy can tell clients not to assign any more work until it completes the work at hand.

Bulkhead pattern: We have discussed this pattern in detail. These are the widely known operations patterns for easing up microservices operations.

Microservices development patterns: The design principle is that a development team should produce the microservices of an application around its essential business capabilities. Microservices, individually or collectively, are for implementing one or more business functionalities. There are established norms, nomenclatures, and patterns for designing and developing microservices. We can extract microservices out of monolithic applications and refurbish them according to the requirement. That is, any legacy modernization leads to the realization of several business-centric microservices. These microservices can then be deployed in cloud environments. That is, microservices and cloud servers combine well to empower legacy applications to be cloud-enabled. On the other hand, microservices are freshly cooked up from the ground up, leveraging all the latest cloud features and these microservices, when choreographed or orchestrated, and result in production-grade applications. These applications are cloud-native. Whatever path we take, as far as the cloud adoption is concerned, the development patterns provide a basic framework and guidelines for building microservices-based applications. Interested readers can get more useful information on various microservices patterns from the IBM blogs page (`https://www.ibm.com/blogs/bluemix/2017/07/using-microservice-application-patterns/`).

Single page application (SPA) pattern: With the emergence and convergence of great browsers, faster networks, and scores of client-side languages (script and markup), we come across multifaceted yet single-page web applications. The beauty of this kind of web application is that it embeds all functionality together in a single page. These applications respond to user requests, clicks, and form inputs through dynamic service calls to various backend REST-based services. This setup updates the specific portions of the screen instead of loading and presenting an entirely new page. This application architecture often simplifies the frontend experience as more responsibility is being delegated to the backend services.

Backend for frontend (BFF) pattern: The preceding pattern works well for single-page applications for single channel users, but it delivers poor user experiences if there are different channels. Recently, we came across multiple input/output devices with different client applications and browsers. The prominent input/output devices include smartphones, handhelds, wearables, portables, such as in—vehicle infotainment devices, sensor-attached physical assets, fixed machines with human-machine interfaces, and the quickly growing ecosystem of IoT devices. This transition sometimes overloads a browser with managing multiple interactions with a growing array of asynchronous REST-based backend services. A backend for frontend pattern, therefore, has emerged and evolved as a well-intended solution approach. This pattern bats for a backend aggregator service that substantially reduces the overall number of calls from the browser. This aggregator service handles most of the communications within external backend services. That is, with an easily managed single request to the browser, a lot of things can happen at the backend silently. This pattern allows frontend teams to develop and deploy their own backend aggregator service for the BFF to handle the entirety of external service calls needed for attaining their specific user experience. The same team builds both the user experience and the BFF, often in the same language, leading to an overall increase in application performance and application delivery. The following diagram illustrates how different entities interact with one another to enhance user experience:

Chapter 3

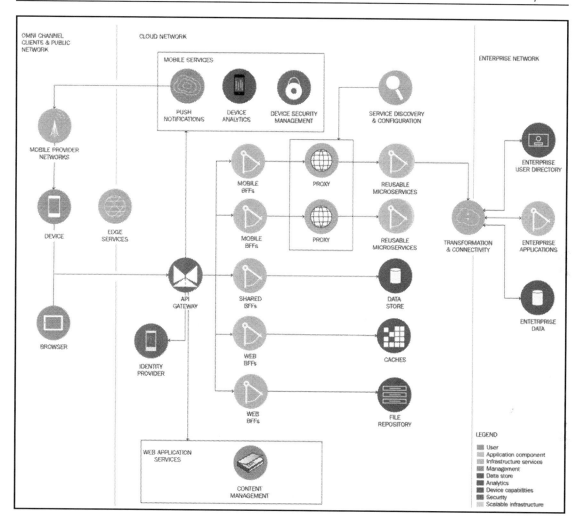

In the preceding architecture, we can see a layer of microservices being reached through the frontend API Gateway. These BFFs (mobile, web, and shared) invoke another layer of reusable Java microservices. Typically, a different team will usually write this. The BFFs and Java microservices communicate with each other using a microservices fabric such as Istio.

Entity and aggregate patterns: An entity is an object that is predominantly differentiated by its identity. Entities are mainly well-defined with a specific and easy-to-grasp identifier. Entities are dependent and not to live independently. Entities combine well with one another to form useful and usable clusters/aggregates to readily cater to varying business requirements. The key challenge here is that the cluster has to maintain the consistency to be right and relevant. For forming viable clusters, the overwhelming route is to choose the root for a cluster, but most of the microservice development teams are not competent enough with all the business details. Herein, the entity and aggregate patterns are useful in identifying specific business concepts that map directly into microservices, which are to implement the distinct business functionalities.

Services patterns: There can be operations that do not directly belong to any specific entity or aggregate. Services patterns offer a way forward to map such kinds of operations. We can model such objects as standalone services with interfaces. These are typically stateless services to be used by any entity and cluster. The services internally use the entity and value objects.

Adapter microservices pattern: There are legacy applications built using SOAP and RESTful services. During the transformation and modernization stage, these kind of adapter microservices is needed greatly. This specialized microservice bridges and adapts between business-oriented APIs, which are built using RESTful or any other lightweight messaging techniques and the traditional microservices, whose interfaces are built using legacy APIs or the SOAP API. An adapter microservice typically wraps and translates existing and function-based services into entity-based REST services. In many cases, converting a function-based interface built using SOAP into a business-based interface is straightforward. It is all about moving from a verb-based (functional) approach to a noun-based (entity) approach. Most of the time, the functions exposed in a SOAP endpoint correspond to the CRUD operations (create, read, update, delete) on a business object. This correspondence enables the faster realization of a REST interface.

Strangler application pattern: The strangler pattern helps to speed up the refactoring process of a monolithic application in a step by step manner. This pattern plays out a central role in transforming any existing legacy and massive applications into nimble and supple microservice-centric applications. The praiseworthy thing about using this pattern is that it creates incremental value faster than doing everything in one big migration. It also gives an incremental and risk-free approach for adopting microservices architecture.

Chapter 3

There are microservices development frameworks, languages, platforms, processes, practices, and patterns. Microservices can be built from the ground up. Also, microservices can be extracted out of legacy applications and refined to suit the evolving needs. Microservices play a vital role in legacy modernization and migration to powerful cloud environments. These patterns bring a lot of optimizations for microservices engineering, deployment, and operations.

Microservice design and implementation patterns: The following diagram clearly presents the list of resiliency patterns for designing, developing, and deploying resilient microservices. This section is being added to explain the various microservice patterns. The interested readers can gather more information on these microservices design patterns from the Microsoft website (https://azure.microsoft.com/en-in/blog/design-patterns-for-microservices/):

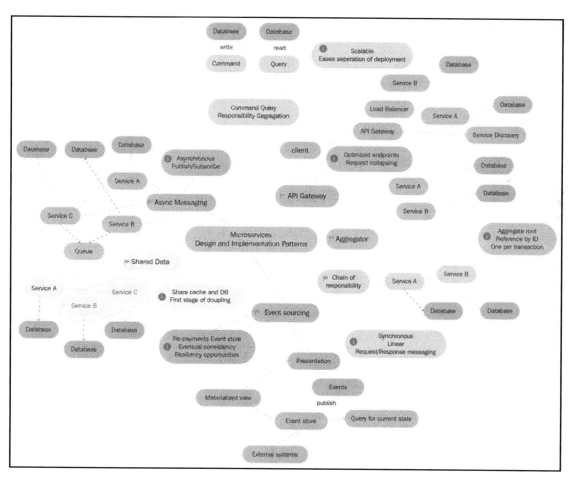

Microservice Resiliency Patterns

Ambassador pattern: This pattern creates some important helper services that send service requests to the remote service on behalf of a consumer service or application. This pattern acts as an out-of-process proxy, and this service is co-located with the client application. This pattern helps the client application immensely by offloading the most common client tasks that include authentication, monitoring, circuit breaking, logging, routing, and security enablement. The resiliency aspect is also being taken care of by this proxy pattern service. This pattern is implemented as a common service (in the microservice parlance, the common service is a collection of multiple microservices) that can be called by any client, which is coded in any programming language. For legacy modernization, this pattern is definitely a boon. All of the common connectivity tasks can be abstracted and implemented by the ambassador service while keeping up the specific tasks with the legacy application. The high-level architecture is shown here:

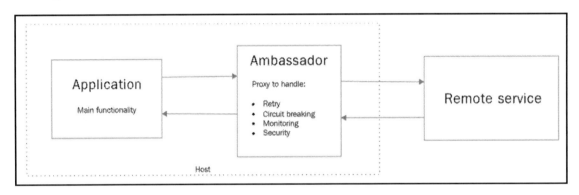

The horizontal tasks can be presented as an ambassador service, which is totally carved out of the legacy application. Any modification or advancement can be incorporated into the ambassador service without disturbing the application's functionality.

Anti-corruption layer pattern: This pattern is also an enabler of legacy modernization. This pattern pitches for implementing a facade or adapter layer between a modern and a legacy application. Due to deeper integration, legacy applications greatly depend on modern applications to be useful for customers and consumers. This added layer precisely translates requests between the participating applications. This pattern does not impose any limitations on application design that depends on legacy systems. The macro-level architecture of this pattern is given as follows. This newly incorporated layer brings the much-needed decoupling between legacy and modern applications so that the previously problematic dependencies get solved once and for all:

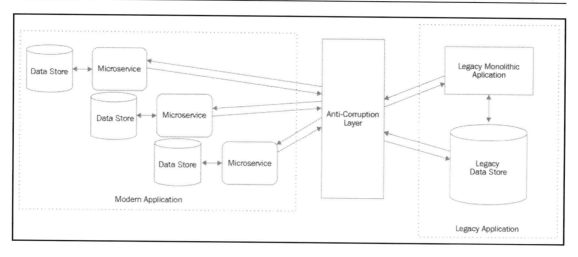

The application's data model and architecture are used to enable the communication and integration between the modern application and the pattern layer. Similarly, the communication from the pattern layer to the legacy system happens based on the system's data model. The anti-corruption layer is stuffed with all the implementation logic to translate the communication requests among the participating systems. The layer can be implemented and inserted as a component within the application, or it can be exposed as an independent service to be availed by the participating systems.

Bulkhead pattern: This pattern is an indispensable mechanism for achieving resiliency. An application service gets many instances that get deployed in different and distributed containers, or VMs. Each instance is being accessed and implemented through multiple connection and execution threads. That is, there are several pools, and each pool has many threads. If there is an error with one pool, it does not catastrophically impact other pools. The isolation is the main thing for application resiliency. Experts advise it is prudent and paramount to partition service instances into different groups based on user and data loads. Network latency is another criterion to be considered seriously. This unique design helps to isolate failures and ensures the service availability. Similarly, a consumer can also partition resources in such a way that the resources used to call one service don't affect the resources used to call another service. The pattern isolates service consumers from service providers so that any failure does not permeate into others.

The following diagram illustrates bulkheads getting structured around connection pools that call individual services:

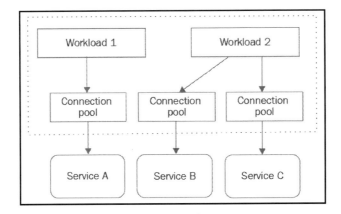

The following diagram depicts how multiple clients call a single service. As indicated in the diagram, the service has many instances so that each client can call a separate service instance. The first client has made too many requests and the service instance is overloaded. With such a neat separation, the other clients can go ahead without any problem:

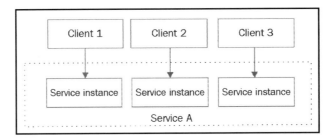

Gateway aggregation pattern: Aggregation of several individual requests into a single and consolidated request can be accomplished through this pattern. This pattern is highly useful when a client has to make several calls to multiple backend systems to complete a business task. The client application sends requests to each service (1, 2, and 3). Each service receives and processes the client request and responds to the application (4, 5, and 6), as per the following diagram. Sending multiple requests delays the process, along with the network bandwidth wastage.

Chapter 3

By putting a gateway in-between the client and the services, most of the issues can be solved:

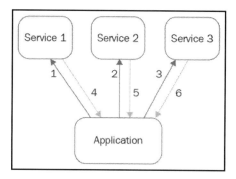

As per the following diagram, the client application sends only a single yet consolidated request to the gateway:

- Intuitively, the request has to embed all the additional requests inside. The gateway then receives and decomposes it and processes each request separately by sending it to its relevant service.
- Each service then does the appropriate task and returns a response to the gateway.
- The gateway then combines the responses from various services together and sends them back to the client application with the consolidated report and reply.
- Thus, multiple traverses back and forth get reduced to just one call and reply. The security surface area has come down sharply:

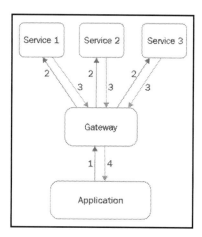

Gateway offloading pattern: There are several shared and specialized service functionalities in the quickly growing service ecosystem. These capabilities can be meticulously offloaded to a gateway proxy. As shared services are getting offloaded to a gateway, the microservices-based application development and deployment becomes simpler and smarter. Security services (authentication, token validation, SSL certificate management, data encryption, and decryption) are generally shared, and these are delegated to the gateway. There are other complex tasks mandating for highly skilled team members. There are tasks that need to be repeatedly and redundantly configured, verified, and validated. By employing the gateway pattern, the operational complexity of various services can be reduced considerably. In large-scale IT environments, the services such as authentication, authorization, logging, monitoring, measurement, management, and throttling have to be implemented and controlled across. Thus, identifying and consolidating the specialized and shared services together to be handled by a gateway service (software or hardware) to reduce overhead and the chance of errors is reduced. The following diagram shows an API Gateway that terminates inbound SSL connections and requests data from any HTTP server upstream of the API Gateway:

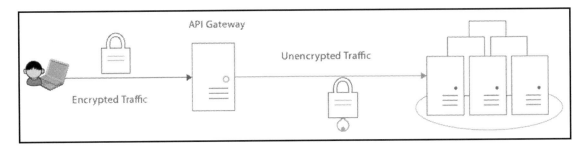

Gateway routing pattern: This pattern recommends a gateway in-between the client and the backend services. This gateway facilitates the routing of client requests to multiple services. The gateway serves as a single endpoint. This pattern is useful if multiple services have to be involved to achieve a business task. The well-intended approach is to place a gateway in front of a set of application services running on different and distributed server environments. This gateway uses the multifaceted application layer-7 routing to correctly route the client request to the appropriate services and their instances. With this pattern, the client application has to know the details of the gateway, as it is the only endpoint involved. If a backend service is composed or decomposed, there is no need to inform the client. The backend service can be replaced, substituted, displaced, and advanced without bothering the client. The gateway in the middle takes care of any changes in the backend applications.

A gateway service is just an abstraction of the backend services. This keeps up with the client's simplicity:

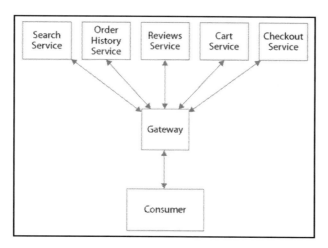

This gateway can also be of help with the deployment process by managing how software updates are being rolled out to users. When a new and advanced version of a service is ready for deployment, it can be deployed in parallel with the currently running version of the service. Routing etched into the gateway enables the choice of the version to be presented to clients. This helps to formulate and firm up various release strategies (incremental, parallel, or full rollouts of updates). Any issues discovered after the new service is deployed can be quickly solved by making an appropriate configuration change at the gateway service. As the gateway bears the changes, clients are not at all affected.

Sidecar pattern: This pattern is famous for achieving resiliency. This pattern bats for partitioning and deploying the different components of an application into a separate runtime/container to guarantee the much-demanded isolation and encapsulation. On the other hand, this pattern can make it easy to stitch polyglot components together to come out with a business-aware composite application. The sidecar is typically attached to a parent application to provide the supporting features for the parent application. The sidecar component also shares the same life cycle as the one being followed by the parent application. This sidecar is being created, sustained, and decommissioned alongside the parent.

If an application is decomposed into services, then each service can be built using different programming languages and technologies. While this mechanism gives a higher-grade flexibility, there are several downsides too. That is, each component has its own dependencies and is in need of a few language-specific libraries to run on the underlying platform. Managing the source code and the dependencies adds considerable complexity while handling application hosting, deployment, and management. The following diagram illustrates how the attached sidecar service brings immense benefits to the primary application:

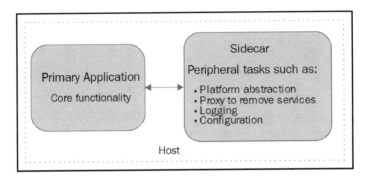

A sidecar service is a separate application, but it is tightly connected to the parent application. It is always attached to the application, and the sidecar goes wherever the parent application traverses. For each instance of the application, a separate instance of the sidecar is also readied, deployed, and hosted alongside the corresponding instance of the primary application. A sidecar is totally independent of its primary application in terms of the runtime environment and the programming language. This non-dependency tells us that there is no need to develop one sidecar for every language. The sidecar application can access the same resources that can be accessed by the primary application. For example, a sidecar can monitor the various system resources being used by both the sidecar and the primary application. Finally, there is no network latency because of their proximity.

We will come across many more microservices-associated design patterns for making microservices simpler to develop and deploy, highly available, assessable, and accessible, scalable, secure, composable, responsive, and resilient. As the density of microservices is all set to escalate in any enterprise IT environment, the complexity mitigation patterns for their optimal deployment, management, governance, orchestration, operations, replaceability, substitutability, and so on will germinate and flourish in the future.

Application decomposition patterns: If we are refactoring a monolithic and massive application into a microservices-based application, then the first pattern that we need to consider is the decomposition. The decomposition process has to be initiated and done based on one or more criteria. The prime criteria for decomposition include task (sub-domain) based responsibility and large-scale business (domain) capabilities. In both cases, the decomposition has to go down to the level of basic business activities such as inventory, warehousing, marking, branding, delivery, sales, and order processing. Now, each of these functionalities can be implemented through a host of microservices. Thus, the decomposition patterns help in identifying the appropriate microservices for each of the business functionalities in the legacy application. With fine-grained microservices in place, the reusability and composability of microservices move toward better and bigger services that are more tuned to business and people-centricity.

Decomposition by use case: It is mandatory to choose the best course of action for application decomposition and service composition. Without an iota of doubt, use cases are the most appropriate way for application decomposition. Use cases are typically the sequences of actions, which one or more users have to follow to finish a standard task. In the digital era, the user or actor need not be a person. Any **input/output (I/O)** device or a client software application can automatically follow the task sequence strictly to complete the initiated task. A use case can be as follows that is in an ATM, a user has to do certain clicks and data submissions to get cash. A use case could be doing something for retrieving and displaying a database record. For complex use cases, it is all about retrieving raw data from multiple devices, and cleansing, massaging, and crunching for extricating actionable insights out of data volumes.

Decomposition by resources: This pattern leads to the realization of a set of common microservices to simplify and speed up the process of legacy modernization. We know that there are different critical resources, such as computing, storing, networking, security, databases, and solutions in the IT world. This pattern recommends that you define and develop microservices to be used as access channels for these IT resources. That is, accessing and using individual resources in an isolated and optimal manner is being accomplished through these specialized microservices. These are horizontal and common microservices, and they can be used by any application for its needs. The service-enablement of IT resources through the service interface and implementation brings the added advantage in easily accommodating changes to any resource. That is, by updating only the resource-mapped and shared microservice, the advancements can be brought in. This resource heterogeneity is also hidden through the expression and exposition of the microservice interface.

Decomposition by responsibilities/functions: Any enterprise application has to have several clearly articulated and accentuated responsibilities. The idea is to pinpoint those responsibilities and create the corresponding microservices. Such responsibility domains might include shopping cart checkout, inventory access, replenishment, or credit authorization. These microservices can be used and reused by many applications.

Massive and monolithic applications need to be partitioned into a large number of interoperable and dynamic microservices. This is the first and foremost activity for embracing the proven and potential microservices architecture. The various decomposition patterns simplify the complex task of legacy application modernization and migration.

Microservices deployment patterns: When enterprise applications are being presented as a collection of interactive microservices, the number of participating and contributing microservices is bound to escalate. The operational complexity of microservices then climbs. Deploying microservices is also an important activity, and a few interesting deployment patterns come in handy for operators to do the clean and automated deployment.

Single host and multiple services: This pattern says that we can deploy multiple instances of a single microservice on a single host/node or that multiple services can be deployed on a single server node. This sharply reduces the deployment overhead and guarantees greater efficiency as microservices and their instances leverage the shared resources in an optimal fashion. The downsides include greater potential for conflict, and security violations. The reason for this predicament is that the isolation of various services interacting with one another, as well as with different clients, is insufficient.

Single service per host: A host can be a BM server, VM, or container. This pattern deploys each service in its own environment. This kind of deployment provides a high degree of isolation and flexibility, thereby there is little scope for any kinds of conflicts, violations, and fights for various system resources. VMs giver better service isolation, whereas containers enable isolation through the controlled sharing of various lower-level system resources while leveraging the unique features of the OS kernel. Deployment overhead may be on the higher side for this single host/multiple services model.

Serverless/abstracted platform: The concept of serverless computing or FaaS is a new abstraction that's emerging and evolving quickly. Various established public cloud service providers, such as AWS, IBM, Azure, GCP, and so on already offer this advanced facility for worldwide software developers. The automation capability level is going up fast in the cloud space. Through a host of automated mechanisms and using the delectable advancements happening in the containerization space, cloud service, and resource providers across the globe help developers to run their software services/modules directly on pre-configured infrastructure. The auto-scaling of the infrastructure is being taken care of by the provider.

Software deployment is extremely simple. It is all about uploading the code, with a small number of configuration settings to the preferred cloud environment. The deployment system places the code in a container or VM, and this is managed by the cloud service provider. Microservices are an easy fit for software deployment. There are microservices-specific software deployment tools. The previously mentioned patterns give the right indication to any cloud administrator on how to go about microservices-centric applications to get the intended success.

Design patterns in API Gateways and microservices: We all know that there is a rush by enterprises to move from monolithic applications to microservices-based applications. The API Gateway solution (software or hardware) is the primary ingredient for the fast proliferation and participation of microservices. The combination of the gateway and the microservice architecture emerges as a potential relief and benefit for the astounding success of microservices. However, we may need to surmount a few significant challenges being posed by this deadly combination. The migration from the monolithic to the microservice world is not straightforward. The extrication of microservices out of monolithic applications is beset with some practical problems. Refactoring is needed in several cases to transition from monolithic to microservices. One verified and validated approach is to zero down the common cross-cutting concerns. The leverage of proven aspect-oriented programming comes in handy when simplifying and streamlining from the legacy to modern software engineering. Here is a list of the often repeated cross-cutting concerns in any software application. Inspired readers are requested to click this link to get more concrete and complete information on the following (https://blog.codeship.com/design-patterns-in-api-gateways-and-microservices/):

- Authentication
- Authorization
- Sessions
- Cookies
- Cache
- Logging
- Dependencies on other services

Authentication: Without an iota of doubt, this is the most widely used task. In the gateway and microservice model, the authentication is being handled by a specialized token-generation service. This unique service is used to produce either a JSON token or some other authentication tokens. The token then gets duly embedded in the subsequent requests for enabling authentication automatically. That is, this service is enabling client applications to get authenticated once for the full session. The token is received and used by the gateway to meticulously evaluate whether the request is appropriately authenticated.

Authorization: This is another common service in the growing microservice ecosystem. It should be possible through this pattern to use a token that's typically sent via a custom HTTP header for enabling authorization. This task has to be finished before a formal request is communicated to the destination microservice.

Sessions: The experts recommend to avoid sessions in favor of tokens, as this helps to avoid looking up user-specific data in microservices. Whenever there is a necessity, the gateway passes the session data from a decrypted token to the microservices. Thus, tokens are being recommended for stateful microservices. This is receiving a special mention here because it is possible to pass only a session identifier. Subsequently, it is all about allowing and asking microservices to look up session data from the attached resource, for example, the Redis **in-memory database (IMDB)**.

Cookies: Like sessions, cookies are also best avoided by microservices, and cookies are easier and cleaner to implement in the gateway. If there is a need for that, microservices can emit cookies, and the gateway has to be configured accordingly to proxy cookies.

Cache: The recommendation here is to ease into caching and start with small expiration times. It is advised to maintain the REST-friendly routes in microservices, and this setup allows for simpler caching at higher levels. Some scenarios have to consider the possibility of cached data as the source of truth. The specialized services, such as event handlers and command-line services, help keep the cache updated consistently.

Logging: This pattern tells us that logging is best done using a log aggregation service. The other easier option is to simply log to stdout and then start doing the log aggregation. A hugely popular logging format such as JSON, with some required fields, is overwhelmingly recommended to enable systematic log aggregation to make sense of it. This guarantees consistent reporting across all of the participating components. There has to be a provision in the chosen log format for a request ID. The ID can then be passed from the gateway into each microservice. This makes it easy to find relevant and right log entries in the services that played a part in receiving and handling a specific request.

Gateway: This has to act as a gated proxy for stringently enforcing the finalized authorization rules so that only the verified requests are allowed to pass through to each microservice. We can attach a dashboard to get a 360 degree view of microservices and their interactions.

Summary

IT reliability contributes immensely to business reliability. IT reliability is being achieved through resilient and elastic IT systems (both software and hardware). With the quicker adoption of microservices architecture, the realization of resilient and elastic software systems is being made easy. Microservices are being touted as the best-in-class application building block, and hence there are enabling patterns for microservices development, deployment, integration, and operations.

In the next chapter, we will focus on DevOps under **Site Reliability Engineering** (**SRE**), since as automation and DevOps play a big role in the SRE journey.

4
DevOps as a Service

This chapter is going to cover various topics related to the DevOps world. We are going to look at DevOps in the context of **Site Reliability Engineering** (**SRE**), as automation and DevOps play an important role in this area. We will be integrating our system with monitoring solutions to collect various metrics to improve our services. This chapter will cover recent trends in this domain and give an idea about the expanding market of DaaS providers. We will also provide a brief introduction to various topics related to DaaS.

We are going to cover the following topics in this chapter. This should give us an idea about what exactly DevOps means to the agile world:

- What is DaaS?
- One-click deployments and rollback
- Configuring automated alerts
- Centralized log management
- Infrastructure security
- Continuous process and infrastructure development
- Continuous integration and continuous development
- Collaboration with development and QA teams

What is DaaS?

DevOps-as-a-Service (**DaaS**) is a service that allows you to get all the compilation, building, and **Continuous Integration** (**CI**)/**Continuous Development** (**CD**) tool chains setup instead of having to setup your own. DaaS can be provided by an internal team. In this case, the development team won't take any direct actions to manage its infrastructure; it will just feed its code to get compile, build, and CI/CD features. Alternatively, DaaS can be provided by external vendors, in a market that is expanding rapidly. These can help with your journey to achieve CI and CD.

In 2016, Gartner declared that 25% of 2,000 global companies that are surveyed will be using DevOps. However, this year, Forrester research has said that this will reach 50%. According to a study by cloud management provider RightScale, *the ratio of enterprises that have adopted some aspects of DevOps principles reached 84% in 2017.*

There are multiple websites that list all the major DaaS vendors. The following are among some of the most well-known names in this market:

- CloudBees
- Happiest Minds
- Shippable
- CloudHesive
- Ranger 4
- Alibaba

A complete list can be found at the following website: `https://www.softwaretestinghelp.com/devops-service-provider-companies/`.

Most organizations trying to setup their own DevOps tool chain still have not reached a level at which they can get end results quickly. This is because of a significant shortage of skilled people in this domain. Also, even if there are people with the necessary experience, it takes time to setup your own mature setup, as there are multiple factors involved in selecting specific tools and using them to setup a DevOps infrastructure.

Selecting tools isn't easy

Selecting tools is quite a complex task. This is why consulting partners and DaaS vendors exist in this market. The following are the major factors that create complexity:

- The cost
- The availability of skilled engineers
- The maturity of tools
- Whether to use open source or enterprise products

The following diagram will give you an idea of how complex the DevOps chain is. It is not easy to decide which specific tools you need to pick:

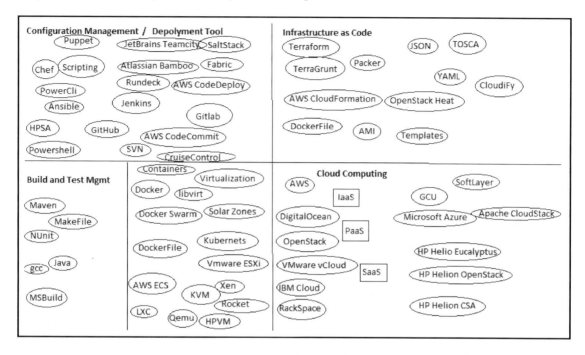

DevOps tool chain

Even if your team is able to setup DevOps, it can still be a struggle to mature your unique toolset and processes. To overcome these challenges, many companies are starting to offer DevOps as a service. It's up to you whether you would like to setup your own DevOps team and tool chain or whether you would like to go with a DaaS approach. To simplify this decision, try to answer the following three questions:

- Where we are?
- Where we are going?
- How do we get there?

For those who would like to act quickly without having the internal capability to develop DevOps, DaaS is a good idea. Then, as time goes by, development teams can gain skills by learning from DaaS providers and start to develop their own internal DevOps process. Contacting DaaS providers for internal problems can take an unnecessary time to solve small problems. Alternatively, you could choose to stick to your DaaS provider.

DevOps as a Service

CloudBees, the the major contributor behind Jenkins, released the **DevOps Quadrant Maturity Model** in 2016. It categorized its implementation as either upstream or downstream and framed this in terms of an x axis and a y axis, where the y axis denotes the level of organization and the x axis denotes the software development life cycle:

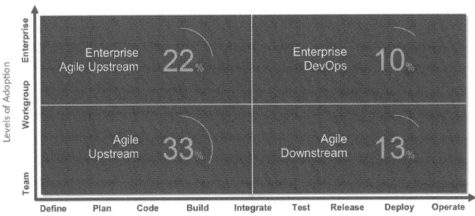

Figure 1: Two axes of DevOps adoption

This screenshot comes from the CloudBees Webinar, Introduction to the Four Quadrants of DevOps maturity, 2016.

Major public cloud vendors are supporting DevOps by providing a tool chain. Companies such as Alibaba have just started providing DaaS, whereas other vendors such as Google's GCP, Microsoft's Azure, and Amazon's AWS don't provide DaaS directly, but they do have tool chains, blogs, and easily available technical documentation that supports DevOps. The term DaaS specifically refers to a situation in which a vendor simply gives us an endpoint, while they will do all the heavy lifting and setup the tool chain for you.

When you will be using build and package like compiling Java code and creating JAR file service in DaaS platform, for example, we just need to input the source code and the concerned DaaS platform component that will build it for you for multiple platforms. It will also package it for multiple operating system varieties. Let's say we build just one microservice in Java. A DaaS platform will compile and build it for you and generate packages, such as Jar, RPM, DEB, and ZIP files. Furthermore, it will deploy it on your configured environment. Tools such as Nexus and JFrog Artifactory provide these kinds of building and packaging services.

Types of services under DaaS

Let's take a detailed look at some of the services that come under DaaS:

- **Azure/GCP/AWS expert guidance and implementation**: Major public cloud vendors don't behave as DaaS vendors, but they do provide you with a toolset for selection and guidance about how to use their services to setup a DevOps tool chain. We can find multiple blogs about how to use tools such as AWS CodeDeploy to deploy code on our infrastructure.
- **Microservices design**: DaaS providers give us options to deploy microservices using different technologies and tool chains. Sometimes, they can even recommend how to design a microservice. For more information, refer to Chapter 2, *Microservice Architecture and Containers*.
- **Blue/green deployment**: Blue/green deployment is a technique in which you keep two sites live. One site receives live traffic and another contains the newest version of your code and undergoes testing. As soon as the second site passes all test cases, you make it live. DaaS vendors provide this feature, and even public cloud vendors have inbuilt support in the tool chains they provide. For example, AWS CodeDeploy gives us the option to select blue/green deployment as a radio button on the CodeDeploy console.

- **Database tweaking and optimization**: DaaS providers have a high level of expertise in engineering and infrastructure. They can provide database tuning and optimization as a service.
- **Infrastructure as code**: This is offered by DevOps professionals and companies such as HashiCorp, which is providing tools such as Terraform and Packer, and AWS, which is providing CloudFormation—like tools in this domain. DaaS providers are using these technologies to build customer infrastructure on the fly or dynamically. An example of this would be provisioning Jenkins or monitoring systems.
- **Dockerizing and scaling applications**: DaaS vendors can provide this thanks to the availability of mature container and orchestrator technologies such as Docker, rkt, Kubernetes, or OpenShift. These are easily available for anyone to use. Scaling is another service in which DaaS vendors play an important role. They can help you scale your infrastructure using options provided from public cloud vendors (such as AWS Auto Scaling or AWS ECS scaling) or your own designed scaling option.
- **Infrastructure design and re-architecture**: This is a consulting service during the initial phase with a client. DaaS vendors learn about the client's setup and recommend customized ways to use the DevOps tool chain.
- **Cloud migrations**: This is another service provided by DaaS in which your own on-premises infrastructure is moved to the cloud or from one cloud vendor to another public cloud. This involves various factors, such as cost, the existing client setup, and the tool chain used.
- **CI/CD pipeline implementation**: This is one of the core services of DaaS providers. They are now mature enough to build a CI/CD infrastructure for you within a few minutes. Behind the scenes, they are using infrastructure as code technologies with their own written script. This involves spinning up tools such as the Docker registry, Jenkins, also TeamCity, such as tool setup, or Check_MK, such as monitoring the auto setup.
- **Configuration management**: Puppet, Chef, and Ansible are the main DaaS services that providers use to manage the configuration of your development or production infrastructure. Sometimes, it is not easy to manage these components, so it can be a good idea to use DaaS vendors.
- **One-click deployments and rollback**: One-click deployment and rollback options are an important feature that all organizations look for because they remove a lot of technical complexity. All deployment tools such as Jenkins, Rundeck, TeamCity, Terraform scripts, or tools such as AWS CloudFormation or CodeDeploy provide one-click deployment and rollback options. Some are pretty straightforward to configure and implement, while others have to be customized.

An example of one-click deployment and rollback

Let's say we have a task to deploy version 1.0 of an application to the east and west regions of the US, and version 1.5 of the same application to a region of the EU. Somehow, however, we mistakenly deployed the US version to the EU, so we have to rollback using the single-click rollback option. The tools we will use are Jenkins, Bash, Terraform, and Git. We will use Jenkins to configure a freestyle job. Our inputs will be the environment, the version, and the region. The following steps show how to setup Jenkins for one-click deployment:

1. Create a new Jenkins job by clicking on new **Item** on the left-hand side of the Jenkins dashboard. It will pop up with a window to create a new job:

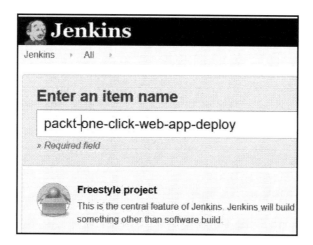

2. Once you create the job, it will open the following window. In **General,** make the project parameterized so that we can input the environment, version, and region:

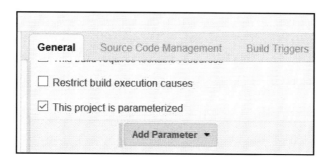

3. In the parameters section, provide the input options for `Region`, such as `us-east`, `us-west`, and `eu-central`:

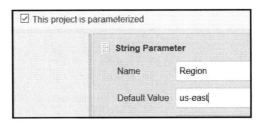

4. Provide the `Version` input option in another parameter option:

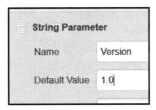

5. Provide the `Environment` input options, such as `production` and `develop`:

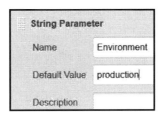

6. The script will have logic to deploy your code according to the provided input parameters. You need to place the `packt-one-click-deploy.sh` bash script on your version control system, such as GitHub or GitLab, and Jenkins will auto-clone it on your Jenkins slave. It will then deploy it from there, as follows:

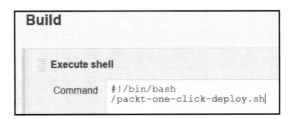

7. Finally, hit the **Build** button to execute your build steps:

The preceding steps can be configured in a Jenkins DSL, such as the Jenkins file, but we kept it more visual so that a novice user can understand how one-click deployment works.

Returning to our previous scenario, in which we deployed the wrong version, we can very quickly and easily redeploy the correct version just by modifying the input files in our job and hitting the **Build** button again.

Configuring automated alerts

This is one of the most important tasks these days, as it is very complex to troubleshoot distributed microservices. SRE is trying to adapt new toolsets and technologies to collect and send automated alerts.

There are multiple tools under the monitoring domain that collect data and send it to automated alerting systems. These include the following:

- SignalFX
- Runscope
- AppDynamics
- Check_MK/Nagios
- Webmetric
- AlerSite

PagerDuty, OpsGenie, and automated emails through CI/CD tools all are widely used to send automated alerts to SREs whenever the preceding monitoring systems reach or cross a configured threshold.

Let's think about some practical examples that we use on a day-to-day basis:

- The AWS RDS CPU utilization surpassed the 80% threshold. You can use AWS SNS to send an automated alert to email IDs. This email ID can be a PagerDuty configured service that will send further alerts to a user on their phone, email, or via SMS.
- Check_MK can be configured to alert a user about expired HTTPs SSL certificates.
- SignalFX can be configured to alert a user when the IIS connection queue is long.
- External monitoring tools such as WebMetric, Runscope, and AlertSite can be configured to send alerts about public-facing websites that are not reachable.

Centralized log management

In a distributed environment, **centralized log management** is a critical component. Otherwise, it is impossible to troubleshoot complex problems. These days, environments are becoming increasingly complex, which is why the DaaS providers market is rapidly expanding. It is important to consider whether you would like to setup your own logging system or whether you would like to go with a DaaS provider.

There are many centralized logging providers on the market, such as Splunk, Logentries, Loggly, Sumologic, or Datadog. It is also important to mention ELK Stack, as this is open source and very popular. We refer to the following terms while talking about the logging management world:

- **Source:** The source is your system. It could be a device such as a server, or a software-defined device such as a firewall or a router. It sends alerts to a logging endpoint such as Logstash or ElasticSearch. The ELK stack gives you the following agents that can be configured according to your requirements: Logstash, Filebeat, PacketBeat, MetricBeat, and Winlogbeat. Logstash is a heavy agent when compared to lightweight agents such as Filebeat or Winlogbeat.
- **Filters:** Filters help you remove unwanted data and send it to your elastic search or Logstash endpoints. Logstash gives you two mechanisms to filter these logs: Grok and regex. For example, if you have the following logs:

```
55.3.244.1 GET /index.html 15824 0.043
```

Your grok filter will look as follows:

```
%{IP:client} %{WORD:method} %{URIPATHPARAM:request} %{NUMBER:bytes} %{NUMBER:duration}
```

- **Output**: This is the final component in your configuration. It updates your final endpoint, where your agents will be forwarding logs. This will be your ElastiCache endpoint, from which Kibana picks logs to show on your dashboard. An example of this is ElasticSearch.

There are many other features provided by log management systems, such as saved queries, dashboards, and automated alerts. These are widely used by enterprises.

Infrastructure security

Security is an important concept for any organization using cloud infrastructure. DevOps professionals are expected to build a delivery pipeline around security. DevOps security is covered by the term DevSecOps, which is not an official word, but one that has been used by a number of different sources to describe this concept.

Security implementation and integration with your DevOps tool chain is a skill that organizations have to learn. This involves categorizing your artifacts and passing them to the security pipeline so that they can be filtered, secured, and verified quickly.

DevOps professionals have some toolsets from the open source world as well as from the commercial world. We have still not yet seen a clear-cut toolset or an easy-to-use implementation in this domain; it is still maturing. However, we should soon get a good set of tools and techniques for DevOps so that we don't have to worry about security in our setup.

Major cloud vendors and world-leading security organizations have started providing new product ranges under this domain. These include the following:

- **AWS**: AWS GaurdDuty, AWS Inspector
- **Microsoft Azure**: MS Azure built-in advanced thread protection
- **Google**: GCP have built-in security at each layer
- **Symantec**: Symantec has some great products for handling security in cloud and on premises, such as the following:
    - Symantec Cloud Workload Protection:
        - Symantec Endpoint Protection
        - Symantec Endpoint Protection Cloud
        - Symantec Endpoint 14.1 (SAEP)
        - Symantec **Cyber Security Services** (**CSS**)

For more information, see my blog about the CIS security benchmark that DevOps professionals have to keep in mind while integrating security in your tool chain: http://blogs.shailendersingh.com/2017/08/26/security-benchmark-implementation-in-aws/

Continuous process and infrastructure development

This is a product development process where product development and product operation teams are in a cohesive relationship that aims at efficient product development. It can be thought of as a development strategy in which developers and operation teams break down their barriers and perform as a single unit.

Before the development of DevOps, there was next to no communication among developers and the business. The traditional life cycles were slow, and **software requirement specifications** (**SRS**) were hard to collect and expensive. Operators would make technically unfeasible promises, which caused damage to companies' reputations. Then, Agile came into the picture and provided product owners with a dynamic mode of collaboration within teams. What was started by Agile was later picked up by DevOps.

In the traditional development style, a product used to run in enhancement mode until it was finalized by a customer. There was a continuous to and fro of code, resulting in a higher cost and time delays in delivery. Large transaction processing domains such as banks were significantly affected by the lack of integration, as large and complex applications often had a fragile supporting hardware, causing unplanned system crashes and a loss of production hours. The loss was never monitored internally. Issues were first reported by end users, and, by the time they were picked up by the technical team, significant damage had already been done.

To avoid this damage, a new strategy was needed. This required the early identification and gathering of development resources, end-to-end product delivery support by developers, and the creation of a reusable deployment procedure.

This gave us the following advantages:

- Faster delivery
- Enhanced product quality
- Better scalability

- Stable environment
- Better collaboration among teams
- Less defects

Nowadays, there is a chain of events between IT teams and customers, where they build and enhance applications continuously. A continuous process, otherwise known as continuous production, is a method that's used to develop a product without any interruptions. In this strategy, resources are provided in a constant flow to meet the product delivery deadline. Here, an operation runs on a 24/7 basis, with only minor maintenance interruptions.

Work flows through a series of interconnected operations where the output of the previous stage becomes the input for the next stage. This helps in reducing storage requirements, and only a minimum inventory is required to maintain workbaskets. This also means that a pending activity is at a minimum and resources are used efficiently. The cost of projects is reduced drastically, and the overall build time is also improved. However, while making a process continuous, we need to be aware of the rigidity of that process. A failure or break in any stage collapses the entire system. We must ensure that the product we are developing is standardized and the work basket is shared equally by every department. Any imbalance in the process will lead to a loss of productivity, ultimately causing a huge cost when working over a large volume of data. Infrastructure is the basic structure or facility required to implement an operations work plan.

In the IT context, infrastructure is a collection of hardware, networks, software, and other tools that are used to develop, deploy, and operate a product or service. The infrastructure must be continuously developed to meet up with the pace in which the product complexity, quality, and cost has been challenged. A product's code is considered as its infrastructure, and it is continuously altered depending on the product enhancements required.

We will further discuss this in the following section, *CI and CD*.

CI and CD

This is perhaps the most well-known strategy of DevOps. CI aims to integrate the work of an individual into a central repository on a frequent basis. This helps to identify code bugs early on and results in a higher-quality product.

Let's take a look at some of the benefits of CI:

- **Maintains code integrity**: Depending upon our code base and applications, multiple teams or developers are working on different features, but, indirectly, they are working on the same part of the code. A higher number of developers will cause more risk to the code's integrity. We should commit or integrate our code on a daily basis to reduce this risk and maintain the code's integrity.
- **Increases code quality**: With a lower integration risk, we can focus more on code functionality and achieve a better quality product application.
- **Easy to troubleshoot code errors**: If any developers commit bad code that breaks the build, it will be easy to troubleshoot these issues and fix them quickly.
- **Improves code testing**: Different builds and versions of the code will help testers trace bugs and issues easily.
- **Quick deployment**: Deploying the latest build can be a very time-consuming process. It also increases the chance of error. Using CI, we can automate this process so that it will take less time to deploy:

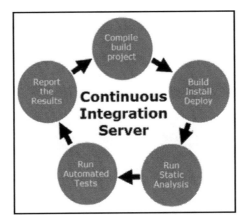

DevOps aims to integrate development and operations teams to enable rapid software delivery. This is achieved through better communication and collaboration of the teams involved, thus resulting in shorter development times, CD, and new innovations. A unified platform is provided to development and QA teams, who perform regress testing.

By simplifying the integration steps, we can achieve the ultimate goal of a cheaper, higher-quality product. As the overall build cycle is reduced, this reduces the cost and provides more opportunity for QAs to analyze and debug the product. CI is not a process that eliminates bugs, but a process wherein new bugs can be detected at an early stage and debugged before they have any negative impact.

CI life cycle

In the following diagram, you can see how CI can help engineering teams to improve the product quality and maintain the code's integrity. As we have already discussed, engineers will commit the code in the repository frequently after code testing. They can commit it on a master code repository, which will trigger the continuous build system at regular intervals. If the build is successful, it will be deployed to various environments. Otherwise, it will notify the engineering team to verify the errors and fix them:

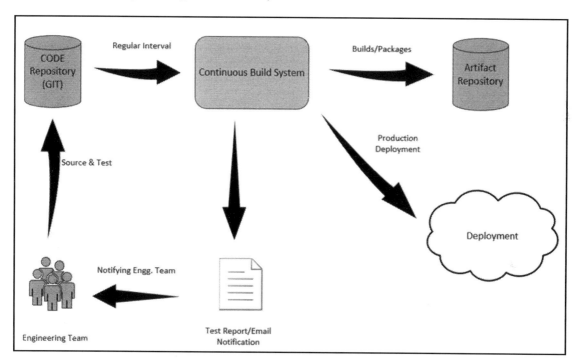

CI tools

There are wide range of CI tools available. These include the following:

- **Code repository**: GitLab, GitHub (with over 24 million users and more than 70 million code snippets in the repository), BitBucket, and SourceForge
- **Continuous build system**: Jenkins, TeamCity, Travis CI, and Bamboo

DevOps as a Service

Let's take a look at how to setup a CI process with Jenkins and GitHub:

1. Firstly, we need to install Java 1.8. with all its dependencies. You can use the following command to install it on Red Hat 7.4:

```
[root@PacktPub ~]# yum install java
Loaded plugins: langpacks, product-id, search-disabled-repos
Resolving Dependencies
--> Running transaction check
---> Package java-1.8.0-ibm.x86_64 1:1.8.0.5.20-1jpp.1.el7 will be installed
--> Processing Dependency: copy-jdk-configs >= 2.2 for package: 1:java-1.8.0-ibm-1.8.0.5.20-1jpp.1.el7.x86_64
--> Processing Dependency: jpackage-utils >= 1.5.38 for package: 1:java-1.8.0-ibm-1.8.0.5.20-1jpp.1.el7.x86_64
--> Processing Dependency: libXext.so.6()(64bit) for package: 1:java-1.8.0-ibm-1.8.0.5.20-1jpp.1.el7.x86_64
--> Processing Dependency: libXft.so.2()(64bit) for package: 1:java-1.8.0-ibm-1.8.0.5.20-1jpp.1.el7.x86_64
--> Processing Dependency: libXi.so.6()(64bit) for package: 1:java-1.8.0-ibm-1.8.0.5.20-1jpp.1.el7.x86_64
--> Processing Dependency: libXrender.so.1()(64bit) for package: 1:java-1.8.0-ibm-1.8.0.5.20-1jpp.1.el7.x86_64
--> Processing Dependency: libXtst.so.6()(64bit) for package: 1:java-1.8.0-ibm-1.8.0.5.20-1jpp.1.el7.x86_64
```

2. Before going further, we need to validate whether Java has installed successfully:

```
[root@PacktPub ~]# java -version
java version "1.8.0_181"
Java(TM) SE Runtime Environment (build 8.0.5.20 - pxa6480sr5fp20-20180802_01(SR5 FP20))
IBM J9 VM (build 2.9, JRE 1.8.0 Linux amd64-64-Bit Compressed References 20180731_393394 (JIT enabled, AOT enabled)
OpenJ9   - bd23af8
OMR      - ca1411c
IBM      - 98805ca)
JCL - 20180719_01 based on Oracle jdk8u181-b12
```

Installing Jenkins

Jenkins will be packaged in a `WAR` file. We can deploy it on any server. Take a look at the following steps:

1. In this example, we are using Apache Tomcat 7.0.42. Let's download Tomcat using the following command:

```
[root@PacktPub ~]# wget https://archive.apache.org/dist/tomcat/tomcat-7/v7.0.42/bin/apache-tomcat-7.0.42.zip
--2018-10-04 12:33:55--  https://archive.apache.org/dist/tomcat/tomcat-7/v7.0.42/bin/apache-tomcat-7.0.42.zip
Resolving archive.apache.org (archive.apache.org)... 163.172.17.199
Connecting to archive.apache.org (archive.apache.org)|163.172.17.199|:443... connected.
HTTP request sent, awaiting response... 200 OK
Length: 8463515 (8.1M) [application/zip]
Saving to: 'apache-tomcat-7.0.42.zip'

100%[======================================================================>] 8,463,515   7.64MB/s   in 1.1s

2018-10-04 12:33:57 (7.64 MB/s) - 'apache-tomcat-7.0.42.zip' saved [8463515/8463515]
```

2. After that, we need to download the latest Jenkins WAR file and copy it to the Tomcat/WebApps folder:

```
[root@PacktPub webapps]# wget https://updates.jenkins-ci.org/latest/jenkins.war
--2018-10-04 12:43:08--  https://updates.jenkins-ci.org/latest/jenkins.war
Resolving updates.jenkins-ci.org (updates.jenkins-ci.org)... 52.202.51.185
Connecting to updates.jenkins-ci.org (updates.jenkins-ci.org)|52.202.51.185|:443... connected.
HTTP request sent, awaiting response... 302 Found
Location: https://updates.jenkins-ci.org/download/war/2.144/jenkins.war [following]
--2018-10-04 12:43:08--  https://updates.jenkins-ci.org/download/war/2.144/jenkins.war
Reusing existing connection to updates.jenkins-ci.org:443.
HTTP request sent, awaiting response... 302 Found
Location: http://mirrors.jenkins-ci.org/war/2.144/jenkins.war [following]
--2018-10-04 12:43:08--  http://mirrors.jenkins-ci.org/war/2.144/jenkins.war
Resolving mirrors.jenkins-ci.org (mirrors.jenkins-ci.org)... 52.202.51.185
Connecting to mirrors.jenkins-ci.org (mirrors.jenkins-ci.org)|52.202.51.185|:80... connected.
HTTP request sent, awaiting response... 302 Found
Location: http://ftp-nyc.osuosl.org/pub/jenkins/war/2.144/jenkins.war [following]
--2018-10-04 12:43:08--  http://ftp-nyc.osuosl.org/pub/jenkins/war/2.144/jenkins.war
Resolving ftp-nyc.osuosl.org (ftp-nyc.osuosl.org)... 64.50.233.100, 2600:3404:200:237::2
Connecting to ftp-nyc.osuosl.org (ftp-nyc.osuosl.org)|64.50.233.100|:80... connected.
HTTP request sent, awaiting response... 200 OK
Length: 75820252 (72M) [application/x-java-archive]
Saving to: 'jenkins.war'

100%[======================================>] 75,820,252  16.9MB/s   in 4.4s

2018-10-04 12:43:13 (16.6 MB/s) - 'jenkins.war' saved [75820252/75820252]
```

3. Start Apache tomcat and access the following URL: `http://your_Public_IP:Port/jenkins` i.e in our case its `http://23.96.21.153:8080/jenkins/login?from=%2Fjenkins%2F`
4. The first time you use the Jenkins browser, it will ask for a password, which you need to copy from the Apache Tomcat logs and paste into the browser, as follows:

```
*************************************************************
*************************************************************
*************************************************************

Jenkins initial setup is required. An admin user has been created and a password generated.
Please use the following password to proceed to installation:

127cff69efa448ef9e44f2abb1c4c76d

This may also be found at: /root/.jenkins/secrets/initialAdminPassword

*************************************************************
*************************************************************
*************************************************************
```

5. The following screen shows what our Jenkins portal will look like. It is suggesting that the initial password has been written to the log and the **/root/.jenkins/secrets/initialAdminPassword** file:

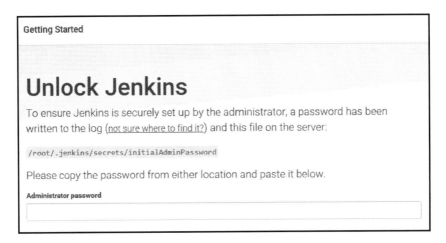

Jenkins setup for GitHub

Let's take a look at how to set up Jenkins for GitHub:

1. After completing the Jenkins installation, you will be able to see the following screen:

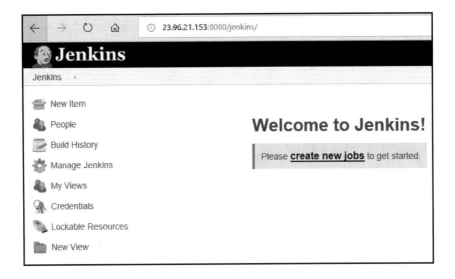

2. In this example, we are using GitHub as a code repository, so we need to enable the GitHub plugin from Jenkins. This will allow us to connect GitHub to Jenkins, and we can easily build our code with just one-click. We need to click on **Manage Jenkins** | **Manage Plugins**:

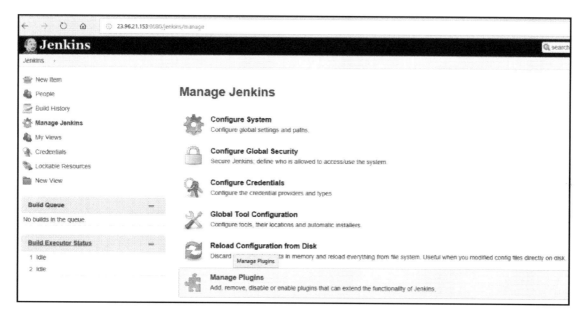

3. Click on the **Available** tab and search for the `GitHub plugin`. Download and install the plugin:

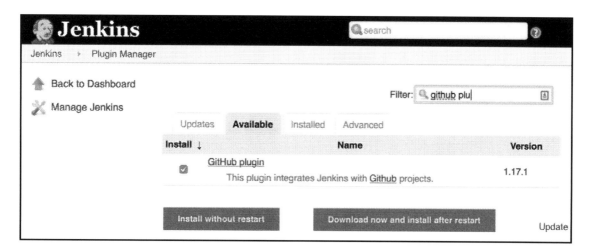

Setting up the Jenkins job

Importantly, we need to create a Jenkins item job. Follow the given steps:

1. Click on **New Item** and write any item name. Click on **Freestyle project** and press **OK**:

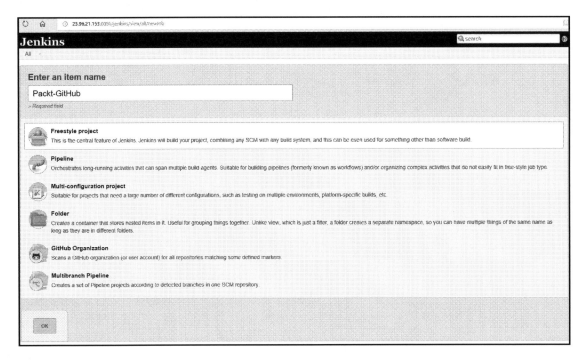

2. In the next step, you need to provide your GIT project URL. Under **Source Code Management**, we should select **Git | Repository URL**, along with its credentials, as follows:

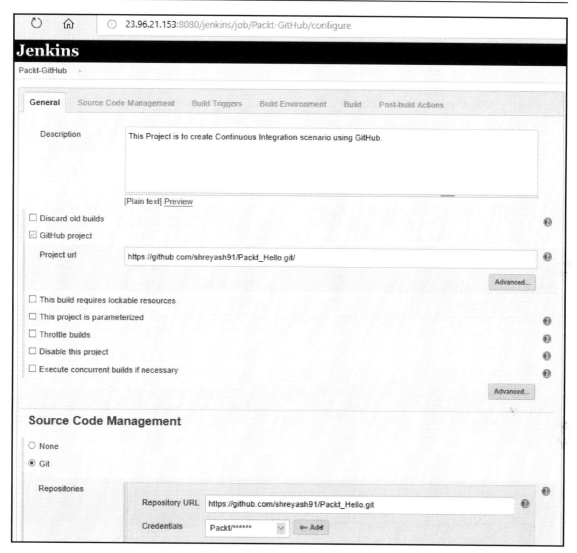

DevOps as a Service

3. We can trigger **Build periodically** based on our schedule. In our case, it will be running every night at **12:01:26**:

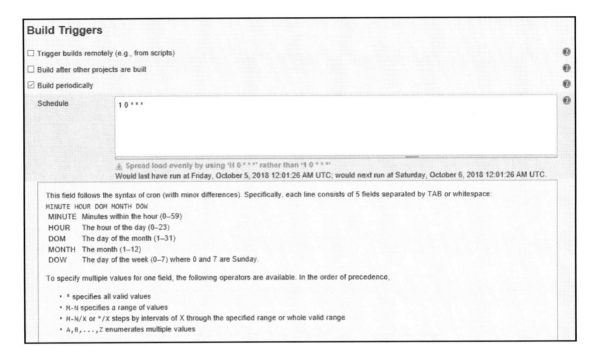

4. Click on the **Save** button and try to run the job. We can also configure JUnit to run the test cases after they have been built and share the report.

Installing Git

Before running the Jenkins job, make sure that Git is installed in our Jenkins box locally. Our job will actually connect to GitHub and perform some Git operations such as fetch, pull, or push, so Git should be up and running.

Starting the Jenkins job

Refer to the following steps:

1. To start the Jenkins job, click on **Build** on the right side. Check for the Jenkins logs:

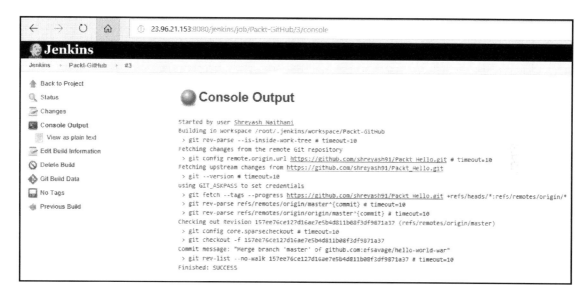

In our example, every time a developer merges any changes into the GitHub repository, it is going to trigger the job from Jenkins and build the latest version of the code. After it is built, we can also configure JUnit to automate test cases in the Jenkins job. Doing this improves the development life cycle and makes our process robust.

CD

CD is closely tied to CI. It refers to the process of releasing a piece of code that has passed a QA test to production. A successfully passed code must be shared to the end user as soon as possible. This helps in promoting new innovations and technology growth within a project.

By utilizing the CI/CD strategy, not only can we carry out rapid development, but we can also make quality checks on the products we develop. We can use inter-department collaboration and business ideas, which can be quickly developed into working products.

An example of a DevOps practice is developing an application with version control. With version control, when we develop an application, we do so in multiple versions, enhancing a new feature after every release. When we deploy the code, an image of the code is saved and a checkpoint is created as a failback procedure. Now, whenever a new enhancement is needed in a system, we simply access the code image and add the new code logic to it. This reduces redundant work, makes efficient use of our resources, and also provides faster delivery. This procedure helps us to restore the application to the last successful checkpoint if the code breaks during release. This concept is described in the following diagram:

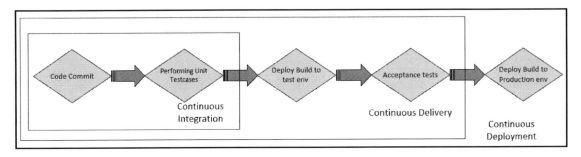

Collaboration with development and QA teams

As the name *DevOps* suggests, DevOps refers to a combination of development and operations teams who come together to complete a business project successfully. DevOps refers to the collaboration of teams that are involved in the development, delivery, and maintenance of a project to make it faster and more efficient in every dimension. Our main focus in DevOps is on the development and quality analysis teams. This is due to the CD and the delivery of new builds.

In today's competitive world, a new innovation or idea is hot property, that everyone wants to cash in on quickly. This need to deliver a new product rapidly leads to an additional load on developers to create new features that need to be optimal in every sense. This may lead the code to break, causing the entire application to shut down. A faulty deployment, in turn, may cause the application's configuration to break, which may be non-recoverable.

The role of developers in DevOps

Developers are the brains behind the success of a product. Their aim is to innovate and enrich a current product based on business requirements. They continuously strive to optimize applications and make them more efficient. They are always working on developing different variations of applications, which can improve the performance of a product by miles. Once updated in the repository, code is picked up in parallel by developers, who apply different logic and methodology to achieve the common goal of performance enhancement. Using version control, they add or remove features based on customer feedback.

The role of QA teams in DevOps

In DevOps, developers and testers play an equally important role. The responsibilities of both are tangled in such a way that outsiders see them as a single team. A QA brings a developer closer to the operations teams, thus enabling transparency throughout the process. They act as a bridge where teams can collaborate and check the feasibility of a product. Once a product is deployed, the entire team works on enriching, supporting, and keeping products running, to ensure long-term success. Product reality checks are done on a real-time basis. If a QA fails to deliver, any new functional updates are a disaster waiting to happen. These quality checks help businesses to intensify the building stages of a product. QA teams bring developers and operations to a single framework, where developers are made aware of operations requirements, and operations are made aware of the developers' work. Developers share code details to testers, who in turn share them to operations teams and perform functionality tests on the code. If any bugs are detected, these are quickly highlighted and resolved in real time before impacts are made on production. Testers share their knowledge with developers, who analyze their code, thus reducing any defects. This results in high quality, fewer version changes, and increased customer satisfaction.

DevOps is a strategy to reduce time delays in the delivery of a product. When a tester and a developer are not synchronized, the product will have to conform to the requirements of one team and then the other team. The continuous deployment of an application with the latest functionality and logic needs to be intensively tested. Testers need to be made aware of code changes and prepare test cases accordingly.

With the introduction of QA teams, DevOps has successfully reduced this delay. DevOps has made it possible for developers to share their build process with testers, who, in turn, share their knowledge with developers, thus creating a system in which everyone is aware of any updates made. Operations teams are made aware of technical details that help them better understand the process. Internal flows and backend processes are now made available to testers, who can use these to pinpoint exactly where and why an issue might pop up. The QA tester is responsible for providing code fixes if any workarounds are required.

QA practices

A QA tester must be willing to be a part with the technical team to understand and analyze work. Their aim must be on automating test cases that can pick up new enhancements and verify their impacts.

They must aim to deliver a satisfactory product over a perfect product. They must maintain quality check metrics, where defects must be checked at the earliest possible opportunity. Product-related requirement gathering must be a one-time activity. The QA teams need to focus on providing a means to continuous testing, wherein any new integrations need to be picked up by automated testing tools.

Summary

DevOps as a service is an emerging philosophy in application development. There's not one path to setup DevOps as a service. It varies from organization to organization, and you need to decide what works in your organization. Many organizations adapt DaaS to manage their application to the cloud. By using DevOps as a service, we can automate build, test, and deploy processes. We can achieve this by implementing effective CI and CD process. In this chapter, we have learned how to setup one-click deployment and rollback using the Jenkins tool. Throughout this book, we have been focusing on microservices, and we have seen how to collect and send automatic monitoring alerts. We learned how to setup Jenkins and GitHub to achieve CI and deployment end to end. This is going to help us improve the engineering pipeline and improve the delivery process. We have also discussed collaboration between development and QA teams.

Chapter 4

We can conclude that the DevOps life cycle contains development, testing, integration, deployment, and monitoring. DevOps certifications are available from Amazon Web Services, Red Hat, Microsoft academy, and the DevOps institute. DevOps helps organizations shift their code deployment cycles to weeks and months, instead of years.

In the next chapter, we will discuss the concepts of clustering, container orchestration, and managing containers using Kubernetes. We will also cover topics such as resilient microservices and share-volume containers.

5
Container Cluster and Orchestration Platforms

Reliable applications and environments can be created through emerging concepts such as containerization, **microservices architecture** (**MSA**), container management, and clustering. Container clustering and orchestration is a highly demanded skill nowadays, as more and more organizations are moving toward microservices to make their services better. At the moment, we have mature products that fulfil the demands of customers, and solutions exist in both the enterprise domain and the open source domain. The latter category is dominating in this respect, with products such as Docker, Kubernetes, and OpenShift.

This chapter intends to provide a detailed explanation of the preceding technologies to ensure the goals of Site Reliability Engineering. The prime topics to be covered in this chapter include the following:

- Resilient microservices
- Application and volume containers
- Clustering and managing containers
- Container orchestration and management

Resilient microservices

We touched on microservices briefly in the previous chapter, but we'll just go through a quick summary again here to remind ourselves. Microservices is an architecture style in which large, complex software applications are composed of one or more smaller services. Each of the services are called microservices and deploy independently of one another, without us needing to know the implementation behind the other microservices. Each service works as a single business function that is loosely coupled, small, focused, language-neutral, and has a bounded context.

Resilient microservices can be defined as having the ability to recover back to a working state after a failure or outage. Resilience is one of the main advantages of microservices. Unlike monolith systems, where if something breaks, it will damage the whole application, in microservices, it will only impact that particular functionality, and other services in the application will run as usual.

Application and volume containers

As we all know, last year was the year of containers (such as Dockers and Kubernetes). You can think of these as methods that package an application's code so that it can be run with its dependencies, isolated from other processes. There are two main types of containers, that is, **stateful containers** and **stateless containers**. In stateless containers, data generated from one application will not be available for another application. Stateful containers, on the other hand, will store or record the data somewhere, so that it is available. In real-world applications, it is likely that we need to use stateful containers, based on our application's requirements.

Let's see the steps behind sharing the disk storage among containers. In this example, we will use a Kubernetes pod named **PacktPod**. This pod will contain two containers: **Container- PacktContainer_first** and **Container-PacktContainer_second**. Let's look at what this will look like:

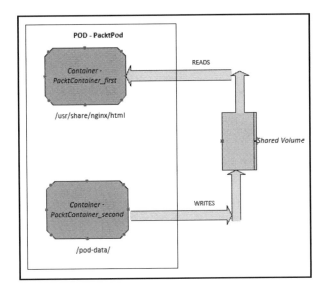

Let's look at how we can setup the shared volume in Kubernetes:

1. First, we need to create a pod definition. This will create a pod name, `PacktPod`; a volume as shared data; and two containers: `PacktContainer_first` and `PacktContainer_second`. Our new file, `PackContainer.yaml`, will look as follows:

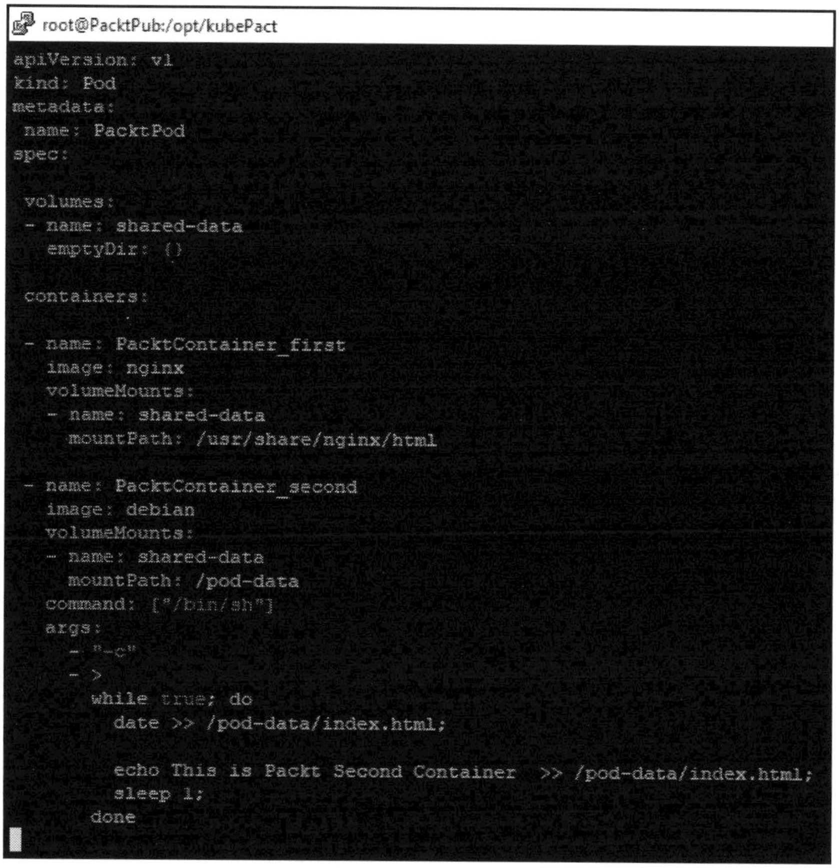

```yaml
apiVersion: v1
kind: Pod
metadata:
  name: PacktPod
spec:

  volumes:
  - name: shared-data
    emptyDir: {}

  containers:

  - name: PacktContainer_first
    image: nginx
    volumeMounts:
    - name: shared-data
      mountPath: /usr/share/nginx/html

  - name: PacktContainer_second
    image: debian
    volumeMounts:
    - name: shared-data
      mountPath: /pod-data
    command: ["/bin/sh"]
    args:
      - "-c"
      - >
        while true; do
          date >> /pod-data/index.html;

          echo This is Packt Second Container >> /pod-data/index.html;
          sleep 1;
        done
```

2. Use the following command to create the pod:

```
# kubectl create -f PackContainer.yaml
```

Container Cluster and Orchestration Platforms

3. Run the following command to execute a shell, and update the `index.html` file with the date and our echo message, `This is Packt's Second Container`:

   ```
   # kubectl exec -it PackContainer.yaml -c PacktContainer_first -- /bin/bash
   ```

4. You can verify the `index.html` file using the following command:

   ```
   # tail /usr/share/nginx/html/index.html
   ```

   This will be the output:

   ```
   [root@PacktPub kubePact]# tail /usr/share/nginx/html/index.html
   Tue Oct 16 08:42:41 UTC 2018
   This is Packt Second Container
   Tue Oct 16 08:42:51 UTC 2018
   This is Packt Second Container
   ```

5. To expose our `pod PacktPod` using the Kubernetes service, use the following command. This will create a new service on the node port:

   ```
   # kubectl expose pod PacktPod --type=NodePort --port=8080
   ```

6. Finally, using the `curl` command, you can check that the first container works and handles HTTP requests on that port. In our case, the container's port is `30691`:

   ```
   # curl http://localhost:30691/

   Tue Oct 16 08:42:41 UTC 2018

   This is Packt Second Container

   Tue Oct 16 08:42:51 UTC 2018

   This is Packt Second Container
   ```

Chapter 5

Clustering and managing containers

In this section, we are going to cover a definition of clusters and look at some trending container clustering solutions available on the market. There are many mature solutions available. We will be using architectural diagrams in this section, as pictures can often help us understand these concepts more clearly.

A recent survey by CNCF (https://www.cncf.io/) shows that organizations are increasingly using containers. We can see that more organizations are using 250+ containers in production-level deployment compared to previous years:

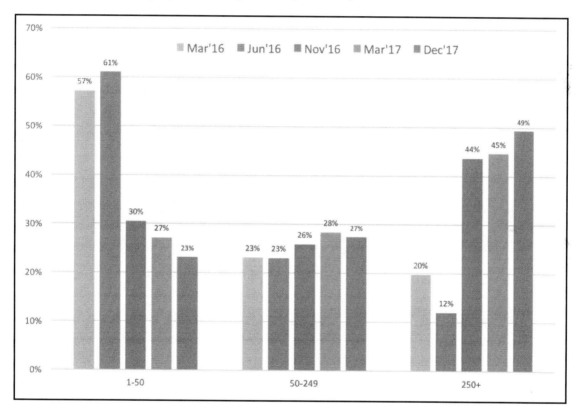

The preceding screenshot can be found at the following link: https://www.cncf.io/blog/2017/12/06/cloud-native-technologies-scaling-production-applications/.

[147]

Container Cluster and Orchestration Platforms

As container adoption is increasing, old concerns are diminishing, and new challenges are coming to the forefront of container management. We should keep these new challenges in mind and proactively focus our efforts on this area before other competitors take the lead in the market.

In the following screenshot, we can see that monitoring and scaling are more important concerns nowadays than in previous years:

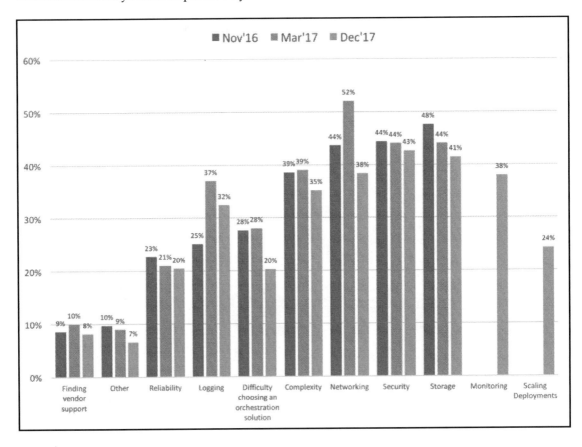

The preceding screenshot can be found at the following link: https://www.cncf.io/blog/2017/12/06/cloud-native-technologies-scaling-production-applications/.

What are clusters?

A **cluster** is a group of resources, which can be anything from memory, CPU, disk, and network interfaces. In the container era, the resources can be containers themselves that contain memory, CPU, a disk, and a network, with the addition of applications either in a single image or configured as code in a Docker-like file.

In this section, we are not going to cover the traditional clustering of servers, using tools such as Veritas Cluster, Red Hat cluster, HP, SUN, or AIX-like clusters, but we are going to talk about container clustering and management, as this is much more important nowadays. The container cluster managers available in the market include the following:

- Docker swarm
- CoreOS fleet
- AWS ECS
- Apache Mesos

Docker swarm: Docker swarm is the clustering solution from the Docker community and is available in both community and enterprise editions. To achieve clustering on Docker containers, we need to start Docker in swarm mode on all managed hosts. It can work in either master or slave mode. Docker calls native clustering a swarm. This is available from Docker 1.12 onward:

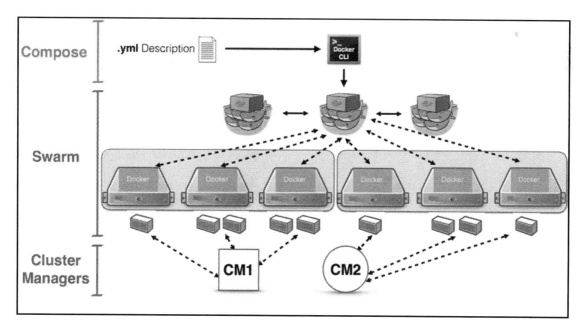

Container Cluster and Orchestration Platforms

Whenever we need to extend a cluster, we simply need to initialize a new node and add it to the cluster so that the swarm master can start scheduling jobs on it. The following is a list of various quick commands that you can refer to:

```
#docker service init

#docker service join

#docker service create

#docker service scale

#docker service update

#docker service deploy
```

For more information, please consult the following link: `https://blog.docker.com/2015/11/deploy-manage-cluster-docker-swarm/`.

CoreOS fleet: CoreOS is the operating system that was primarily developed and contributed to by Google. It originally had functionality for container cluster management, but it was depreciated in February 2018, and now CoreOS is focusing on Kubernetes for all solutions, so we aren't going to cover any further information about this here:

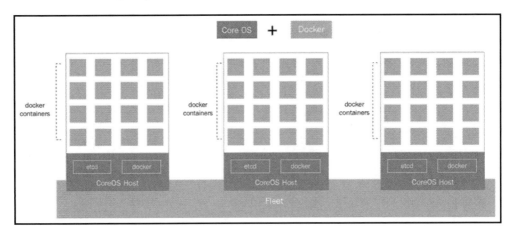

More information can be found at the following link: `https://blog.appdynamics.com/product/4-cluster-management-tools-to-compare/`.

Chapter 5

AWS ECS and ECS service as a cluster manager: Amazon provides an **elastic compute service** (**ECS**) to help you to deploy your containers in the AWS environment. ECS has three components:

- Cluster
- Service
- Task

An ECS cluster is a group of EC2 instances that can be entirely customized; you can configure any instance type category.

We can use an ECS service to combine multiple microservices. Each service will contain our container definition in the form of tasks, and we can easily set the minimum count, the desired count, and the maximum count of containers. Similarly, we can increase the web interface count to handle more load.

Tasks are the Docker YAML configuration files in which we configure the image name, the version, the memory, the CPU, and the volume. Tasks can be written in YAML or JSON format, and task files are very similar to Dockerfiles.

AWS ECS provides us with a nice dashboard on which we can see a summary of the cluster's usage. Normally, EC2 nodes configured on clusters are managed through AWS EC2 **auto scaling groups** (**ASGs**) so that, when required, we can easily increase the horizontal capacity of the cluster.

Often, people don't understand the resource requirements of a cluster and unknowingly start adding more services or tasks on existing clusters without increasing the cluster's capacity. Keep an eye on your AWS ECS dashboard to see your compute capacity, and carefully analyze your memory allocation strategy. Over-commitment can create issues during peak load hours. Make sure you are adding enough instances with the correct instance type to handle your production load. AWS are currently developing Fargate services that will remove this management and enable us to add capacity on the fly.

The traffic flow in ECS starts from Route 53, continues to ELB and the ASG Target Group, and ends with the AWS ECS service name.

The following diagram shows the following components:

- AWS ECR (the container registry)
- Task definition (the actual JSON file, similar to Dockerfile, which contains container resource specifications such as RAM or CPU)

- Service description (the number of different microservice containers running, such as the application or the web server)
- AWS ECS cluster

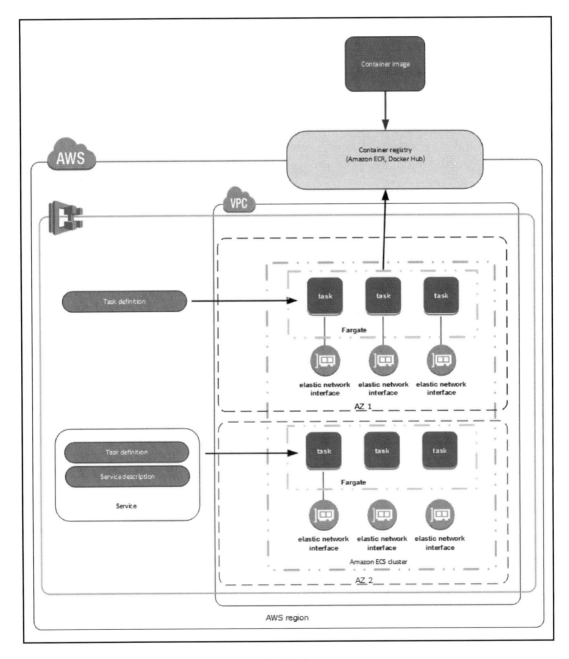

Chapter 5

 The preceding image can be found at the following link: `https://docs.aws.amazon.com/AmazonECS/latest/developerguide/Welcome.html`.

All of these components are fenced under AWS VPC. The cluster is built on EC2 instances that are deployed in two availability zones: **AZ 1** and **AZ 2**. Whenever a service starts, it reads the task definition and pulls the concerned Docker images from the AWS ECR repository. You can also fetch images from the Docker registry (hub) or your own deployed private registry.

Apache Mesos: Apache Mesos is not exactly a container clustering or management solution, but it can help to combine resources from a hybrid environment. It allows us to create a pool of memory and CPU resource capacity that can be utilized by other container solutions. Marathon is a solution that organizations use in conjunction with Mesos to provide this service. Refer to the following diagram to understand the concept in detail:

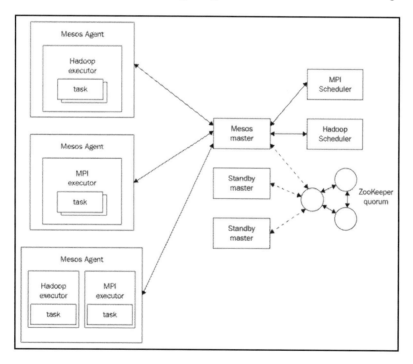

 The preceding diagram can be found at the following link: `http://mesos.apache.org/documentation/latest/architecture/`.

[153]

Container orchestration and management

Container orchestration is a technology that is significantly changing the horizon of companies. We are seeing more and more companies adapting these technologies on a daily basis. Red Hat and Google are the major players that are directly providing these technologies and helping other organizations to develop similar products. Currently, the most mature products include Kubernetes and OpenShift, and many organizations are using these at a production scale. We are going to cover most of the available solutions on the market and will try to give you an insight into their architecture.

A recent survey conducted by CNCF shows some useful statistics about how companies are managing containers. We can clearly see that Kubernetes is leading in terms of container management:

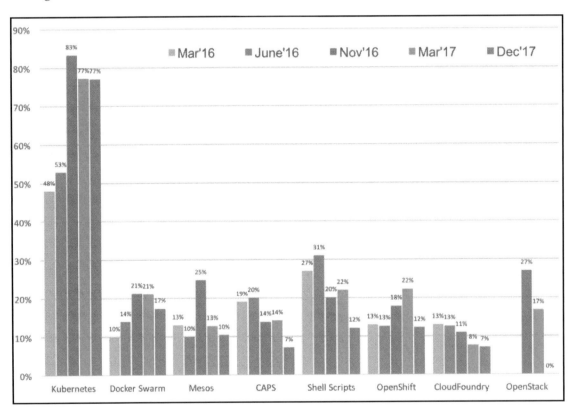

The preceding screenshot can be found at the following link: `https://www.cncf.io/blog/2017/12/06/cloud-native-technologies-scaling-production-applications/`.

What is container orchestration?

Container orchestration is the automated management, coordination, arrangement, and monitoring of computer resources so that they can be provided to engineers with enterprise quality without taking much time to setup. The most popular container orchestration software available on the market is as follows:

- Red Hat's OpenShift
- Google's Kubernetes or AWS EKS
- Mesos and Marathon
- CoreOS Tectonics
- Docker compose
- OpenStack Magnum

Red Hat's OpenShift: Red Hat is early starter in the container orchestration market and includes the majority of Kubernetes clusters. OpenShift is a container orchestration solution that helps to deploy containerized microservices into pods. Red Hat has developed a UI layer and integrated other products to provide this solution. It has the following components:

- Web UI/dashboard/namespaces
- Pods
- Router
- Services
- Deployment management

You can configure any physical, cloud, and virtual servers under OpenShift. It uses the Kubernetes nodes and Docker as a base container platform to give you an OpenShift cluster form. We can increase the application capacity simply by increasing the pod count configuration by modifying a replica key value pair in a `YAML` file. It uses the `oc` command, which is just a wrapper around `kubectl` commands.

Container Cluster and Orchestration Platforms

The traffic flow in the OpenShift cluster starts from Route 53 (DNS) and continues on to ELB (or not, if there is no load balancer). The proxy is configured to redirect traffic to specific pod instances before sending traffic to OpenShift. Here, the service module routes your traffic to the correct pod and then finally to the container inside the pod.

> The flow can be represented as follows: DNS | load balancer (optional) | proxy/router | services | pods | configured container inside the pod.

The following architecture diagram shows the various components of the OpenShift platform. These include the following:

- **Enterprise Container Hosts** (any physical, virtual, or cloud-based server)
- **Container Orchestration and Management**
- **Application Lifecycle Management**
- **CONTAINER**

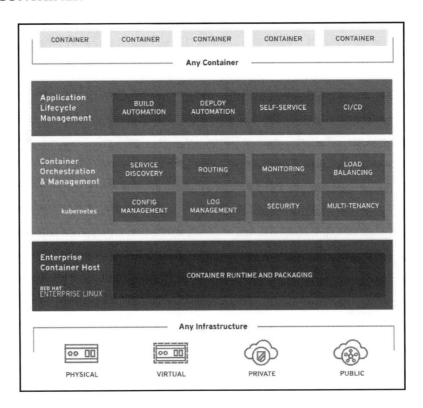

[156]

This screenshot can be found at the following link: `https://www.openshift.com/learn/what-is-openshift/`.

An OpenShift cluster requires servers, on which it will install the required cluster components, such as Kubernetes, an internal load balancer, internal log management, security, and multi-tenancy functionality. These come as bundled software. The application life cycle management layer is a layer in which you can use your own in-house tool to deploy your application using `oc` APIs or commands. We can also use any CI/CD tool, such as Jenkins.

The following example code shows some of the most commonly used commands, including how to log in to your ACP (OpenShift) endpoint, access your pods, and log in to a running container:

```
# Packt Pub example to access your container running in ACP cluster:

# Following command will help you to login inside your Openshift setup
#oc login -u 'Shailender' -p 'YOURPASSWORD'
#oc project <Project name to switch >

# Following command will help you to list all container running inside your POD with name and resource specification.

#oc describe pods packtpub-app-1-dvj4b|egrep -i "name|image:|started|mem|cpu"
#oc describe pods |egrep -i "^name:"


# Following command will help you to login inside a container running under POD

#oc exec -it packtpub-app-1-dvj4b -c 'packtpub-webserver' bash
```

NOTE: packtpub-app-1-dvj4b is randomly generated name so after each new deployment this name will change so make sure you are using current running POD name value during running above mentioned commands.

Container Cluster and Orchestration Platforms

Take a look at the following screenshot, which shows the OpenShift dashboard:

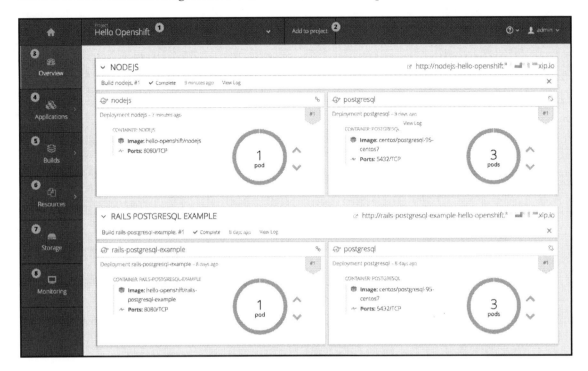

 This screenshot can be found at the following link: `https://docs.openshift.com/container-platform/3.5/architecture/infrastructure_components/web_console.html`.

The preceding screenshot shows almost all the features of this product. On the right-hand side, we can see all the menus that allow us to navigate to all of the previously mentioned components. The environments and projects are separated through namespaces.
Here, **Hello Openshift** is our namespace or project name, under which we will deploy or configure our pods. In the circle, we can see the currently running pod count for a specific service that can be increased or decreased easily by pressing the up or down arrows.

We can clearly see the container names in key value form. For example, in the **postgresql** pod, the value is **POSTGRESQL**. We can also see the image used to build each pod and the port number on which it is listed. We can automatically scale these pods using the scaling option. By default, we can only scale using the CPU threshold, and there is no default option for the memory or the number of network connections supported. If we want to implement this functionality, we need to come up with our own custom solutions.

Google's Kubernetes or AWS EKS: Kubernetes is the open source version of Google's clustering solution, which is named Borg, and Omega and was donated by Google to the open source community CNCF in 2014. Kubernetes is dominating the container orchestration market and extends far beyond the Docker swarm solution in terms of its usage. Docker took the lead in the container market, whereas Kubernetes took the lead in the orchestration market. Kubernetes gives you the option to configure any container platform, which means you can use it to configure Docker or rkt containers as well. Kubernetes is commonly known as Kubernetes and is written in Go language. It includes both a master server and a nodes server (minions).

The master node runs a REST-based kube-apiserver service that behaves as a frontend to the Kubernetes cluster and consumes JSON. The internal workings of the Kubernetes cluster are handled by internal architectural components, including kube-clusterstore, kube-controller-manager, and kube-scheduler. `kubectl` is the command that is used on a day-to-day basis to manage activities on this cluster.

Most third-party vendors and DaaS vendors have now started to provide Kubernetes as a service, and it can be found in almost all cloud vendors, including AWS, Google's cloud, the Aliababa cloud, and MS Azure. It has similar components to those that we described in OpenShift:

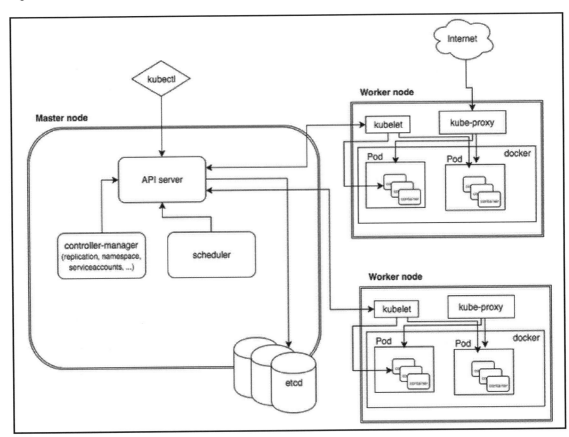

Chapter 5

 This screenshot can be found at the following link: `https://x-team.com/blog/introduction-kubernetes-architecture/`.

Apache Mesos and Marathon: Marathon is a container orchestration solution for DC/OS. To deploy applications, it is common to use a combination of Mesos and Marathon. Mesos includes resource nodes, while Marathon uses its scheduler to deploy jobs. For more information, consult the following diagram:

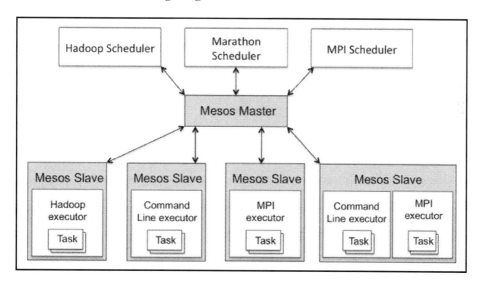

 This screenshot can be found at the following link: `https://www.ericsson.com/research-blog/mesos-meetup-hosted-ericsson-research/`.

[161]

Container Cluster and Orchestration Platforms

CoreOS Tectonics: CoreOS is currently developing its tool chain to become a real container operating system with orchestration solutions. The following diagram shows how CoreOS has combined various technologies with the Tectonics orchestration solution. The following diagram contains some of the most important components, including the following:

- The container image registry layer
- The host layer on which your workload will run
- The monitoring and security toolset
- The container environment

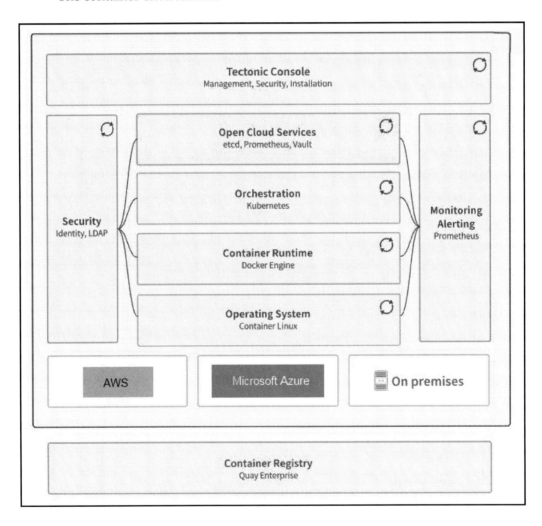

This screenshot can be found at the following link: `https://coreos.com/tectonic/`.

It has the following components, which can be deployed on any cloud vendor. This helps us avoid vendor lock-in issues:

- A Tectonic console interface
- Prometheus as a monitoring solution
- Kubernetes as an internal orchestration solution
- Docker as a container engine
- CoreOS as an operation system

Docker compose: Docker compose is an orchestrator as well as a command. `docker compose` is used to configure your application. For example, a web server and a database server can be configured under a single file, called a linked container, and the `docker compose` command will be used to run the setup. The following code is an example of how to create a `.yml` file and how to run configured containers:

```
# vim packtpub-deployment.yml
version: '2'
services:
  packtpub-web:
    build: .
    ports:
      - "80:80"
  packtpub-postgres:
    image: "postgres:alpine"
# Run docker compose from your project folder
#docker-compose up
```

OpenStack Magnum: Another option in the private cloud setup market is OpenStack. This is an orchestration solution, which uses existing Docker and Kubernetes technologies with the Magnum service, through which you can interact with APIs.

Container Cluster and Orchestration Platforms

The left-hand side of the image shows you the compute capacity of your cluster, where you can configure any virtual or physical machine running on any container-supported platform. Docker runs as a container engine and containers work as specific service instances that Kubernetes or Swarm can use as worker nodes according to your scaling requirements.

On the right-hand side of the image, we can see that the Magnum components are running in conjunction with the OpenStack Heat template. Here, it interacts with OpenStack services, such as **Glance**, for image management; **Cinder**, a block storage service; **Neutron**, a network service; and **Nova**, a compute service. Whenever you require more capacity for your application, it interacts with the components on the left to spin up more Docker containers to fulfil the demand requirements through the Magnum conductor.

For cluster management, Magnum provides APIs through which we can interact with the **Magnum Client**. An example of one of these APIs is the python-magnum client:

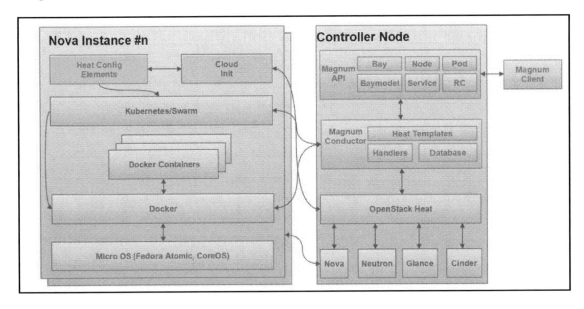

This screenshot can be found at the following link: `https://wiki.openstack.org/wiki/Magnum`.

Summary

In this chapter, we covered various concepts related to containers, container management, and container orchestration. We looked at application resiliency with persistent volumes and considered the technologies that can be used. This will help you a lot in regards to selecting the appropriate tools. It is very important to choose, setup, configure, and monitor these kinds of complex solutions. If it is coming from DaaS or as an enterprise version, it gives us some sort of monitoring and management options. If we try to setup our own solution, however, we have to configure and integrate other solutions to make it a production-ready endpoint for your organization.

In the next chapter we will be learning about Software architecture and design is a process that includes several contributory factors, such as business strategy, human dynamics, quality attributes, design, and IT environment.

6
Architectural and Design Patterns

Architecture and design are the foundation blocks of everything during service or microservice development, and they give you clarity and the direction to implement any logic in the cloud era. It was not only used in tradition monolithic setup, but will be used for future setups and will always remain a building block that will continue to help you build your service from scratch. I see it as a kit given to interns to build their initial system and continue to rebuild and redesign by keeping these architecture and design statements in their minds. Software architecture and design is a process that includes several contributory factors, such as business strategy, human dynamics, quality attributes, design, and IT environment.

Architecture pattern

Some of the following points provide clarity about an architectural pattern definition:

- It serves as blueprint for your system
- It is general and reusable in nature
- It gives you a functional understanding about how components are going to interact with one another
- Architecture styles are also known as *architecture patterns*
- Non-functional decisions are formed and divided by the functional requirements
- A well-laid architecture reduces the business risks associated with the building solution and helps you define a clear-cut understanding between business and technical requirements, and it also builds relationships among those components

The following mind map diagram gives different types of **Architectural Patterns** used in the IT world where you have easily heard about the **Client Server Pattern**, the **Master Slave Pattern**, the **Model-View-Controller Pattern**, and **Peer to Peer Pattern**:

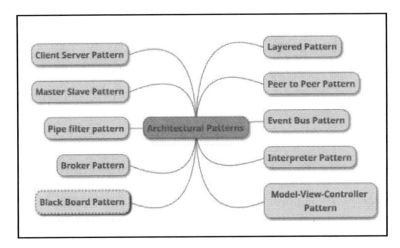

Design pattern: Functional requirements are defined in it, and it helps you decompose a system into components and defines their interaction to meet the functional and non-functional requirements of your system. There are many design patterns such as **Execution**, **Computational**, **Structural**, **Algorithm Strategy**, and an **Implementation Strategy Patterns** that you can use to build your system, and you can pick one pattern at a time to focus more on one part and move on to another pattern once you have almost achieved the previous pattern's implementation. The following diagram describes a design pattern more closely to build software:

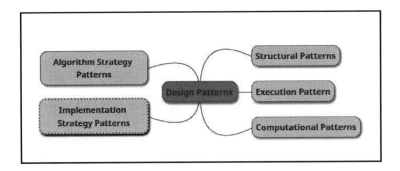

Senior technicians, such as solution architects, application architects, and enterprise architects help you use architecture and design patterns in an initial phase for any software development or in your infrastructure setup.

In our chapter, we will focus on distributed computing and the operational aspects, where we will be looking at the new trends where people are considering security, reliability, resiliency, performance optimization, and passing the message in a distributed world in async application, management, and monitoring of critical infrastructure components where we are having different design patterns altogether.

Design pattern

It is very important to consider all design patterns before designing any service, as it helps you build a predictable service that is secured, resilient, performant, scalable, available, and reliable with the following foundation pillars that gives maturity to your application. Traditionally, these patterns were not considered formally, but in the cloud era, we have much more flexibility to choose and consider these patterns during our design process, as these patterns are the building blocks for the cloud vendor service, and even they use the same pattern in designing their own infrastructure.

We are going to cover the following six design patterns. These topics are so broad that we can write a complete chapter on them, but we are going to give you a glimpse into these subtopics so that we can consider them while we are performing some practical implementation:

- Security
- Resiliency
- Performance
- Scalability
- Availability
- Reliability

Architectural and Design Patterns

The following diagram shows the design pattern pillar for new generation services:

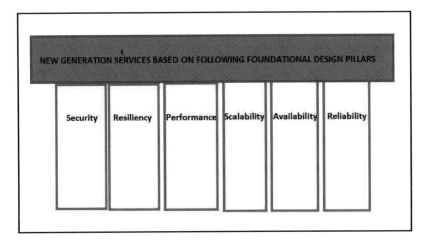

All of the preceding topics are so important in distributed, multi-tenant, cloud-hosted environments, where you have to consider these patterns while designing your services. Some of the frequently used patterns under these topics are API throttling, **Single Sign On (SSO)** using federated authentication, rate limit, and sidecar container. **Messaging, Management, and Monitoring** are also the design patterns that are shown in the following mind map, but their subtopics are covered in our six pillars, as some show all of these overlaps:

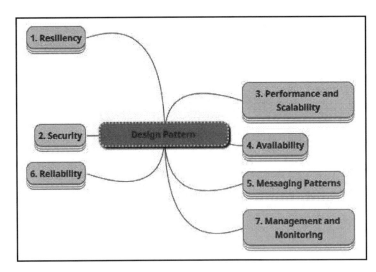

The toolsets available on the market have all the functionality and configuration to practically implement them and take these design patterns in to a real, practical world. Very few organizations are aware of these topics, and those who have exposure to it have started building scalable massive applications and lead in their domain industry. AWS, Azure, and GCP are tried and tested, and they are leading the cloud market, whereas Netflix and YouTube are the top companies in the video streaming domain, and behind the scenes you will find that they have implemented these same design patterns while implementing their services.

Most of the cloud vendors release their well-architected framework, guidelines, and design patterns that they use to consult their customers and tell them to build their services. For example, Amazon has released the **well-architected framework** (**WAF**). The five pillars that are used during any design discussion whenever you will be building your services around AWS cloud are as follows:

- Security
- Reliability
- Performance Efficiency
- Cost Optimization
- Operational Excellence

Mind maps are very useful for showing the relationship among these patterns so that you can get a good glimpse in a single view, and we tried to put them all together in the following design map. The following 32 are the broadly classified design patterns by Microsoft that you will find categorized under the previous seven design patterns. The next page shows a mind map of the design pattern:

Architectural and Design Patterns

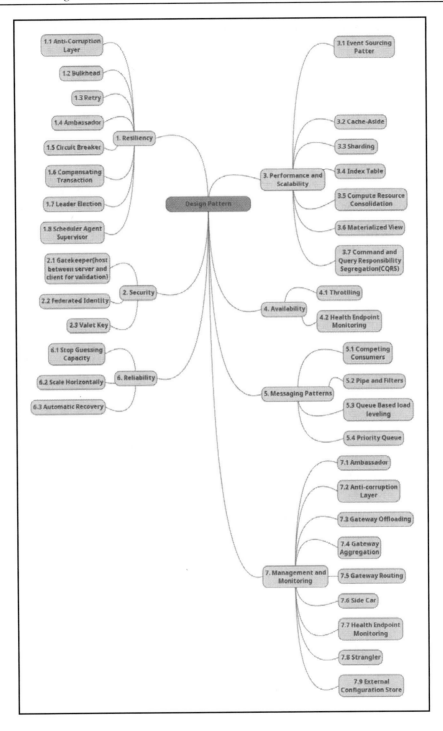

The following are some brief descriptions about these design patterns:

Design pattern	Summary
Ambassador	Helper service that sends network requests on behalf of consumer services or agents.
Anti-corruption layer	It helps you create a layer between a traditional legacy application and a newly designed application.
Backends for frontends	It helps give you an idea about how to create backend services that will be directly consumed by frontend services or UI.
Bulkhead	This gives an idea about how to isolate your application into pools so that one service failure doesn't impact the other service.
Cache-aside	Keeping data ready in the cache for fast access.
Circuit breaker	It helps you to design your service to handle failures where a service fix requires some time, and using a circuit breaker, you can implement logic about how you can delay or handle agent requests gracefully.
CQRS	**Command and query responsibility segregation (CQRS)** is a pattern that defines segregation operations to read data by using separate interfaces.
Compensating transaction	There are many conditions where your logic fails in the middle during execution, and you should implement functionality to gracefully roll back transactions to their original state.
Competing consumers	Enables multiple concurrent consumers to process messages received on the same messaging channel.
Compute resource consolidation	Consolidates multiple tasks or operations into a single computational unit.
Event sourcing	Uses an append-only store to record the full series of events that describe actions taken on data in a domain.
External configuration store	Moves configuration information out of the application deployment package to a centralized location.
Federated identity	Delegates authentication to an external identity provider.
Gatekeeper	Protect applications and services by using a dedicated host instance that acts as a broker between clients and the application or service validates, and sanitizes requests and passes requests and data among them.
Gateway aggregation	Uses a gateway to aggregate multiple individual requests into a single request.

Gateway offloading	Offloads shared or specialized service functionality to a gateway proxy.
Gateway routing	Routes requests to multiple services using a single endpoint.
Health endpoint monitoring	Implements functional checks in an application that external tools can access through exposed endpoints at regular intervals.
Index table	Creates indexes over the fields in data stores that are frequently referenced by queries.
Leader election	Coordinates the actions performed by a collection of collaborating task instances in a distributed application by electing one instance as the leader, who assumes responsibility for managing the other instances.
Materialized View	Generates pre-populated views over the data in one or more data stores when the data isn't ideally formatted for the required query operations.
Pipes and Filters	Breaks down a task that performs complex processing into a series of separate elements that can be reused.
Priority Queue	Prioritizes requests sent to services so that requests with a higher priority are received and processed more quickly than those with a lower priority.
Queue-based load leveling	Uses a queue that acts as a buffer between a task and a service that it invokes to smooth intermittent heavy loads.
Retry	Enables an application to handle anticipated temporary failures when it tries to connect to a service or a network resource by transparently retrying an operation that's previously failed.
Scheduler agent supervisor	Coordinates a set of actions across a distributed set of services and other remote resources.
Sharding	Divides a data store into a set of horizontal partitions or shards.
Sidecar	Deploys the components of an application into a separate process or container to provide isolation and encapsulation, such as running log and metric agent containers as a sidecar with your main application.
Static-content hosting	Hosts static contents on cloud provider services, such as AWS S3.
Strangler	Incrementally migrates a legacy system by gradually replacing specific pieces of functionality with new applications and services.
Throttling	It helps you limit requests on your service to avoid any DoS or DDoS attacks, and also gives clear implementation logic about how to handle multiple clients' traffic gracefully in a multi-tenant environment.

| Valet key | Uses a token or key that provides clients with restricted direct access to a specific resource or service. |

Reference: https://docs.microsoft.com/en-us/azure/architecture/patterns/.

Note: There are possibilities that the design pattern sub topic may fall into multiple categories, so keep hold of the *design pattern mind map* in your mind, as we have given more broad and random definitions under a specific design pattern topic and will not duplicate the definition of those design patterns.

Design pattern for security

Security is one of the important points while moving into the cloud or within your organization to protect yourself from external attacks. Security at each layer is a must and more important to secure your infrastructure, thus protecting confidential information. Security has the following broader design patterns that are also covered in AWS WAF:

- Identity and access management
- Detective control
- Infrastructure protection
- Data protection
- Incident response

Some detailed examples of the preceding points are as follows:

- Protecting identities using roles, for example, AWS IAM roles, implementing fine-grained authorization
- Blocking traffic using ports/IP ranges, such as AWS Security Groups and separating internal and external traffic using a CIDR range
- Latest trend using network flow log analysis to detect behavior such as AWS VPC flow log analysis using AWS GaurdDuty, Symantec Cloud Workload Protection

[175]

- Endpoint protection using anti malware/antivirus agents, such as Symantec Endpoint Point Protection, Symantec Cloud Workload Protection Agent, also known as a CAF agent
- Centralized log analysis around your IT infrastructure to detect anomalies or DDoS attacks by observing traffic trends or abnormal sources of traffic
- IDS/IPS approach by having all traffic forwarding through the gateway to such a system and then blocking/allowing traffic
- Security in transit and an at-REST approach such as using SSL implementation and encrypting your disk at storage
- You should have systematic process to handle any security incident, and you should have the available information to detect such incidents so that timely action can be taken on such incidents

Design pattern for resiliency

Resiliency is the ability of a system to gracefully handle and recover from failures. It is one of the most important factors when designing services so that it can recover either its high load, or the failure of internal or external components, during any condition:

- **Building services**: In microservices and implementing microservice design principle discussed in this book.
- **Retry logic**: It helps an application to handle anticipated, temporary failures if any endpoint or transaction fails, and it helps to retry the same transactions to recover from a specific issue.
- **Supervisor agent**: Installs a supervisor-like service that continuously monitors your application/daemons/services and restarts them if they fail. SupervisorD is an available free tool that companies use to recover their services, as it helps to configure multiple services monitoring using a simple configuration.
- **Health monitoring**: Each application/service should expose its health status so that it can be monitored using an external tool so that an action can be taken to notify and recover automatically. Most web applications expose/health. (php,aspx)-like pages that are continuously getting monitored by systems like AWS ELB and provides you *health status* mechanism to check instant status before forwarding traffic to registered nodes. Some of the external monitoring systems such as Runscope, AlertSite, and Webmetric systems monitor specific strings or HTTP 200 status codes to get the health status of your application.

- **Circuit breaker**: To protect your application from cascading failures these days, we are implementing logic that blocks traffic or send and delay messages to a connecting app that protects your application by blocking traffic to your downstream components. For example, if you already know that you are hitting your peak limit of scalability and you can't handle more traffic than if you send back a delay message to your agent if agents are provided by you, but if agents are provided by you, then you just block such traffic.
- **Queue-based system**: To handle temporary failures or to handle asynchronous loads, we are using a queue-based mechanism to handle traffic to avoid any failure of your service and to help with parallel processing without spiking your microservice CPU or memory. AMPQ implementations in the form of RabbitMQ are used in an industry for such a queuing system where multiple microservices listening to channels are configured under exchanges.
- **Compensating transaction**: There are many conditions when your logic fails in the middle during execution and you should implement functionality to gracefully roll back a transaction to its original state.
- **Master or leader selection**: There are many systems in a distributed environment or in a microservices world, where an infrastructure component assumes a master or a leader role so that functionality can be made compliant, according to guidelines. For example, Docker swarm uses a manager node, and Kubernetes uses a master node to manage other worker nodes.

Design pattern for scalability

Scalability is the ability of a system either to handle an increase in load without an impact on performance or that we can readily increase scaling on resource utilization for the available resources:

- Avoid, a single point of failure
- Scale, horizontally, not vertically
- Move work away from your core service
- Implementation of caching system
- Keep, your cache up to date
- Asynchronous system
- Statelessness
- Make, your system able to handle any failure

Scalability is one among many AWS WAF components. When scaling to handle load, you will find the preceding design principles in the following points. We usually see these in practical implementations in our real cloud and container worlds:

- **Scaling on CPU utilization**: Monitoring the CPU utilization of your service then scaling up or scaling down, Kubernetes, AWS **Elastic Container Service (ECS)**, **Elastic Container Service for Kubernetes (EKS)**, or other cloud systems use similar approaches to scale client infrastructure as they collect this information from hypervisors and expose CPU utilization to external apps.
- **Scaling on memory utilization**: Services can be scaled using memory monitoring, but AWS ECS, EKS, and Kubernetes don't have it as a default functionality, and you must write your own wrappers around it.
- **Scaling on a number of connection requests**: You can scale your service by a number of connections because there are some systems such as proxy systems and load balancers that just forward clients requests to downstream microservices that require the capacity to handle a specific number of connections.
- **Scaling storage capacity**: Scaling storage capacity or a filesystem is another requirement in a scalable system where you must scale your hard disk/file systems so that it can handle your requirements.

Design pattern for performance

Performance can be measured using the responsiveness of your system on any given period of time. These are the following design principles for the efficiency described in AWS WAF:

- Democratize advanced technologies
- Go global in minutes
- Use Serverless architectures
- Experiment more often
- Mechanical sympathy

Here are some more detailed explanations of the mentioned design principles:

- **Democratize advanced technologies**: It's better to take complex technology from external vendors or as a service instead of reinventing the wheel at your end, because it's hard to implement complex technologies in a short duration, and other competitors can get an edge if you are unable to implement them in-house.
- **Go global in minutes**: The cloud helps you to reach out to a wider community in a short duration of time or even in minutes.

- **Use Serverless architectures**: In the cloud, Serverless architectures remove the need for you to run and maintain servers to carry out traditional compute activities. For example, storage services can act as static websites, removing the need for web servers, and event services can host your code for you. This removes the operational burden of managing these servers and can also lower transactional costs because these managed services operate at a cloud scale.
- **Experiment more often**: The cloud helps you to experiment more, as more often you can try different designs and architectures.
- **Mechanical sympathy**: It gives you a more aligned approach about how you would like to implement your design.

Design principles for availability

Availability is the term used to refer to the uptime of your system. It is one of the most requested features by most of the companies during their SLA agreement, as availability is directly propositional to income:

- Business drives high availability
- Keep it simple strategy
- Configuring for higher availability

Here is a more detailed implementation of availability at a very granular level:

- **HA at region level**: Make sure you deploy your infrastructure in multiple regions, such as deploying some infra in the US and Asia so that you can failover if one region goes down. For example: AWS regions.
- **HA at zone level**: Usage of multi availability zones, such as availability zones.
- **HA at network level**: Major vendors enterprise networking gears come with high available functionality where it can failover traffic to an other router/switch. In case they don't detect any heartbeat, then you can perform maintenance.
- **HA at load balancer level**: Using highly available services, such as AWS **Elastic Load Balancing** (ELB) or deploying redundant load balancers using a clustering solution.
- **HA at hypervisor level**: VMware ESXi or other hypervisor platforms come with HA protocol, where they make another system the leader when one of the systems goes down.
- **HA at service/at microservice level**: Deploying your service on highly available systems, such as Kubernetes pods, AWS EKS, ECS, and Docker swarm.

You can keep eye on your incident trends, and you can have a look on **mean time to resolve (MTTR)** and **mean time in-between failure (MTBF)** to get an idea about the availability of your services and whether you have implemented the preceding mentioned key concepts so that your incident should be low on counts.

Design principles for reliability

People are moving toward the cloud because it guarantees to provide you with a more reliable system compared to an in-house setup. Cost is one of the major factors in achieving the right amount of reliability:

- Test recovery procedures
- Automatically recover from failure
- Scale horizontally to increase aggregate system availability
- Stop guessing capacity
- Manage change using automation

The following gives more information about the previous points:

- **Test recover procedures**: Practice recovery procedure for your services data so that you can handle any incident and recover your system in a short period of time to make your system more reliable.
- **Automatically recover from failure**: Monitor your **key performance indicators (KPI)** to automatically take action during failure, for quick recovery.
- **Scale horizontally to increase aggregate system availability**: Scaling horizontally is fast in comparison to vertical scaling, and the horizontal scaling cost is going linear, whereas vertically scaling cost goes exponential.
- **Stop guessing capacity**: Provide data and facts to your system so that it can take a decision to scale instead of guessing your customer traffic. Guessing is a short-term temporary fix, and this situation comes when people don't have metric collection about their services. In the absence of data/facts, if you choose to guess the load, it leads to failure and decreases reliability. We see more unreliable infra during DDoS attacks on a guessed system compared to a fact/data-based scaled system.
- **Manage change using automation**: Avoid human intervention in change implementation, and try to automate this process as much as possible.

Some time back, I was working to achieve reliability for my company, and I developed a project reliability maturity KPI matric that was very useful for telling people about the maturity or reliability implementation in the project using various KPI categorized under it.

Design patterns – circuit breaker

In this section, we will discuss the circuit breaker pattern. Before that, let's think about any microservice architecture in which one service is synchronously invoked by other services. What if one service breaks down? This could be due to high latency, a code issue, or limited resources. The failure of one service can lead to other services failing throughout the application. To manage this problem and prevent a cascading service failure, we can use a circuit breaker. This is more than a design pattern; we can think of it as a sustainable pattern, which means that it can help prevent our microservices from dying.

Everything fails, accept it! A circuit breaker can help us solve our problems.

Think about your own personal electricity supply. You might get power from the main grid, and it might come through a circuit breaker. If a lighting strike causes additional power to surge on the power grid, it will break the circuit breaker. The circuit breaker will therefore protect your internal wiring and the electrical system in your home. In the microservice world, circuit breakers work in exactly the same way that is if a service goes down or fails: it will stop all the calls and requests to that particular service and instead return cached data or a timeout error.

Advantages of circuit breakers

Here are a few advantages of a circuit breaker:

- **Monitoring**: The circuit breaker is very valuable for monitoring. If a service goes down, it should be monitored, properly logged somewhere, and recovered from a failure state.

Architectural and Design Patterns

- **Fault-tolerant**: When you test various states in your circuit breaker, this helps you add logic to create a fault-tolerant system. For example, if service1 is unavailable, then we can add logic to fetch the service1 page from the cache.
- **Reduced load**: If service1 is slow or down, a circuit breaker can handle this situation by serving a cached page or a timeout page and help the services to recover by reducing their load.

As we can see in the following diagram, the circuit breaker pattern has three states: **Closed**, **Open**, and **Half-Open**:

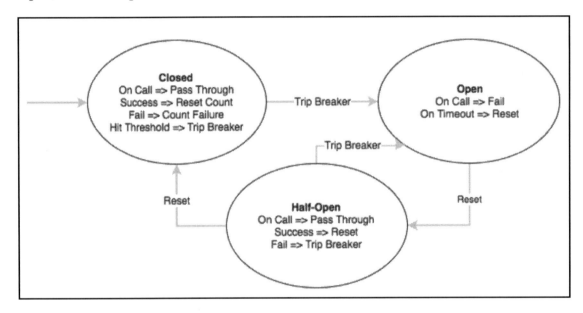

Closed state

The normal state of the circuit breaker pattern is the closed state, which indicates that all services are up and running. It will pass all requests through to the services. If the number of failure requests increases by a predefined threshold, this will turn to the open state:

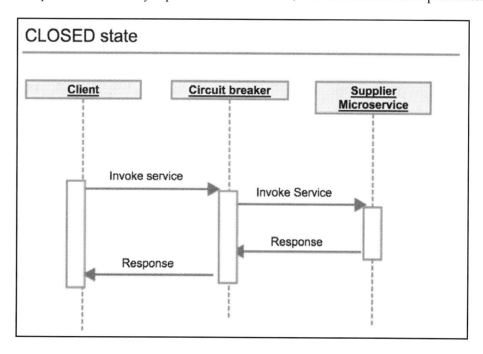

As you can see from the preceding diagram, the **Client** is trying to access the service, and the request is passed through the **Circuit breaker**. In this case, our backend microservice (referred to as the **Supplier Microservice**) is up and running, so it can respond without latency. The **Circuit breaker** passes that request through to the **Client**.

Open state

If our backend service is experiencing slowness or if the service is down for any reason, the circuit breaker receives a failure response for a backend service. Once the number of failure requests increases by a predefined threshold value, it will change the circuit breaker state to open. The circuit breaker can handle this situation by serving a cached page or a timeout page and help those services recover by reducing their load:

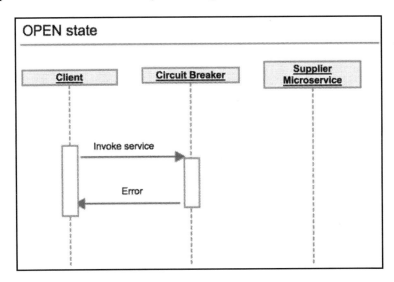

As we can see from the preceding diagram, our backend microservice (**Supplier Microservice**) is unavailable. The **Circuit Breaker** responds with either an **Error** or a cached page to the **Client**. We can add in logic to our **Circuit Breaker** to indicate which response it should send if the backend microservice is unavailable.

Half-open state

We should have proper monitoring in place for the circuit breaker to know whether the backend microservice has recovered. The circuit breaker makes trial calls to a backend microservice periodically to check the status of that service. This state is known as the **half-open state**. It will remain in this half-open state unless all requests return successfully from the backend microservice. Then the circuit will retain its normal status, which is the closed state:

Chapter 6

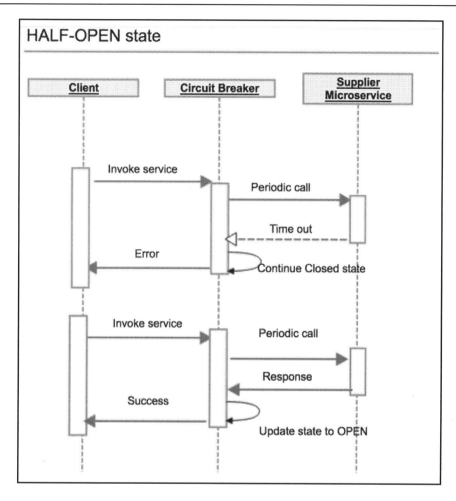

As shown in the preceding diagram, the **Client** request failed due to the unavailability of the backend microservice (**Supplier Microservice**), and the **Circuit Breaker** went into the open state. After a time, the circuit breaker continues to check the backend service status using trail calls. Once the **Circuit Breaker** receives a successful request from the trail calls, the circuit will be switched to the closed state.

Architectural and Design Patterns

Summary

In this chapter, we covered architectural patterns, design patterns, software-inclined design patterns, and patterns that are currently distribute as cloud-dominated **Software as a Service (SaaS)** inclined markets, and they are trying to explore more patterns that can be easily achieved and implemented. We have given an overview of how to design your application around those patterns, and we have provided a good pictorial view, using mind maps that can be easily referred to during such discussion and implementation. We covered circuit breakers, rate limit, and throttling, which will help you build resilient services that can handle any distributed attacks and give a good experience to customers hosted on a multi-tenant environment. We covered circuit breakers thoroughly to give you an idea about how to implement them and how to use them in a situation where you are experiencing a heavy load or your backend-serving services are down. We have given tips for availability and reliability that you can use in your live project.

In the next chapter, we will be learning about reliability implementation techniques, which will include rust programming and ballerina programming.

Reliability Implementation Techniques

This chapter hopes to reassure you that the future is bright that is things are changing in the cloud era, and we will soon be able to use the right programming language to support our thinking. We will be able to write code using FaaS, microservices, and endpoints, to which IoT devices will send data. Almost everything will go through gateways and hit your services through APIs. In the last three decades, we have seen the development of many programming languages, which have been worked on by numerous programmers. Are all these programming languages meant for the future? We would say no; very few languages provide appropriate support for the world of integration through APIs. Node.js is perhaps the only one that is trying to fulfil the principles of REST programming.

In this chapter, we are going to cover the language of the future. It has been referred to as the first cloud-native programming language and lauded as flexible, powerful, and beautiful. Yes, we are going to cover Ballerina, is a totally new programming language, that is compiled, static, rich in data types, and strongly typed. It has support for XML, uses JSON, and has a textual and graphical syntax. Yes, a graphical syntax! Be prepared to be amazed by this language. It will provide you with a complete overview of your logic when coding in your IDE.

We are also going to cover a second programming language, which is Rust. We are going to cover the following topics:

- Ballerina programming
- Rust programming
- Concepts related to reliability

Ballerina programming

My first impression of Ballerina was that it was an amazing language that would vastly improve the world of SRE. It provides everything we need in the decentralized world: libraries, IDEs, compilers, builders, deployers, documentation, and tools. In Ballerina's first demo, the developers created a REST endpoint listening on a network port, implemented communication with Twitter on their API, and embedded a `hello` function with the same code file as the `main()` function of their services, and all in a maximum of 15 minutes. They continued to show more examples, including how to use a circuit breaker with Ballerina in a few very simple steps.

Ballerina evolved from the Apache Synapse project in 2005. It was developed by WS02 architects in response to integration implementations using existing languages. It is a simple programming language and was released under the Apache License v.2.0

Its syntax and runtime address the hard problems of endpoint integration. It is a Turing complete language, and it enables agility, with fast edit, build, and run cycles. Ballerina code is compiled in services that include transactions, embedded brokers, and gateway runtimes.

It has the following features:

- It is a programming language for the network world
- It is optimized for integration in the distributed world
- It is very simple to understand and write, like a simple C program with if and else conditions
- It uses simple syntax with no indentation, unlike languages such as Node.js, Go, Python, or Java, which are not very developer-friendly
- It has data, network, and security-aware programming inspired by Maven, Go, Java, and Node.js
- It helps to increase developer's productivity by improving clarity and allowing developers to review code logic at a single glance
- It has low latency, uses little memory, and has a fast startup time
- It supports JSON, XML, and tables as a data type
- It provides connectors for single sign-on authentication. It also provides connectors for BasicAuth, SOAP, AmazonAuth, and OAuth
- It has deep integration with HTTP, REST, and Swagger
- It provides client connectors for major web APIs such as Twitter, LinkedIn, Facebook, Gmail, and Lambda functions
- It has a patent pending

- It integrates well with Docker
- It integrates well with Kubernetes and can deploy code using it
- It can understand your test-case requirements
- It can understand your package repository requirements and provide a similar model to Go, **Node Package Manager** (**NPM**), or Maven dependency management
- It is available on most widely used IDEs, including Vim, VC, IntelliJ IDEA, and PyCharm
- It uses the parallel worker concept, where workers are non-blocking, and no functions can lock the execution of other parallel functions defined in the same file

While the preceding list is already very long, there are another couple of important features that are worth highlighting. One of these is the Ballerina composer tool, which is a browser-based tool that can be used to write code and draw sequential diagrams in an innovative way. We can easily switch between the sequence diagram view and the source code view. The composer source code is available in GitHub, so download it and try it in your development work. Another amazing feature is that a single program has a `main()` function and service endpoints that can listen to any valid network port (from 0 to 65,535) and you can have concurrent processing in a single program. This is the first language that has this kind of innovative feature and that also keeps REST API endpoints in mind.

In this section, we are going to look at the following examples:

- A `hello` program example
- A sequential diagram example
- A simple example with Twitter integration
- A circuit breaking code example
- A data type and control logic expression statement

A hello program example

The following is the standard Ballerina `hello` program that shows how to print. Create a file using `vim` and run the `hello.bal` command:

```
//#vim hello.bal

//Ballerina base library for Input/Output messages
import ballerina/io;
```

```
// function main()
public function main()
{
     io:println("You are reading PacktPub Hello example! ");
     io:println("-------- Program End -------");
}
```

A simple example with Twitter integration

The following program is an example of how to integrate with the Twitter API. We are going to pass the Twitter API credentials for your account through a configuration file. This program will be listening on TCP port:9090, and it will post a tweet through your account.

Run the following command to execute the following code:

ballerina build packt-twitter-example.bal

```
    // NOTE 1: Use Linux VIM editor to edit file and copy following code
    mentioned after vim line
    // NOTE 2: Make sure you get twitter's client id, secret, access and tokens
    before running this code and you can refer
    https://developer.twitter.com/en/account/get-started

    #vim packt-twitter-example.bal

    //Example shown during Ballerina demo
    //Created for Ballerina example and similar reference can be taken from
    their github
    //Github: https://github.com/ballerina-platform/ballerina-lan

    import ballerina/config;
    import ballerina/io;
    import wso2/twitter;

    endpoint http:Listener listener {
       port:9090
    }

    endpoint twitter:client tweeter {
       clintId: config:getAsString("YOUR_CLIENT_ID");
       clientSecret: config:getAsString("YOUR_CLIENT_SECRET");
       accessToken: config:getAsString("YOUR_ACCESS_TOKEN");
       accessTokenSecret: config:getAsString("YOUR_ACCESS_TOKEN_SECRET");
       clientConfig: {}
    }
```

Chapter 7

```
@http:ServiceConfig {
   basePath: "/",
}
service<http:Service> hello bind listener {
 @http:ResourceConfig {
 basePath: "/",
 methods: ["POST"],
 body: "person",
 consumes: ["application/json"],
 produces: ["application/json"]
 }
     hi (endpoint caller, http:Request request, Person person) {
     string payload_body = check request.getTextPayload();
     var status = check tweeter ->tweet("Hello" + payload_body + "PacktPub
#ballerina example" )
     int id = status.id;
     string createdAt = status.CreatedAt;
     json jason_content = {
         twitterID: id,
         createdAt: createdAt,
         key: "value"
     };
     _ = caller -> respond(jason_content);
   }
}
```

This will generate a graph that looks as follows (note that the text is different, as we used different code for the graph):

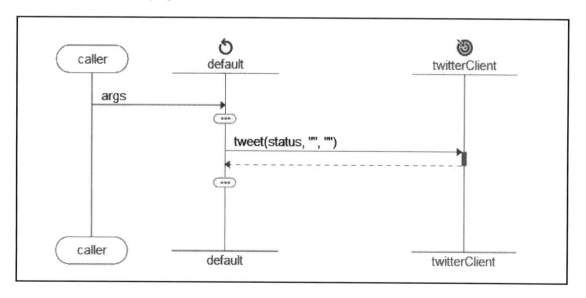

Reliability Implementation Techniques

The -> arrow mark is very important. The graph generator tool uses it to generate the endpoint graph from the caller to the endpoint with information about the communication direction, and it is very useful to developers when writing their code.

Using Ballerina, we can add service endpoints directly to our code and make them co-exist with the main function. This makes Ballerina a completely cloud-native programming language that supports gateways and REST API endpoints with minimal code lines.

Kubernetes deployment code

The following code will generate a Docker image with the Kubernetes deployment file in YAML format. It is very well organized by the Ballerina source code folder tree structure, referenced here:

```
// -------------------------------------
@kubernetes:Deployment {
   image: "demo/ballerina-packt-image",
   name: "ballerina-packt-image"
}

// secretes.toml is file in which we defined our secure or other variables
@kubernetes:ConfigMap {
   ballerinaConf: "secretes.toml"
}
@http:ServiceConfig {
 basePath: "/"
}
// -------------------------------------

//Following is just same code that we given in above twitter example to
give you reference about where you can place your deployment code
service<http:Service> hello bind listener {
  @http:ResourceConfig {
      path: "/",
      methods: ["POST"]
   }
   hi (endpoint caller, http:Request request, Person person) {
     string body = check request.getTextPayload();
     var status = check tweeter ->tweet("hello" + body + "PacktPub #ballerina example" );
     int id = status.id;
     string createdAt = status.CreatedAt;
     json js = {
       twitterID: id,
       createdAt: createdAt,
```

```
        key: "value"
    };
}
```

In the preceding code block, the `Deployment` and `ConfigMap` lines will convert your code into easily deployable code on a Kubernetes cluster. After writing those lines, you should be in a position to run the rest of the commands.

If you build and compile your newly modified code, you will see some Kubernetes related messages. It will also generate a Kubernetes folder structure in which you can find your deployment configuration in YAML. This can be directly deployed on Kubernetes or on an OpenShift cluster by using the `kubctl` command on the generated `ConfigMap` files under the Kubernetes folder. An example of this is as follows:

```
@kubernetes:ConfigMap – complete 1/1 - Referring that it has successfully generated Kubernetes config map files

$ ballerina build packt-twitter-example.bal
@kubernetes:Service                   - complete 1/1
@kubernetes:ConfigMap                 - complete 1/1
@kubernetes:Docker                    - complete 3/3
@kubernetes:Deployment                - complete 1/1
```

The following `tree` command shows the file and folder structure generated after the `build` command:

```
$ tree
.
├── packt-twitter-example.bal
├── packt-twitter-example.balx
├── kubernetes
│   ├── packt-twitter-example_config_map.yaml
│   ├── packt-twitter-example_deployment.yaml
│   ├── packt-twitter-example_svc.yaml
│   └── docker
│       └── Dockerfile
└── secretes.toml
```

Once you run `kubectl apply` on the generated configuration map YAML file or on the folder structure, it will deploy your Twitter code as a running pod on which you can redirect network traffic:

```
# Following kubectl command will deploy YAML configs on your kubernetes cluster

$ kubectl apply -f kubernetes/
configmap "packt-twitter-example_config_map" created
```

```
deployment "packt-twitter-example" created
service "packt-twitter-example" created

#Run following commands to see your deployment status

$ kubectl get pods
```

A circuit breaker code example

The following code is an example of a circuit breaker using Ballerina. It will be listening on the `port:9090` TCP, as well as on `port:9091` TCP. The code is much more readable for programmers than the code for other languages:

```
//Circuit breaking example from https://ballerina.io/
import ballerina/http;
import ballerina/io;

string previousRes;

endpoint http:Listener listener {
port:9090
};

// Endpoint with circuit breaker can short circuit responses under
// some conditions. Circuit flips to OPEN state when errors or
// responses take longer than timeout. OPEN circuits bypass
// endpoint and return error.
endpoint http:Client legacyServiceResilientEP {
url: "http://localhost:9091",
circuitBreaker: {
// Failure calculation window
rollingWindow: {
// Duration of the window
timeWindowMillis: 10000,

// Each time window is divided into buckets
bucketSizeMillis: 2000,

// Min # of requests in a `RollingWindow` to trip circuit
requestVolumeThreshold: 0
},

// Percentage of failures allowed
failureThreshold: 0.0,

// Reset circuit to CLOSED state after timeout
```

```
    resetTimeMillis: 1000,

    // Error codes that open the circuit
    statusCodes: [400, 404, 500]
    },

    // Invocation timeout - independent of circuit
    timeoutMillis: 2000
};
```

The preceding code is for `legacyServiceResilientEP` with various circuit breaker definitions. The following code is a further extension of this, in which we are defining various paths and methods with circuit breaker condition definitions, according to which the code will respond:

```
@http:ServiceConfig {
basePath:"/resilient/time"
}
service<http:Service> timeInfo bind listener {

@http:ResourceConfig {
methods:["GET"],
path:"/"
}
getTime (endpoint caller, http:Request req) {

var response = legacyServiceResilientEP ->
get("/legacy/localtime");

match response {

// Circuit breaker not tripped
http:Response res => {
http:Response okResponse = new;
if (res.statusCode == 200) {

string payloadContent = check res.getTextPayload();
previousRes = untaint payloadContent;
okResponse.setTextPayload(untaint payloadContent);
io:println("Remote service OK, data received");

} else {

// Remote endpoint returns an error
io:println("Error received from "+"remote service.");
okResponse.setTextPayload("Previous Response : "
+ previousRes);
```

Reliability Implementation Techniques

```
}
okResponse.statusCode = http:OK_200;
_ = caller -> respond(okResponse);
}

// Circuit breaker tripped and generates error
error err => {
http:Response errResponse = new;
io:println("Circuit open, using cached data");
errResponse.setTextPayload( "Previous Response : "
+ previousRes);

// Inform client service is unavailable
errResponse.statusCode = http:OK_200;
_ = caller -> respond(errResponse);
        }
    }
  }
}
```

The following screenshot shows the circuit breaker code flow diagram:

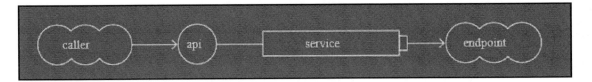

Ballerina data types

Ballerina provides similar data types to those that we have seen in traditional programming languages. However, it also provides some other useful types, such as XML, JSON, and Table. The following hierarchical chart shows the different supported data types:

Chapter 7

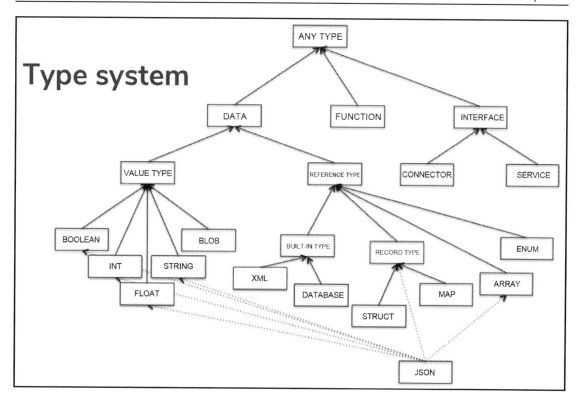

Control logic expression

Similar to other programming languages, Ballerina has control logic statements, such as the C programming language, and these are very simple. The available control statements are as follows:

1. while
2. if ..else if .. else
3. foreach
4. Match
5. Match expression
6. Elvis

The following code shows an example using `while` that will run this loop twice and print an `i` value:

```
//while example
while (i < 2) {
        io:println(i);
        i = i + 1;
}

//Output:
1
```

The following code is an example using the `if ... else if ... else` statement. It will print values according to the provided value of b. For example, if you set b=2, it will print b > 0:

```
// if ..else if..else example
if (b < 0) {
        io:println("b < 0");
} else if (b > 0) {
        io:println("b > 0");
} else {
        io:println("b == 0");
}
```

The following example will provide all the names in the boys' names list:

```
//foreach example
string[] boys = ["Shailender", "Shreyansh"];
foreach v in boys {
        io:println("boys: " + v);
}

//Output:
Shailender
Shreyansh
```

There are many other statements and expressions and operators available in Ballerina, such as the `Elvis` operator and the `match` and `match expression` flow control statements.

All referenced examples can be found by going to the following link:
https://ballerina.io/learn/by-example/.

[198]

There are many components that we should discuss when describing Ballerina, including its runtime environment, how it can deploy code on most of the latest orchestration tools, such as Kubernetes and Docker, and its life cycle, from writing the source code to production and deployment.

The building blocks of Ballerina

Ballerina has the following three foundational building blocks:

- Runtime
- Deployment
- Life cycle

Let us take a look at each point in detail:

- **Ballerina runtime environment**: The complete definition of runtime is described on the right-hand side of the following screenshot:

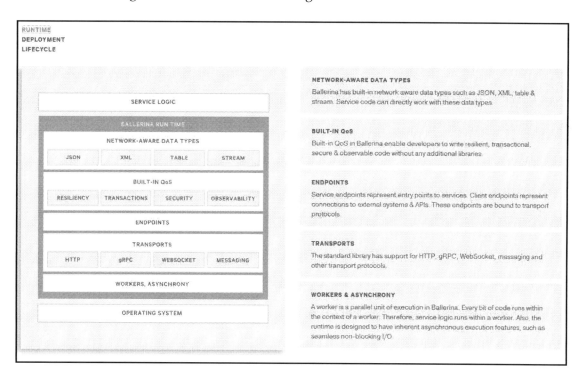

Reliability Implementation Techniques

   This screenshot can be found at the following website: `http://ballerina.io`.

- **Ballerina deployment**: We can deploy Ballerina code directly from your developer Command Prompt, and this option supports DevOps and easy CI/CD. The following screenshot shows the platforms on which you can deploy the Ballerina service:

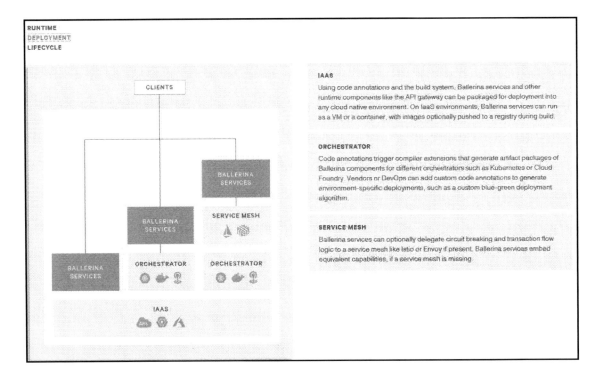

- **Life cycle:** Ballerina has multiple tools, including source code compilation for test-case generation and helps build various different deployment platforms. We can write the Ballerina source code with the `.bal` extension in most famous IDEs such as Visual Studio, VIM, PyCharm, and IDEA, and then we can use the `ballerina build` command to compile the source code into byte code with the `.balx` extension. After that, we use `ballerina run<binary_name>.balx` to execute our code. The following diagram shows the life cycle of our source code through the **CI/CD** process:

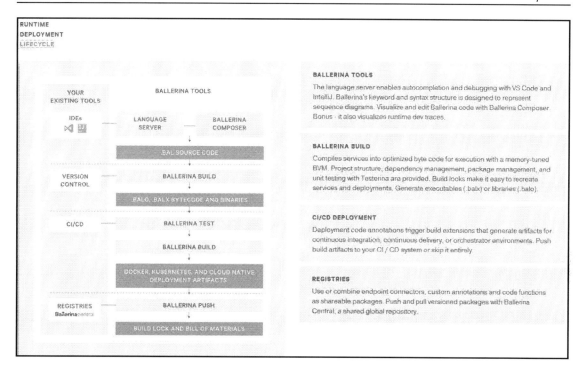

Ballerina command cheat sheet

The following code is a command cheat sheet that you use for your reference:

```
#ballerina init
#ballerina build <source_code>.bal
#ballerina run <byte_code>.balx

#ballerina search <library>
Example: #ballerina search twitter

#ballerina help
#ballerina push
#ballerina pull
#ballerina test
#ballerina version
#ballerina swagger
#ballerina list
#ballerina doc
#ballerina encrypt
```

Reference: https://ballerina.io/philosophy/.

Reliability

This section is about the reliability of applications. A circuit breaker is an important concept in reliability, as it helps us to avoid cascading failures as a result of third-party failed endpoints or failed components within your application. We may well have faced situations in which one component failure has taken our complete system down. Even though we already had DR setup and multiple availability zones, our application still failed. To solve this problem, we can implement a circuit breaker, which helps to make our services more reliable and predictable.

It helps to either degrade your service or reply with your own HTTP code, requesting that the client helps you to implement a reliable service in which your application responds with some valid return code. In our Twitter example, we can easily embed a circuit breaking code. There are numerous examples available on the internet for your reference.

It is very important to embed reliability in your code so that it can handle failures and exceptions gracefully and make you a more reliable vendor in the market. Reliability affects your reputation, and reputation is related to money, so it is important to design your application with the future in mind.

Rust programming

Let's get started with the Rust language. Before going into detail about Rust programming, it is important to consider why we need it, bearing in mind we already have several other languages such as Java, C/C++, and Python. In C/C++/C# we have a lot of control over the hardware that we are running on, so we can optimize it properly. In C/C++/C# languages, we can have more control, as we can translate them directly to assembly code, but they are not very safe, as small mistakes can create big segfaults. On the other hand, we have the Python and Ruby languages, which give us more safety, but very little control over what's going on. This is where Rust comes into play. Using Rust, we have all the control, plus all the safety as well.

The official definition given by (rust-lang.org) is that *Rust is a systems programming language that runs blazingly fast, prevents segfaults, and guarantees thread safety.*

Rust is a systems programming language, which means you can utilize some interesting features such as fine-grained control over allocation or its not-required garbage collection (memory leaks are rare) or minimal runtime. Rust runs blazingly fast, which makes this language everyone's favorite, as you can run and compile your code very quickly. It can provides us better performance than C/C++. Rust prevents almost all crashes and segfaults. It's just safe by default. It has no null pointers and no dangling pointers, it's just a sophisticated type and the last part is that it eliminates data races, which means it guarantees thread safety and ownership.

Installing Rust

Installing Rust is very simple; you just need to run the following installation script, and it will automatically install. This rustup script is shared by https://www.rust-lang.org/en-US/:

```
curl -sSf https://static.rust-lang.org/rustup.sh | sh
```

Once you have completed the installation, just try to run `rustc -v` to verify the installation version. `rustc` is a rust compiler.

Lets get started by using a simple `hello` code:

```
// This is the main function
fn main() {
    // The statements here will be executed when the compiled binary is called
    println!("Hello. This is PacktPublisher!"); //println is Macro which prints text to console.
}
```

Concept of Rust programming

Lots of you may be wondering why we need another language when we already have many of them: JAVA, C/C++, Python, and so on. Before going deep into rust programming, let's see why need it in the first place and why we are calling it the future of programming. In C/C++/C#, we have a lot of control over the hardware that we are running on so that we can optimize it properly. In these languages, we can have more control, as we can translate it directly to assembly code, but it's not very safe, and a small mistake can create a big segfault. On the other hand, we have the Python or Ruby language, which gives us more safety but very little control over what's going on. But now we have Rust, and Rust gives you all the control, plus all the safety. The Rust language first appeared around 2010; it was developed and designed by Graydon Hoare.

Rust language won the *Most Loved Programming Language* in the stack overflow survey in 2016, 2017, and 2108:

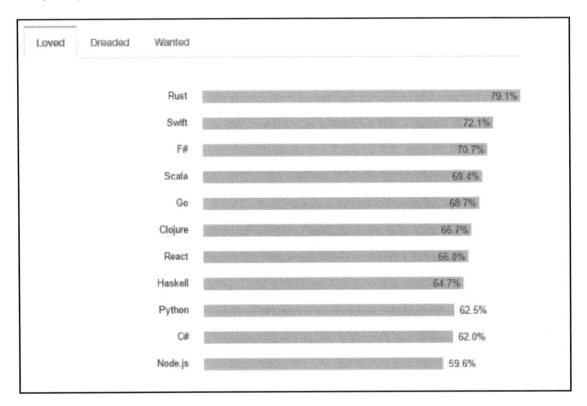

The following diagram shows how Rust has evolved over time:

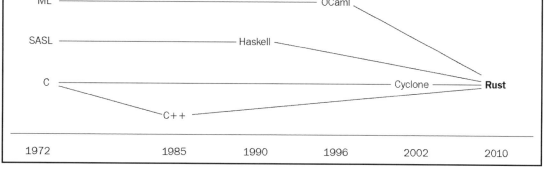

The ownership of variables in Rust

Variables are moved to new locations, preventing the previous location from using them. We need to define the owner of the variable, so we can't just create a new variable randomly and use it.

In the following code, Box is the allocation operation. We are passing it to the helper function. As we can see in the following example, in the first helper function call with the first slot value, the ownership is moved under the helper function. During the second call, it fails, because the second call has the Box<int> type, which can't be copied:

```
fn main() {
    let slot = Box 1;
    helper(slot); // moves the value
    helper(slot); // error: use of moved value
    }
fn helper(slot: Box<int>) {
    println!("The Number was: {}", slot)
    }
```

Borrowing values in Rust

Owned values can be borrowed in Rust to allow them to be used for a certain period of time. Borrows can be nested, and borrowed values can become owned values through cloning (using a command such as v.clone).

The following code snippet shows an example of borrowing. The & symbol means *borrowed reference*:

```
fn helper(slot: &Vec<int> { /* ... */ }
fn main() {
  let a = Vec::new();// doesn't move!
  helper(&a);
  helper(&a);
   }
```

Borrowed values are only valid for a particular lifetime:

```
let a: &int;
{
    let b = 3;
    a = &b; // error! 'b' does not live long enough
}

Let a: &int;
let b =3;
a = &b; // ok, 'b' has the same lifetime as 'a'
```

Memory management in Rust

Rust has a fine-grained memory management, but it is automatically managed once created. Each variable has a scope in which it is valid, and it is automatically de-allocated when it goes out of scope.

The following code snippet shows an example of memory management:

```
fn main() {
       // 'Slot' is an *owned* value
       let slot = box 3i;// The Slot goes out of scope here, it is owner if its data
   }
```

Mutability in Rust

Values are immutable by default in Rust and must be tagged to be mutable:

```
Let a = 10;
a = 11; //Error
//Lets see how mutability can help here
Let mut a =10;
a = 11; // It will work fine!
```

Mutability is also a part of the type of a borrowed pointer. Variables are immutable only by default; we can make them mutable by adding mut in front of the variable name:

```
fn inc(i: &mut int) {
    *i +=1; //It will work fine!
}
```

Concurrency in Rust

Concurrency involves using ownership to prevent data races. Parallelism, which refers to the ability for different parts of a program to execute at the same time, is becoming increasingly important as more computers take advantage of multiple processors. Concurrency allows you to write code that's free of subtle bugs and is easy to refactor without introducing new bugs. Safety is achieved by ensuring that proc owns the captured variables. Threads can communicate with channels as follows:

```
//Spawn a child thread to be run in parallel
spawn(proc() {
    expensive_computation();
} );
other_expensive_computation();
```

Error-handling in Rust

Irrespective of the programming language, errors will occur. We need to be able to handle these errors. In Rust programming, we have two types of errors:

1. **Unrecoverable errors**: Like Macro in Clang, Rust has a similar panic! function. Take a look at the following example, which shows how we can handle unrecoverable errors using the panic! function inside the main:

    ```
    fn main()
    {
        panic!("Something is wrong... Check for Errors");
    }
    ```

2. **Recoverable error**: This is a standard part of programming and is nicely handled by Rust. Take a look at the following example. When you call File::open and an error occurs, it will call the panic function:

    ```
    use std::fs::File;
    fn main() {
        let _E = File::open("PacktDocument.txt");
        let _E = match _E
    ```

```
    {   Ok(file) => file,
        Err(why) => panic!("Something is wrong with the Document
{:?}", why),
    };
}
```

The future of Rust programming

Rust is good at large-scale maintainable systems and is easy to embed in other languages. While Rust is still maturing, there are already many projects that use it. For example, Redox is an operating system written in Rust; Iron is a concurrent web framework written in Rust; and Microsoft Azure IoT Edge, a platform used to run Azure services and artificial intelligence on IoT devices, has components that are implemented in Rust as well. Other projects developed in Rust include Servo Mozilla's parallel web browser engine, which was developed in collaboration with Samsung and Quantum. This project, composed of several sub-projects, improves the Gecko web browser engine of Firefox, which was developed by Mozilla. You can get more details about Rust on the following website: (`rust-lang.org`, `github.com/rust-lang/rust`).

Summary

In this chapter, we covered a couple of great languages. We have looked at their complete runtime environment, deployment commands, service graphs, and a cheat sheet for easy reference. We also defined how important these languages are in the existing cloud era, where everything is being converted to API endpoints and REST. These languages are very important from an SRE point of view, as we can easily see how communication happens between various endpoints and services in the cloud environment. This helps with the planning, implementing, and real-time troubleshooting of applications.

In the next chapter we will be leaning about the best practices included in Realizing Reliable Systems.

8
Realizing Reliable Systems - the Best Practices

System reliability is defined as the combination of system resiliency and elasticity. With the proliferation of web-scale, data-intensive, and process-intensive applications across industry verticals, the application reliability has to be ensured at any cost to fulfil varying business expectations. Similarly, cloud environments emerge as the one-stop IT solution for business process and operation automations. All kinds of personal, professional, and social applications are being meticulously modernized and moved to cloud centers to reap all the originally expressed benefits of the software-defined cloud infrastructures. Thus, cloud reliability is also guaranteed through the leverage of highly pioneering technologies and tools. Thus, the reliability of applications and IT infrastructures is very important to encourage customers to retain their confidence and continuity on the various innovations and improvisations happening in the IT space. This chapter will pin down the best practices accrued out of the expertise, experience, and education of site reliability engineers, DevOps people, and cloud engineers.

The world is increasingly becoming connected. With the competent technologies and tools continuously abound for establishing and sustaining deeper and extreme connectivity, our everyday entities and elements are getting connected with one another (locally, as well as remotely) to interact and collaborate decisively and deeply. All kinds of physical, mechanical, electrical, and electronics systems in our personal as well as professional environments are connected to and integrated with the faster maturity and stability of digitization/edge technologies. There are powerful communication and data transmission protocols emerging and evolving fast to systematically link up everything and to empower them to team up together in a purpose-driven manner.

Furthermore, the power of digital technologies (cloud infrastructures and platforms for hosting and managing operational and transactional applications, big, fast, and streaming data analytics platforms, groundbreaking **artificial intelligence** (**AI**) algorithms and approaches to bring forth prognostic, predictive, prescriptive, and personalized insights out of the **Internet of Things** (**IoT**) data, the pervasiveness of the **microservices architecture** (**MSA**) pattern, enterprise mobility, and social networking, the surging popularity of fog or edge computing, blockchain, and so on) leads to the realization of knowledge-filled, service-oriented, event-driven, cloud-hosted, process-aware, business-centric, and mission-critical software solutions and services, which have been directly enabling business automation and augmentation. The technologically enabled IT adaptivity, agility, and affordability enhancements overwhelmingly lead to the setting up and sustaining of intelligent business operations and brings forth premium offerings.

With the unprecedented adoption of the cloud paradigm, the arrival of programmable, open, and flexible IT infrastructure is being speeded up. Previously, it was primarily closed, inflexible, and expensive IT infrastructures in the form of mainframe servers and monolithic applications. With the cloud-enablement strategy gains prominence, we have additional infrastructural assets in the form of **virtual machines** (**VMs**) and containers. Cloud IT infrastructures are highly optimized and organized through the smart application of cloud technologies and tools. Because of segmenting physical machines/bare metal servers into multiple VMs and containers, the number of participating infrastructural modules is bound to go up rapidly. This sort of strategically sound partitioning of IT infrastructures (server machines, storage appliances, and networking solutions) into a number of easily maneuverable and manageable, highly scalable, network-accessible, publicly discoverable, composable, and available IT resources. This transition definitely brings forth a number of business, technical, and user advantages. However, there is a catch. That is, the operational and management complexities of modern IT infrastructures have gone up significantly. Also, for the connected world, the software solutions have to be made out of distributed and decentralized application components. To succulently meet evolving business requirements, software packages have to be nimble and versatile. Thus, hardware, software, and services have to be creatively modernized and innately insights-driven.

Software complexity is on the rise consistently, due to requirements, changes, and additions. The functional requirements of software applications are being widely fulfilled, but the challenge is how to build software applications that guarantee the **non-functional requirements** (**NFRs**), which are alternatively termed as the **quality of service** (**QoS**) and **quality of experience** (**QoE**) attributes. The well-known QoS properties are scalability, availability, performance/throughput, security, maneuverability, and reliability.

For achieving reliable systems, we need to have reliable infrastructures and applications. Increasingly, we hear and read about infrastructure-aware applications and applications-aware infrastructures. Thus, it is clear that both infrastructure and application play a vital role in rolling out reliable software systems. This chapter is dedicated to detailing the best practices that empower software architects and developers to come out with microservices that are resilient. When resilient microservices get composed, we are to enjoy and experience reliable software systems.

Reliable IT systems – the emerging traits and tips

Businesses across the globe mandate for reliability. IT reliability is the foundation for enabling business reliability. IT pundits have released a series of steps to be followed to arrive at reliable systems. There are architectural and design patterns, best practices, platform solutions, technologies and tools, methodologies, and so on, to produce reliable systems that are resilient and elastic. Let's discuss them in detail in the subsequent sections. Before doing that, let's focus on the various noteworthy advancements happening in the IT space.

MSA for reliable software

MSA is being viewed as the next-generation application architecture style and pattern. There are several proven techniques for faster software development through a host of agile programming methodologies, such as pair and extreme programming, Scrum, and so on. However, there is a lacuna on accelerated design of enterprise-class applications. MSA is being presented as the new agile application design method. Furthermore, developing applications is also sped up through the careful partitioning of legacy as well as modern applications into a number of easily implementable and manageable application components and services. That is, every software application gets segmented into a set of interactive microservices. Building microservices can be independently accomplished. Applications can be quickly formed out of distributed microservices through composition (orchestration and choreography) platforms. In other words, the era of software development from the ground up is gone forever. Instead, sophisticated applications are being made out of microservices through configuration, customization, and composition techniques.

Thus, application design and development gets accelerated through the smart leverage of the MSA concepts, tools, frameworks, design and integration patterns, and best practices. Now, with the DevOps movement gaining a strong foothold across the IT industry, the goal of swift deployment of developed and tested application components is being fulfilled. With microservices being positioned as the most optimal unit of software design, development, and deployment, we will see microservices-centric applications ruling the business and IT services.

The accelerated adoption of containers and orchestration platforms

The faster proliferation of containers, especially the Docker containers, is accelerating the widespread usage of microservices. That is, containers offer the best packaging format and runtime/execution environment for microservices. Due to the lightweight nature of containers and microservices, which are generally fine-grained, the number of containerized microservices and their instances for redundancy for an application is quite high. Even a small-scale cloud center hosts several thousands of application and data containers. Thus, the operation, observation, and management complexities are bound to escalate rapidly. As an automated solution for this predicament, there are container life cycle management solutions, such as Kubernetes, Docker swarm, and Marathon. These solutions simplify and speed up container clustering, orchestration, and management activities.

The emergence of containerized clouds

With the growing tool ecosystem of Kubernetes, setting up and sustaining containerized cloud environments are being greatly simplified and streamlined. With the emergence of **configuration management** (**CM**) tools, such as Chef, Puppet, and Ansible, and cloud orchestration tools, such as Terraform, the concept of **infrastructure as code** (**IaC**) is gaining a lot of attention and attraction. The automated provisioning of IT resources (bare metal server, virtual machine, and containers), application delivery and deployment, configuration, management, and placement eases the accelerated realization of appropriate cloud infrastructures for efficiently running platforms and applications to guarantee business productivity. Containers and Kubernetes can run on OpenStack clouds and directly on **bare metal** (**BM**) servers. The amalgamation of OpenStack and Kubernetes platform solutions brings forth a litany of business and technological benefits for the future of cloud environments (local as well as remote).

Thus, the combination of microservices, containers, and container orchestration platforms in association with multi-cloud environments (edge, private, public, and hybrid) is to lead to competent and cognitive IT that can easily fulfil the evolving business requirements in an adroit fashion. Thus, the resilient and elastic infrastructure lays out a stimulating and sparkling foundation for realizing and running reliable systems. The onset of containers is a good sign for fulfilling the dream of reliable infrastructures.

Service mesh solutions

It is an indisputable truth that the resiliency of microservices leads to reliable systems. For crafting process-aware, business-centric, and composite applications, several microservices have to be fused together. Resilient and scalable microservices are collaborating with one another, leading to the realization of reliable software systems.

The service resiliency is being achieved through the leverage of service mesh solutions, such as Istio, Linkerd, and Conduit. Forming service meshes is the way forward for ensuring the much-demanded service resiliency while services interact with one another. The faster maturity and stability of service mesh-enabling solutions goes a long way in establishing resilient microservices, which, when composed together, form reliable systems. Thus, containerized microservices, container orchestration platforms such as Kubernetes, and the incorporation of service mesh solutions blend well to put a robust and versatile foundation for producing and deploying reliable systems.

Microservices design – best practices

As microservices get established and elevated as the next-generation application building block, microservices design has to be done leveraging the various patterns, practices, and platforms. This section throws some light on some of the best practices recommended by highly accomplished and acclaimed software architects. There are articles and blogs explaining the various best practices for the efficient design of microservices.

Precisely speaking, with the unprecedented adoption of microservices architecture and the steady growth of the tool ecosystem, the risk-free realization of modular, service-oriented, extensible, event-driven, cloud-hosted, process-centric, business-critical, insights-filled, scalable, and reliable applications is gaining momentum.

It is a widely accepted fact that MSA guarantees the much needed agility in application design, development, and deployment. However, there are a few challenges. Microservices can be weighed down due to the feebleness of distributed processing. For any worthwhile application, there is a need for integration between all the participating microservices, legacy applications, data sources, and so on. To overcome the previous limitations, there are fresh approaches being recommended and rolled out.

The relevance of event-driven microservices

To enhance the scalability and reliability of microservices-centric applications, a number of options are being looked into. The combination of **event-driven architecture** (**EDA**) and **microservice architecture** (**MSA**) is being found to work wonders in the pursuit of designing and deploying reliable applications. This section throws some light on the importance of event-driven microservices and how they can be implemented and composed to produce reliable systems. Let's start with the need for asynchronous communication.

Events have become an important ingredient to have not only scores of integrated systems, but also intelligent systems for succulently automating business activities and people tasks. Enterprise applications are increasingly event-driven. For examples, we have varied events through various business operations. An airline service provider delays a flight, a doctor prescribes a medicine, a consignment has just arrived, an invoice is not paid in time, a threshold break-in in electricity meter, and so on. Events link different and distributed applications and services to do integrated operations. A monitoring, measurement, and management service can receive and analyze a stream of events being emitted by other applications to discover whether the pattern of events stick to its normal course. If there is any deviation, then it has to be detected and used for taking any appropriate counter measures.

Why asynchronous communication?

Microservices can communicate in a synchronous and asynchronous manner. However, as things evolve, there is an insistence for event-driven microservices, which, in turn, ask for asynchronous interactions. In this section, we are going to discuss some of its motivations.

We have been fiddling with synchronous communications. We are more comfortable with TCP, HTTP, and FTP protocols, which intrinsically support synchronous communication, which has certain advantages. The overwhelmingly used interaction model of request and response is being accomplished through synchronous communication pattern. However, the world tends toward an asynchronous communication pattern. If the server application is heavily loaded, then clients have to wait to get the response from the server. How can this situation be handled? That is, how can a long-running business process on the server machine can be elegantly communicated to the client? If a server-side service is not available due to one of the typical reasons, then how can the client handle this scenario? As there are redundant service instances, how can the client be empowered to take a different route to the functioning service to handle the client request? How can a guaranteed server or service response time can be ensured to the client is another huge challenge in this extremely connected world? There are other challenges, too.

The asynchronous communication is expected to relieve us from these pains. Long running tasks, unavailable or unresponsive servers, service transparency, request reordering and prioritizing, and so on, can be easily accomplished through asynchronous communication. Now, let's discuss the nitty-gritty of the EDA pattern.

An EDA consists of event producers that generate a stream of events, and event consumers that listen for the events. Events are delivered in near real-time, so consumers can respond immediately to events as they occur. Producers are decoupled from consumers. An EDA can use a pub/sub model or an event stream model. Refer to the following points:

- **Publish/subscribe**: We have detailed this further on. Due to the production of a staggering amount of events, competent messaging middleware solutions abound to precisely keep track of event subscriptions. That is, when a tangible event gets published, the messaging infrastructure sends the event to each of its subscribers. Once an event is received, it cannot be replayed again. Furthermore, new subscribers can't see the event.
- **Event streaming**: Events are streamed and written to a log in an orderly manner. Events are persisted to be durable. Clients don't subscribe to the event stream. Instead, a client can read any part of the stream. A client can join at any time and replay events.

Events may be simple or complex. Lately, there has been a number of streaming analytics platforms and event processing engines being made to make sense out of event streams. These days, the application design is increasingly event-centric. Events have acquired such a dominant position in the business and IT worlds. Data-centricity is steadily tending toward event-centricity. The enterprise and cloud IT teams are tasked with having event platforms in place to succulently extricate beneficial associations and patterns, fresh possibilities and opportunities, outliers/anomalies, risks and rewards, and so on. Refer to the following points:

- **Simple event processing**: An event immediately triggers an action in the consumer.
- **Complex event processing**: Complex events are typically a series of events and a consumer is supposed to process complex events searching for actionable insights in the event data.
- **Event stream processing**: It is all about using an event-streaming platform, such as Apache Kafka, as a pipeline to ingest events and feed them to one or more stream processors. The stream processors process or transform the stream accordingly.

Why event-driven microservices?

There is a connect between asynchronous communication and event-driven microservices. Events are emerging as the unit of integration in the increasingly decentralized and distributed IT world. Microservices and their applications have to be deftly enabled to capture and crunch event messages to be intelligent in their actions and reactions. Business and people-centric applications are expected to be **sensitive and responsive (S and R)**. The mode of pulling information from servers is to be replaced with servers pushing their information and capabilities to several clients across. That is, the push mode is getting star attraction these days. Client agents and services fire and forget until the server services respond back with all the requested details. There are simple and complex events, and the IT systems have to have the appropriate competency to intelligent respond to various events in time. Simple events are being clubbed together to create complex events.

To attain the real agility through microservices, there is a need to embrace the distinct capabilities of the EDA pattern. That is, it is all about getting the right event to the right service to produce the right response at the right time. Events have to be systematically captured and acted upon immediately and intelligently to produce real-time, situation-aware, people-centric, and adaptive applications. Thus, microservices, to generate real-world applications, have to be sensitive to all kinds of events.

While designing next-generation systems and environments, the event-centric thinking has to be the key for the renowned success as the device ecosystem continuously evolve with the addition of a dazzling array of slim and sleek, handy and trendy wearables, implantable, handhelds, and mobiles, portable, nomadic and wireless devices, edge and digitized entities, and so on. As we prepare ourselves for the ensuring era of IoT systems and environments, there is a need for knowledge-filled, event-sensitive, and device-centric microservices aplenty. For fulfilling any useful activity, there is a need for microservices to find, bind, and leverage one another in an insightful manner. Thus, for integrating microservices, the proven and potential methods of service orchestration and choreography play a very bountiful and beautiful role.

Event-driven design is a way of extending applications without modifying them. In a microservices architecture, each microservice is designed as a fine-grained and self-sufficient software, which fulfils a single business activity. That means, for implementing a use case or process, there may be a need to visit many microservices several times. That is, for integrating and composing microservices, eventing and asynchronous messaging are being preferred, as they are guaranteeing scalability and resiliency. There are message-oriented middleware and message brokers from the open source community as well as from commercial vendors. For events, there are event stores and hubs to stock events. Events emitted by publishing applications are meticulously captured, stored, and delivered by these middleware solutions to the consuming applications. Because of these intermediaries, events and messages are being kept in a secure place. For internal communications, Apache Kafka is a popular product. For external communications, the HTTP-based middleware solutions such as WebSockets, Webhooks, and so on, are being used.

We have leveraged several enterprise integration patterns for producing integrated systems. However, the distributed nature of microservices demands for decentralized messaging. That is, there is a shift from centralized integration bus architecture to smart microservices with dumb pipes. The required intelligence is stuffed with all the participating services instead of accumulating them in a central integration hub, such as **enterprise application integration** (**EAI**) hub, **enterprise service bus** (**ESB**), and so on.

Today, we have a database for each of the microservices. That is, we are heading toward polyglot and decentralized persistence. On a similar line, we need to embrace the decentralized polyglot messaging infrastructure for enabling microservices to find, bind, and compose to produce process-aware, business-centric, and composite services.

Asynchronous messaging patterns for event-driven microservices

Here are a few popular asynchronous messaging patterns that enable the faster realization of event-driven and asynchronous messaging microservices. Let's refer to the following points:

- **Event sourcing**: Today, events are penetrative and pervasive, and occur in large numbers due to the broader and deeper proliferation of multi-faceted sensors, actuators, drones, robots, electronics, digitized elements, connected devices, factory machineries, social networking sites, integrated applications, decentralized microservices, distributed data sources, stores, and so on. Thus, events from varied and geographically distributed sources get streamed into an event store, which is termed as a database of events. This event store provides an API to enable various consuming services to subscribe and use authorized events. The event store primarily operates as a message broker. Event sourcing persists the state of a business entity such as an order service as a sequence of state-changing events. Whenever there is a change in the state of the business entity, a new event gets triggered and is meticulously appended to the list of events. This is in a way like how the aspect of log aggregation works. Event sourcing is an excellent way to add visibility to what is happening to a service. The application can easily reconstruct a business entity's current state by replaying the events:

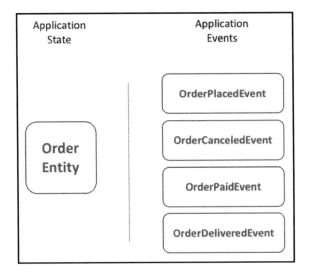

The most common flow for event sourcing is as follows:

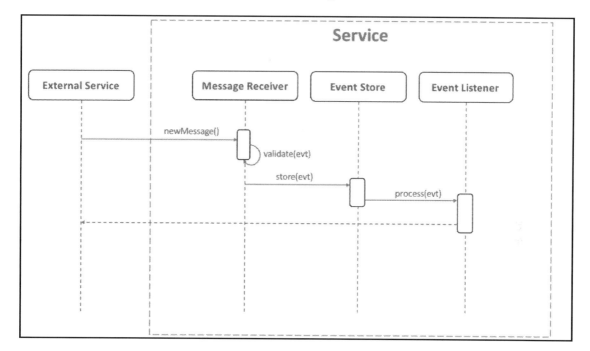

- **Message Receiver**: Receives and converts the incoming request into an event message.
- **Event Store**: Stores the event messages sequentially. It notifies the listeners/consumers.
- **Event Listener**: Represents the code in charge of executing the respective business logic according to the event type.

Apache Kafka is a widely used event store. Events are grouped into multiple logical collections called *topics*. These topics are subsequently partitioned toward parallel processing. A partitioned topic functions like a queue. That is, events are delivered to their consumers in the order they were received. However, unlike a queue, events are persisted to be made available to other consumers. Older messages get automatically deleted based on the stream's **time-to-live** (TTL) setting. Event consumers can consume the event message at any time and replay the messages any number of times. Apache Kafka can scale quickly to handle millions of events per second.

The idea is to represent every application's state transition in a form of an immutable event. Events are then stored in a log or journal form as they occur. Events can also be queried and stored permanently. This ultimately shows how the application's state, as a whole, has evolved over time.

Publisher/subscriber: This is emerging as the way forward to accomplish asynchronous real-time data distribution. The producer does not know about the subscribers. This pattern is used to comprehensively decouple microservices. Subscribers register to receive message without any knowledge of the publishers. This pattern is primarily for ensuring applications to scale handle any number of subscribers. The middleware broker is to guarantee the required scalability. Microservices architecture is capable of creating loosely and lightly coupled microservices. Hence, independently deploying and updating besides horizontally scaling microservices is quite easy. However, while composing microservices using service orchestration, we get sticky microservices, and hence experts bat for service choreography. This pattern is shown in the following diagram:

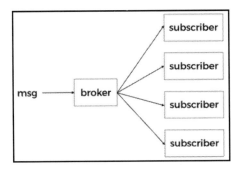

In this example, the **PORTFOLIO** service has to add a stock position. Instead of calling the accounts service directly, the **PORTFOLIO** service publishes an event to the **POSITION ADDED** event stream. The accounts service has subscribed to that event stream, and hence it receives a notification. Rather than calling the accounts service directly, it publishes an event to the **POSITION ADDED** event stream. The accounts microservice has subscribed to that event stream, so it gets the notification. This indirect and intermediary-enabled asynchronous communication ensures that the participating services are totally decoupled. This means that services can be replaced and substituted with other advanced services. The services can be quickly scaled out by additional containerized microservice instances. The only flaw here is that there is no centralized monitoring and a management system is in place:

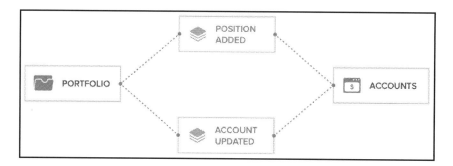

Event firehose pattern: When more events are being produced by several producers and there are many consumers waiting for event messages, there is a need for a common hub for messages exchange. The event messages get exchanged via topics. As indicated, in the case of asynchronous command calls, the exchange happens via queues. The common implementation of this pattern looks a little something like this:

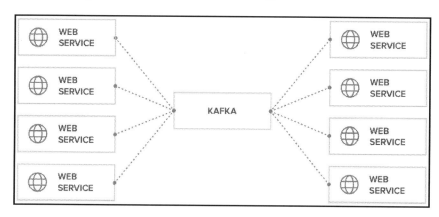

Asynchronous command calls: There are certain scenarios mandating for proper orchestration over asynchronous calls. These are usually done for local integration use cases. The other prominent use cases include connecting closely related microservices to exchange messages with a delivery guarantee. Here, microservices interact in an asynchronous manner. In this pattern, messages are typically exchanged using queues. Queues facilitate messages to be exchanged in a point-to-point manner. Most of the conversations here are short-lived. It is a traditional broker-centric use case, but reliably connecting endpoints through asynchronous communication.

This pattern is demanded when one microservice has to publish an event for a second microservice to process and then has to wait to receive and read an appropriate reply event from that second microservice. Consider the previously mentioned portfolio example. A standard REST API call tells the portfolio service to add a stock position. The portfolio service posts an event to the position-added queue for the accounts service to process. The service then waits for the accounts service to post a reply event to the account updated queue so that the original REST API call can return data received from that event to the client service.

Saga pattern: We all know that each microservice is being empowered through its own database. However, some business operations involve multiple services. Each atomic business operation that spans multiple services may involve several transactions on a technical level. The challenge here is how to ensure data consistency in a multi-database environment. That is, when multiple databases are to be accessed, the traditional local ACID-compliant transaction is not sufficient. That is, the situation here demands distributed transactions. One viable option to solve this problem in a hassle-free manner is the leverage of an XA protocol implementing the **two-phase commit** (**2PC**) pattern. But for web-scale applications, 2PC may not work well. To eliminate the disadvantages of 2PC, experts have recommended to trade ACID for **basically available, soft state and eventually consistent** (**BASE**).

The experts say to implement each business transaction that spans across multiple services as a saga. That is, a saga is presented as a sequence of local transactions. Sagas are viewed as an application-level distributed coordination of multiple transactions. Each local transaction updates the database and publishes an event message to the next local transaction in the saga. If a local transaction fails due to one or other reasons, then the saga executes a series of compensating activities that undo the changes that were made by the preceding local transactions.

Chapter 8

The role of EDA to produce reactive applications

These are also event-driven applications. Predominantly, instead of service orchestration, service choreography is preferred for building event-driven applications. As per the Reactive manifesto, reactive applications have to have the following characteristics. They have to be responsive, resilient, elastic, and message-driven. Reactive systems are bound to respond instantaneously to any kind of stimulus. This is just opposite to the traditional **request and response** (**R and R**) model, which is generally blocking. This pattern turns out to be an excellent way for using the available resources in a better manner. Also, the system responsiveness gets a strong boost. Instead of blocking and waiting for computations to be finished, the application starts to handle other user requests in an asynchronous manner to make use of all the available resources and threads.

Command query responsibility segregation pattern

This is an important pattern that's used to realize decoupling at a database level. This pattern actually helps us to use different models to update and read data, as depicted in the following diagram. This segregation comes in handy as we embrace microservices, which are event-driven:

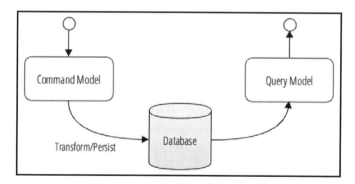

Command query responsibility segregation (**CQRS**) is acquiring a special significance because domain events are the inputs in the EDA era. However, the database expects a domain object, which is structurally different than a domain event. Here is a domain model object representing an account. The example is taken from an article (http://www.kennybastani.com/2017/01/building-event-driven-microservices.html).

Example 1, account aggregate:

```
{"createdAt": 1481351048967,"lastModified": 1481351049385,"userId":
1,"accountNumber": "123456","defaultAccount": true,"status":
"ACCOUNT_ACTIVE"}
```

When a service is to query for an account, the database expects this model to be input. However, the requirement at hand is to update the current status to ACCOUNT_SUSPENDED by using a domain event. There is a need for a kind of transformation. The following is a snippet of a domain event to transition the state of the account from ACCOUNT_ACTIVE to ACCOUNT_SUSPENDED.

Example 2, account event:

```
{"createdAt": 1481353397395,"lastModified": 1481353397395,"type":
"ACCOUNT_SUSPENDED","accountNumber": "123456"}
```

The need is to process this domain event and apply the update to the query model. The command contains the model of the domain event and uses it to process the update to the account's query model:

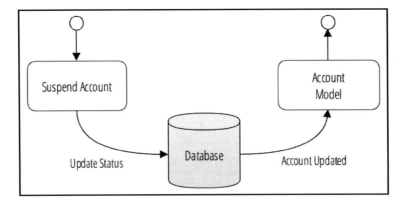

When CQRS combines with microservices, things become complicated as shown here:

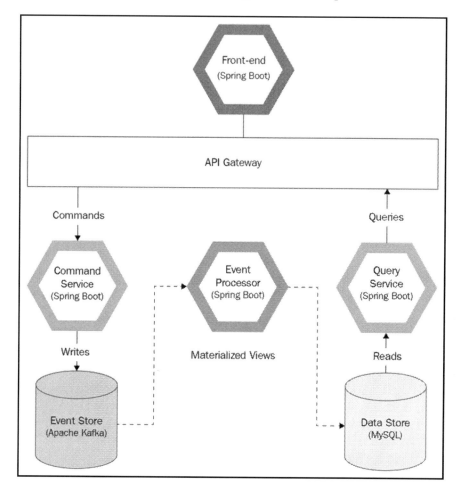

A single microservice is partitioned into three services (command, event processor, and query services). These services can be deployed independently. CQRS is vital for the increasingly event-driven microservices world.

Serverless is another interesting phenomenon. With containers gaining the most optimal runtime environment, cloud service providers are able to bring in additional automation in infrastructure provisioning, configuration, and management. Serverless, which is also termed as **FaaS** (**Function as a Service**), assists with deploying code as functions quickly. That is, there is no need for developers to worry about optimally setting up and managing appropriate application infrastructures for running functions. What is the relationship between microservices and Serverless functions? A microservice can be realized through a smart composition of Serverless functions, as indicated in the following diagram:

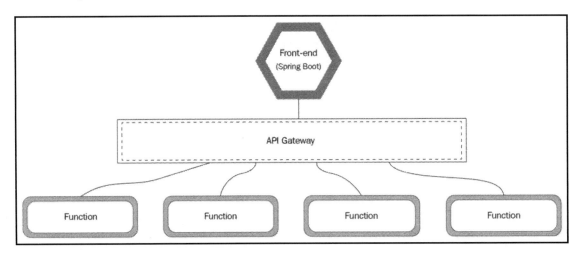

Serverless lends well to increasing the velocity with which microservices get updated and deployed in production. It does so by moving much of the workflow management out of the core components and into small composable functions that can be independently upgraded and deployed. Thus, faster deployment of microservices gets fulfilled through Serverless computing.

In conclusion, we are heading toward a deeply and extremely connected world. Any noteworthy event and incident, state or status changes, threshold break-ins, and so on, are being collected and conveyed to all the consuming systems in time to take immediate counter measures with all the confidence and clarity. That is, our applications have to be designed to appropriately respond and reciprocate for varied events from distributed sources. That is, event-driven application architecture is gaining a strong foothold in the IT and business worlds. Integrated systems such as business workloads, operational systems, and IT services are adequately empowered and stuffed with required logic to be sensitive and responsive to events.

There are event stores and hubs, **message-oriented middleware (MoM)**, message brokers, and event-streaming platforms and databases to facilitate the EDA goals. As we have described in the previous sections, microservices emerge as the unique and nimble building block for building and deploying event-driven applications. For truly enabling the digital transformation initiatives, business houses and IT organizations have to meticulously invest their time, talent, and treasures on event-driven microservices to harvest handsomely in the due course of time.

Reliable IT infrastructures

As indicated at the beginning of the chapter, to arrive at reliable systems, we need to have reliable applications and infrastructures. We have discussed the various ways and means of bringing forth reliable applications already. Now, we need to dig deeper and detail the best practices to be followed to craft and use reliable infrastructures.

High availability

Regarding redundancy toward higher availability, the first and foremost tip is to architect software applications to be redundant. Redundancy is the duplication of any system to substantially increase its availability. If a system goes down due to any reason, the duplicated system comes to the rescue. That is why we often hear and read that software applications are being generally deployed in multiple regions, as indicated in the following diagram. Lately, applications are being constructed out of distributed and duplicated application components. Thus, if one component or service goes down, then its duplication comes handy in sustaining and elongating the application lifetime.

Microservices architecture eventually leads to distributed systems, which are highly available and scalable:

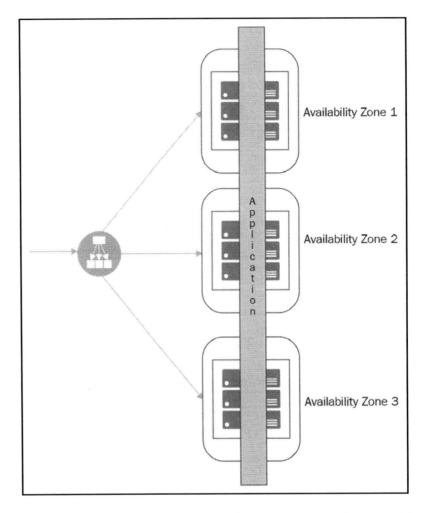

The following table clearly insists why the redundancy turns out to be a crucial need for business and IT systems. With duplication in place, we can easily attain **99.999%** availability of systems and software:

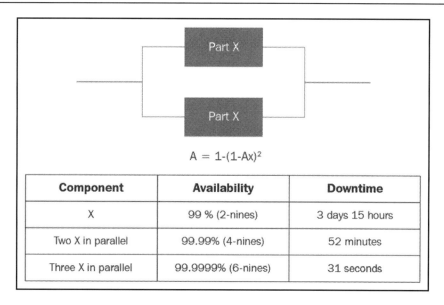

Component	Availability	Downtime
X	99 % (2-nines)	3 days 15 hours
Two X in parallel	99.99% (4-nines)	52 minutes
Three X in parallel	99.9999% (6-nines)	31 seconds

That is, if a component is guaranteed to fulfil **99%** availability, then if we have the component in two geographically different places, then the total availability goes up to **99.99 %**. With more instances, we are bound to get higher availability of systems. To design such an architecture across multiple availability zones and regions, applications have to be stateless and there is a need to use an elastic load balancer (cluster to avoid single point of failure) to intelligently route requests from different sources to the backend applications and their clones. Not all requests are going to be stateless. Some requests demand stickiness, and hence there are several options being rolled out to involve stateful applications.

Fault-tolerance towards higher availability: Fault tolerance relies on a specialized mechanism to proactively detect a fault/risk in one or more of the components of any IT hardware system and instantaneously the system gets switched to a redundant component to continue the service without any delay. The failed component may be the motherboard, which typically comprises the CPU, memory, and connectors for input and output devices, power supply, or a storage component. Software downtime is another issue due to faults in software packages. Recently, there is a litany of techniques and tools helping out our developers to build fault-tolerant software systems.

Besides this, there are software testing and analysis methods through automated tools, which comes handy in eliminating any kind of deviations and deficiencies in software libraries. In the recent past, with the faster maturity and stability of containers, errors or attacks on containerized microservices could be easily identified and contained within their containers, toward the goal of fault isolation. That is, through this isolation, any kind of misadventures and misdemeanors can be stopped on their way preemptively. That means, a compromised component need not affect other components within the system. This avoids the complete shutdown of the system. Failed services can be rectified and restarted or the redundant service instances can be leveraged to ensure the business continuity. The fault-tolerance capability of IT systems guarantees that there is no service interruption. Systems are being innately empowered to continuously deliver their assigned functionalities in the event of internal failures and external attacks.

Auto-scaling

As defined elsewhere in this book, reliability is resiliency plus elasticity. That is, IT infrastructures ought to be extremely elastic. They have to be application-aware, and to meet up any kind of spikes in user and data loads, infrastructure modules and assets have to be elastic. The popular compute instances such as virtual machines and containers have to be automatically provisioned in addition to the existing ones to tackle the extra load. Similarly, other infrastructural components such as networking solutions and storage appliances have to be enabled to be auto-scaling in times of need. These are coarse-grained IT resources. The fine-grained IT resources such as memory, processing power, and I/O capability also have to have the power to be self-scaling in an on-demand manner. Thus, any spike in load can be met by IT resources in an automated manner with less intervention, involvement, and interpretation of human resources. In the cloud era, additional IT modules can be provisioned across nearby availability zones by taking the location constraints into account. The intelligent capacity planning and management acquires special significance here. Not only infrastructures, but also applications have to be architected and designed in such a manner to support auto-scaling intrinsically. There are patterns, procedures, and practices aplenty to come out with highly scalable applications and services. With the deployment of web-scale applications and as the traffic varies very frequently in a big way, the auto-scaling feature is being insisted these days.

Real-time scalability: Provisioning additional resources to meet up increasing demands is being sped up through the leverage of application containers. Containers, as articulated in other chapters, are lightweight and hence bringing forth additional containers concurrently is faster and easier. Thus, the goal of real-time scalability facility is being realized through the containerization movement. Containers typically take a couple of seconds to be alive whereas virtual machines consumer a few minutes. Bare metal servers take several minutes to be ready for receiving client's requests. Thus, considering the limitations of physical and virtual machines, horizontal scalability gains prominence these days.

Infrastructure as code

The widely quoted benefit of **infrastructure as code** (**IaC**) is repeatability and reproducibility. There are a number of components (server, network, security, storage, and so on) in a data center that need to be configured to deploy applications. In cloud environments, there are thousands of such components to be configured. If all is being done manually, the time taken is very huge and error-prone. There are possibilities for the creeping in of configuration differences and drifts. Humans aren't great at undertaking repetitive and manual tasks with 100% accuracy. But machines are very good at doing repetitive, redundant, and routine tasks in scale and speed. If we produce a template and input it into a machine, the machine can execute the template thousand times without any errors. The template-centric approach for infrastructure provisioning, configuration and application deployment gains wider attraction and attention these days. Infrastructure optimization and management get elegantly simplified through the leverage of well-designed templates. With the concept of IaC picking up steadily, the infrastructure setup and sustenance is being streamlined with ease. With the enhanced visibility, controllability, and observability, IT infrastructures are being manipulated as we do programming software applications. The infrastructure life cycle management activities are being automated through a host of advancements happening in the pioneering IaC space.

Immutable infrastructure: Instead of getting updated, immutable components are being replaced for every deployment. That is, no updates are being performed on live systems. It is all about provisioning a new instance of the resource. Containers are the best example of an immutable infrastructure resource. Similarly, fresh instances of various AWS images are being created and deployed instead of updating the existing instances.

To support application deployment in an immutable infrastructure, the canary deployment is being recommended. The canary deployment reduces the risk of failure when new versions of applications go to production environments. The canary deployment helps to gradually roll out the new version to a small set of users and then expands it to make it available to everyone. This is illustrated in the following diagram:

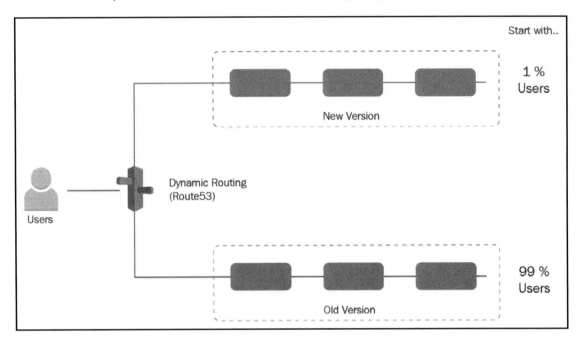

The real benefit of canary deployment is it is possible to roll back the new version if there are any issues. Thus, faster yet safer deployment of applications with real production data is facilitated through the canary deployment model.

Stateless applications: As mentioned previously, for enabling auto-scaling, applications have to be stateless. For immutable infrastructures, the stateless feature is important. That is, any request can be expertly handled by any resource. Stateless applications respond to all client requests independent of prior requests or sessions. There is no need for the applications to store any information in memory or in local disks. Keeping state information in the application server may lead to performance degradation when there is a huge number of requests from different users. Generally, sharing state information with any resources within the auto-scaling group has to be accomplished through **in-memory databases (IMDBs)** and **in-memory data grids (IMDGs)**. The popular products are Redis, Memcached, and Apache Ignite. Thus, to have reliable infrastructure and application, we need IaC, stateless application, immutable infrastructure, automation through DevOps tools, and so on.

Avoiding cascading failures: Generally, any error/misbehavior in one component of any system gets quickly propagated across the system to bring down the whole system. Thus, it is mandatory to unearth and use competent techniques that intrinsically help to avoid those cascading failures. A classic example of a cascading failure is overload. That is, when one component is stressed due to heavy load and is in utter distress, all the other components depending on the stressed component may be made to wait exorbitantly. That is, precious and expensive resources are being exhausted and resultantly, the whole system may be out of work. Thus, fault identification and isolation in a preemptive manner is vital for the intended success of any complicated and sophisticated system. There are a few widely accentuated approaches and algorithms to avoid cascading failures.

Back-off algorithms: Due to various business evolutions, we are heading towards distributed computing. Firstly, due to the varying size, speed, structure, and scope of business, social, and device data getting generated and collected, we need highly optimized and organized IT infrastructures and integrated platforms for efficient data virtualization, cleansing, storage, and processing. We aspire to have groundbreaking platforms and infrastructures for performing big, real-time, and streaming data analytics. Secondly, we have highly integrated and insights-driven applications in plenty. That is, we are destined to have both data and process-intensive applications. Distributed computing is the way forward. Large-scale complex applications are meticulously partitioned into a number of easily producible and manageable application components/services, and these modules are being distributed and decentralized.

The key IT components for distributed applications include web/application servers, load balancers, firewalls, sharded, and dedicated databases, DNS servers, and so on. There are a few crucial challenges being associated with distributed systems. Security, service discovery, service integration, service availability and reliability, network latency, and so on, are the widely circulated issues of distributed computing. Experts and evangelists have studied these problems thoroughly and have recommended a series of best practices, evaluation metrics, architecture and design patterns, and so on. In `Chapter 3`, *Microservice Resiliency Patterns*, we detailed a set of resiliency patterns to come up with reliable systems. Besides, there are resiliency-enablement frameworks, platform solutions, programming models, and so on to sufficiently enhance system and service reliability.

Retry: The one standard technique for tackling issues related to the famous distributed computing is to apply the proven retry method. The service requesters attempt to redo the failed operation as soon as an error occurs. The issue is when there is a large number of requesters, and the network can start to feel the stress. That is, the network bandwidth will be completely drained and resultantly the system is bound to collapse. To avoid such scenarios, back-off algorithms such as the common exponential back-off are recommended to be used. The exponential back-off algorithms gradually increase the rate at which retries are being performed. This way, the network congestion can be greatly avoided.

In its simplest form, a pseudo exponential back-off algorithm looks as follows:

```
retries = 0
DO
    wait(2^retries * 100 milliseconds)

    status = do_request() OR get_async_result()

    IF status = SUCCESS
        retry = false
    ELSE
        retry = true
        retries = retries + 1
WHILE (retry AND (retries < MAX_RETRIES))
```

Timeouts: This is another resiliency-guaranteeing method. Suppose there is a steady baseline traffic and, all of a sudden, the database slows down and INSERT queries take more time to respond. The baseline traffic is not changed and hence the reason for the sudden slow down is that more request threads are holding the database connections. As a result, the pool of database connections has shrunk significantly. There are no connections left out in the pool to serve any other API, and hence other APIs start to fail. This is a classic example of cascading failure. If the API had timed out instead of clinging on to the database, the service performance could have gone done instead of the unwanted complete failure. Thus, there has to be the timeout phenomenon to achieve service resiliency.

Idempotent operations: This is an important facet in ensuring data consistency and integrity. If there is a client request being sent out as a message over HTTP to an application and due to a transient error, there is the timeout reply from the application. The request message could have been received and processed by the application. Still, because of the timeout response, the user goes for the retry option.

Suppose the request is an INSERT to the backend database. When the retry option is applied again, there is a possibility for a repeat insertion of the same data. These errors can be avoided if the application implements idempotent operations. An idempotent operation is one that can be repeated any number of times and this repetition does not affect the application in any way. Importantly, the same result will be delivered even if repeatedly tried.

Service degradation and fall backs: Instead of a complete shutdown, an application can be allowed to degrade to provide a lower-quality service. That is, the application response may be a bit slow, or the throughput of the application is on the lower side. This is a kind of trade-off to be made instead of application failure. One or other fall back options have to be employed.

As we all know, enterprise-scale and mission-critical applications are being made out of distributed and decentralized microservices. With the adoption of containerized microservices, the availability of microservices is being significantly increased through the deployment of multiple instances of the services. That is, multiple instances of the same microservice are being deployed through the leverage of containers, which emerge as the most optimal runtime/execution environment for microservices. When one service experiences some difficulties, its instance can be asked to deliver the expected functionality. The API gateway works as the mediator and coordinator of microservices. The location intelligence, along with the network's latency, plays a very vital role in finalizing service instances in place of the service.

Let's see what happens if it is a database. If INSERT queries become slow, then it is prudent to go for a timeout and then fall back to the read-only mode on the database until the issue with the INSERT gets sorted out. If the application does not support read-only mode, then the cached content can be returned to the user.

Resilience against intermittent and transient errors: With cloud environments emerging as the one-stop IT solution for business process and operations regarding automation, augmentation, and acceleration requirements, enterprise-class applications are meticulously modernized and migrated to clouds to reap all the originally expressed and eulogized benefits of the flourishing cloud idea. Building and deploying application components in a distributed manner with centralized governance becomes the new norm as the aspect of hybrid IT is gaining a grip on IT. There are several problems cropping up with large-scale distributed systems in cloud environments. Due to the exorbitant rise in the size and the complexity (heterogeneity and multiplicity-induced) of the systems and the architecture used, the occurrence of intermittent errors is not ruled out. Well-known intermittent errors include transient network connectivity, request timeouts, I/O operations, and the dependency on external services, which become overloaded.

Hence, there is a clarion call for producing resilient systems that can intelligently return to their previous and preferred state if attacked and affected. The best practice is to design systems to fail and not to be fail-proof. The complications of modern IT systems demand that we need to design, develop, and deploy resilient and versatile applications. Applications have to be designed to be extremely fault-tolerant to continuously deliver their ordained functionality. One idea is to collect the statistical data about the various intermittent errors and based on that information, define a threshold that can trigger the correct reaction to errors.

Circuit breaking: This is a widely implemented resiliency technique that's used by various web-scale service providers. This is all about applying circuit breakers to failing method calls to avoid any kind of catastrophic and cascading failure. As we stated earlier, timeout, back-off, allowing service degradation, fall back, and intermittent error handling are the key methods to prevent cascading failures.

A circuit breaker monitors for the number of consecutive failures between a producer and a consumer. If the number passes over a failure threshold, the circuit breaker object trips, and all attempts by the producer to invoke the consumer will fail immediately, or return a defined fall back. After a waiting period, the circuit breaker allows for a few requests to pass through. If those requests successfully pass a success threshold, the circuit breaker resumes its normal state. Otherwise, it stays broken and continues monitoring the consumer. The following is a diagram that shows a circuit breaker with timeouts:

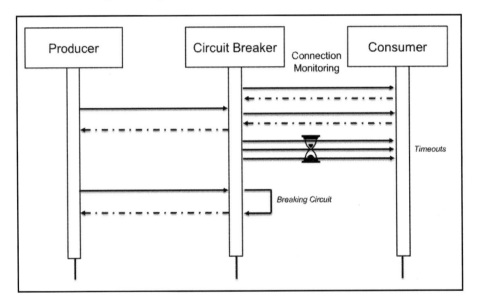

Circuit breaking is being presented as one of the key resilient methods, and such resiliency enabling mechanisms inspire software architects and engineers to incorporate the resiliency measures while designing and building software systems. There are free implementations such as Hystrix, and they can be incorporated in the source code to arrive at resilient applications.

Load balancing: This is another resiliency aspect that's widely used in enterprise and cloud IT environments. With more services and their instances being stuffed in any IT environment, the need for load balancers for distributing application and device requests to multiple instances of one or more application components by understanding the latest load scenario of each application component is on the rise. How every instance is occupied is being taken into consideration by a load balancer to route client requests so as to balance the load. This is clearly helping out in maintaining the system's resiliency.

There are hardware and software load balancers on the market. Consistent and continuous health checks of microservices are very vital for their continued service delivery. Load balancers are capable of doing that, as depicted in the following diagram. Load balancers are continuously probing their service instances, and if a service is not available for fulfilling service requests, then load balancers will redirect service requests to one of the functioning service instances. As mentioned previously, there can be several reasons for services to go down or become unable to fulfil their obligations in time. The service database is not responding, or the service may be overwhelmed with many service requests. The network may not be available transiently:

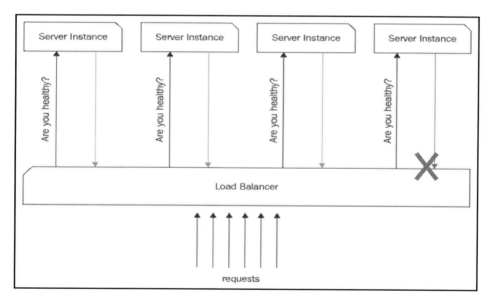

With the multiplicity of microservices, services and their communications have to be guaranteed for resiliency. There are several straightforward ways and means of ensuring service resiliency as discussed in the previous sections. When we have resilient services, through the various composition methods, resilient services lead to reliable systems.

Summary

With the role and responsibility of IT continuously rising in elevating business operations and people tasks, the complexity induced by the multiplicity and heterogeneity of IT systems is on the rise consistently. There are a number of noteworthy advancements in IT, and these have resulted in a variety of business processes getting optimized, simplified, and automated. Business agility is being fulfilled through the IT agility mechanisms. Business deployment and service models have gone through a few transitions in the recent past with the faster maturity and stability of the cloud paradigm. Business transformations are directly enabled through IT transformation. However, with the faster adoption of digital technologies, the new concept of digital transformation is becoming the new normal.

The goal of business reality through IT reliability technologies and tools is to attain the sustainable digital transformation. Reliable systems with resiliency and elasticity characteristics are the need of the hour. This book, especially this chapter, has covered most of the aspects regarding reliable IT. In the next chapter we will be covering how service mesh solutions come handy in fulfilling the service resiliency requirements.

9
Service Resiliency

There is a seamless and spontaneous convergence between containers and microservices. This distinctive linkage brings forth a number of strategic advantages for worldwide businesses in accomplishing more with less. Containers are being positioned as the most appropriate packaging and runtime mechanism for microservices and their redundant instances. Subsequently, microservices are meticulously containerized, tested, curated, and stocked in publicly available container image repositories. Now, with the widespread acceptance of Kubernetes as the leading container cluster and orchestration platform, cloud environments comprising millions of containers (hosting microservices) are being speedily set up and sustained. That is, containers are being insightfully managed by Kubernetes to be hugely constructive and contributive for business automation and acceleration. Kubernetes has laid down a stimulating foundation for creating multi-container composite applications, which are business-aware and process-centric.

However, it has been found that there are some severe shortcomings as far as service-to-service communication is concerned. In other words, the salient features guaranteeing service resiliency are not being natively provided by Kubernetes. Experts and exponents, therefore, have recommended that service meshes are the way forward to ensure service resiliency. This chapter is dedicated to telling you all about the platforms for container enablement and orchestration purposes. Furthermore, how service mesh solutions come handy in fulfilling the service resiliency requirements is illustrated in this chapter.

Delineating the containerization paradigm

Containers have emerged as the efficient runtime and resource for cloud applications (both cloud-enabled and native). Containers are comparatively lightweight, and hence hundreds of containers can be made to run on a physical or a virtual machine. There are other technical benefits such as horizontal scalability and portability. Containers almost guarantee the performance of physical machines. Near-time scalability is seeing the reality with the faster maturity and stability of the enigmatic containerization paradigm.

Service Resiliency

The ecosystem of containerization movement is growing rapidly, and hence containers are being positioned as the perfect way forward to attain the originally envisaged benefits of cloudification.

Containers are being positioned as the most appropriate resource and runtime to host and execute scores of microservices and their instances. The container monitoring, measurement, and management requirements are being sped up with the availability of several open source as well as commercial-grade monitoring and data analytics solutions. The container networking and storage aspects are seeing a lot of traction these days. To be more specific, there are a number of automated tools and viable approaches toward making containerization penetrative, participative, and pervasive.

Why use containerization?

The old way to deploy applications was to install software applications on a bare-metal server/physical machine (node/host) using the **operating system** (**OS**) package manager. This had led to the disadvantage of entangling the application's executables, configuration, libraries, and other dependencies with one another and with the underlying host OS. With the faster maturity and stabilization of virtualization, the overwhelming practice is to build immutable **virtual machine** (**VM**) images to achieve predictable rollouts and rollbacks. But the main challenges include that VMs are heavyweight and non-portable.

The new way is to deploy containers, which implement OS-level virtualization rather than hardware virtualization. These containers are fully isolated from one another and also from the underlying host. The unique differentiations are that containers come with their own filesystems and can't see other container processes. It is possible to bound the computational resource usage of each container. Containers are easier and faster to build than VMs. As containers are totally decoupled from the underlying infrastructure and from the host machine's filesystem, they are extremely portable across local and remote servers. Also, multiple OS distributions aren't a barrier for the container portability.

Containers are extremely lightweight. One application/process/service can be packed and hosted inside each container. This one-to-one application-to-container relationship brings up a bevy of benefits (business, technical, and user). That is, immutable container images can be created at build/release time itself rather than at deployment time. This enables the generation of different images for the different versions/editions of the same application. Bringing in technical and business changes into application logic can be easily accomplished and accelerated.

Each application need not be composed with the rest of the application stack. Also, an application is not tied up with the underlying infrastructure. Therefore, containers can run anywhere (development, testing, staging, and production servers). Containers are transparent, and hence their monitoring, measurement, and management are easier to do. The key container benefits of containers are given as follows:

- **Agile application creation and running**: Building container images through the techniques and tools provided by the open source Docker platform for containerization enablement is faster. Not only development but also packaging, shipping, and running containers are transparent, quicker, and simpler.
- **Continuous integration, delivery, and deployment**: The containerization concept has been hugely contributing for automating the DevOps tasks (continuous integration, delivery, and deployment).
- **Separation of concerns between development and deployment**: As indicated previously, it is possible to create container images at the build/release time itself. The deployment is totally decoupled from the development, and hence applications can run on any system infrastructure without any hitch or hurdle. That is, containerization fulfils the longstanding goal of software portability.
- **Observability**: With the containerization paradigm, not only OS-level information and metrics, but also application-level information such as the performance/throughput, health condition, and other value-adding and decision-enabling details can be collected, cleansed, and crunched to extricate actionable and timely insights.
- **An optimal runtime for microservices**: Both cloud-native as well as enabled applications are predominantly microservices-centric. Containers are being positioned as the most optimal runtime for microservices. The convergence of containers and microservices is to bring a variety of benefits for cloud IT environments.
- **Resource isolation**: Due to the isolation brought in through containerization, application performance can be easily predicted.
- **Resource utilization**: Due to the lightweight nature of containers, accommodating many containers in a single machine is possible. Thus, containerization leads to heavily dense environments. Furthermore, the resource utilization goes up significantly.

Containerization, without an iota of doubt, is being prescribed as the strategically sound tool for resolving most of the ills plaguing cloud environments.

Service Resiliency

Demystifying microservices architecture

Lately, **microservices architecture (MSA)** is gaining a lot of mind and market shares. Monolithic and massive applications are being continuously dismantled to be a pool of easily manageable and composable microservices. **Application development and maintenance (ADM)** service providers know the perpetual difficulties of building and sustaining legacy applications, which are closed, inflexible, and expensive. The low utilization and reuse are other drawbacks. Enabling them to be web, mobile, and cloud ready is beset with a number of practical challenges. Modernizing and migrating legacy applications to embrace newer technologies and to run them in optimized IT environments consumes a lot of time, talent, and treasure. Software development takes the agile route to bring forth business value in the shortest possible time. Software delivery and deployment are getting equally sped up through the DevOps concept, which is being facilitated through a host of powerful automation tools and techniques. Now, the software solution design also has to be accelerated in a risk-free fashion. Here comes the microservices architecture style and pattern.

Microservices is emerging as an excellent architecture style enabling the division of large and complex applications into micro-scaled yet many services. Each one runs in its own process and has its own APIs, and communicates with one another using lightweight mechanisms such as HTTP. Microservices are built around business capabilities, loosely coupled and highly cohesive, horizontally scalable, independently deployable, and technology-agnostic. Each microservice is supposed to do one task well. On the other hand, when these microservices get systematically composed, the realization of enterprise-scale and business-critical applications in which large complex software applications are composed from several services. It is quite easy to deploy newer versions of microservices frequently. That is, any kind of user recommendations, business sentiment changes, and technology updates can be deftly accommodated and delivered. Similarly, designing, developing, debugging, delivering, deploying, and decommissioning newer microservices can be swiftly done. There are enabling platforms and optimized IT infrastructures for the faster realization of microservices, which can be easily and quickly deployed.

Microservices are also innately facilitating horizontal scalability. Microservices are self-defined, autonomous, and decoupled. The dependency-imposed constrictions are elegantly eliminated, thereby faults are tolerated and the required isolation is being achieved. Microservices development teams can independently deliver on business requirements faster. However, there are some fresh operational challenges being associated with microservices-centric applications. Microservices ought to be dynamically discovered. On finding the network location addresses, the control and data flows have to be precisely routed to the correct and functioning microservices. There has to be a controlled and secured access to microservices, which need to be minutely monitored, measured, and managed to fulfil the designated business targets can be attained.

All kinds of logging and operational data have to be consciously and consistently collected, cleansed, and crunched to extricate usable and useful operational insights in time. Microservices are increasingly containerized, and powerful DevOps tools (continuous building, integration, testing, delivery, and deployment) are being used for business empowerment.

In spite of all those top claims, the microservices architecture is simply an evolutionary one. It inherits some of the baggage of the previous incarnation, which is nonetheless the **service-oriented architecture (SOA)** pattern. The **enterprise service bus (ESB)** is the service bus/gateway/broker/messaging middleware in the SOA world. ESB comes with service discovery, mediation, enrichment, resiliency, security, and other concierge-like capabilities. However, in the ensuing microservices era, the ESB-like monolithic software gets expressed and exposed as a dynamic set of interactive microservices. The beauty lies in segregating business capabilities from all kinds of support services. As illustrated in the following diagram, the networking/communication functionalities are separated out of the core activities of microservices. This segregation brings forth a number of business and technical advantages:

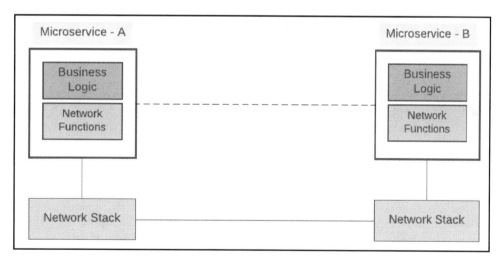

We have discussed the containerization phenomenon and the faster proliferation of microservices as the highly optimized application building block and the deployment unit. Now, there is a greater interest in converging these two strategically sound concepts. The combination is going to be disruptive, innovative, and transformative for business enterprises. The enterprise and cloud IT divisions are going to be the most constructive and contributive. The promising convergence of microservices and containerization is to open up hitherto unknown and unheard possibilities and fresh opportunities for business and IT domains.

Decoding the growing role of Kubernetes for the container era

Kubernetes is a portable and extensible open source platform for managing containerized workloads. Kubernetes automates the end-to-end container life cycle management activities. Configuration requirements are aptly declared, and a host of automation modules of the Kubernetes platform are working together in realizing the desired state. Having understood the strategic importance of Kubernetes, like cluster and orchestration platforms in effectively and efficiently running containers in cloud environments, we can see that tool ecosystem is growing fast. Containers, being the favorite runtime to host and execute microservices, are turning out to be the most tuned resource for the cloud era. For automating the container creation, running, dismantling, stopping, replacing, and replicating the contributions of container cluster and orchestration platform are growing well.

Kubernetes (k8s) eliminates many of the manual activities for deploying and scaling containerized applications. Multi-container composite applications, which are business-centric, process-aware, mission-critical, flexible, event-driven, cloud-hosted, and service-oriented, are the new way of producing enterprise-scale applications. Kubernetes plays a very vital role in producing such kinds of versatile, resilient, adaptive, adept, and dynamic applications. Kubernetes is making its way into every kind of cloud environment (private, public, hybrid, and edge).

As indicated previously, futuristic applications are being derived out of multiple containers being fused together, that is, containers have to be clustered and orchestrated to construct and deploy next-generation workloads in containerized cloud environments. Kubernetes orchestration enables building application services that span across multiple containers, schedules those containers across a cluster of nodes/hosts, scales those containers if necessary, and manages the health of those containers over time. The other important contributions of Kubernetes includes performing a seamless and spontaneous integration with networking, storage, telemetry, and other core services to give a comprehensive yet compact container infrastructures for workloads. The idea is to bring as much automation as possible to empower applications and services to deliver their functions as per the **Service Level Agreements (SLAs)** agreed between providers and users:

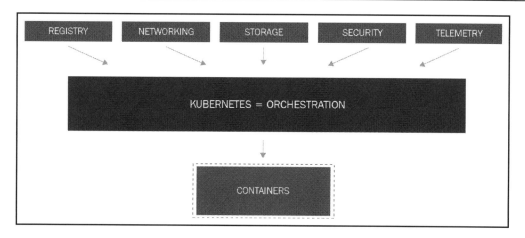

Having realized the strategic contributions of containers for the flourishing cloud era, the container embarkation journey started with clarity and confidence. The lightweight nature, along with high transparency, makes containers more conducive for cloud applications and infrastructures. The fallout is that the number of containers in a cloud center goes up significantly. Therefore, the operational and management complexities of containerized clouds are steadily increasing. The way forward is to bring in deeper and decisive automation through automated tools and platforms. For the sake of simplicity, Kubernetes enables multiple containers to be clubbed together as a pod. In a host/node/machine, there can be a few pods, and each pod comprises one or more containers. Docker networking capabilities can link multiple containers together. Kubernetes follows different mechanisms for container networking. Furthermore, Kubernetes schedules workloads onto container clusters. The load balancing feature of the Kubernetes platform can balance the dynamic loads across pods to ensure that the right number of containers are running all the time to facilitate the workloads so that they are delivered without any hitch and hurdle.

Containers are efficient in the sense that more work can be performed with less resources. The expensive IT resources are being maximally utilized to guarantee the required affordability. Software deployments and upgrades are being taken care of. Kubernetes mounts and adds storage to run stateful applications. It scales containers, and the containers instances to enhance the availability of containerized applications. All of the deployed software applications and their runtimes (containers) are being continuously monitored and managed. Various operational conditions, including the application health condition, are captured to do various appropriate activities, such as auto-scaling, replication, and so on. There are a number of open source tools emerging and evolving to make the leveraging of Kubernetes easy to use. There are several project initiatives and implementations for service and container image registries, networking, security, and so on. Kubernetes has become an automation, acceleration, and augmentation platform for containerized environments.

Describing the service mesh concept

Services ought to be meshed to be versatile, robust, and resilient in their interactions. For an ever-growing microservices world, service mesh-enablement through automated toolkits is being widely recommended. Thus, we come across a number of service mesh solutions that are becoming extremely critical for producing and sustaining both cloud-native and enabled applications. Microservices are turning out to be the most competent building blocks and the units of deployment for enterprise-grade business applications. Because of the seamless convergence of containers and microservices, the activities of continuous integration, delivery, and deployment gets simplified and sped up. As described previously, the Kubernetes platform comes in handy when automating the container life cycle management tasks. Thereby, it is clear that the combination of microservices, containers, and Kubernetes, the market-leading container clustering, orchestration, and management platform works well toward operations automation and optimization. Not only infrastructure optimization but also the various non-functional requirements of applications are being easily attained. This combination also activates and accentuates faster and frequent software deployment in order to satisfy customer, user, business, and technology changes.

However, there are still some gaps for ensuring the mandated service's resiliency. It is widely insisted that the reliability of business applications and IT services (platform and infrastructure) has to be guaranteed to boost cloud adoption. The infrastructure's elasticity and service resiliency together heighten the reliability of software applications. It is widely believed that resilient services collectively result in reliable applications. The underlying infrastructural modules also have to contribute immensely for guaranteeing the application reliability. There are several techniques for enhancing the reliability of cloud infrastructures. The clustering of IT resources such as BM servers, VMs, and containers is one widely accepted and accentuated approach toward IT reliability.

With the faster proliferation of virtual machines and containers in our data centers, the aspect of auto-scaling is seeing reality. Then, there are these powerful techniques such as replication, partition, isolation, and sharing, which are contributing immensely to the higher availability of IT services and business applications. The distributed computing has come as a blessing to ensure high availability. However, the distributed nature of IT systems and business service components brings forth its own issues. Remote calls via fragile networks is troublesome. The predictability aspect is greatly lost when distributed and different systems and services are being leveraged to accomplish business goals. Thus, we need a fresh approach to solve the service resiliency problem for the ensuing service-oriented cloud era. As indicated previously, service resiliency leads to reliable applications. Cloud infrastructures are being continuously upgraded through a host of pioneering reliability-enablement technologies to realize the IT reliability vision.

A service mesh is an additional abstraction layer that manages the communication among microservices. In traditional applications, the networking and communication logic are built and inserted into the code. Now, we tend toward microservices, which focus on just business logic alone. All other associated actions are being separated out and presented as horizontal and utility services. Such kinds of partitioning legacy applications as a dynamic pool of fine-grained and single-responsibility services guarantees a number of benefits for service providers and consumers. In traditional applications, the resiliency logic is built directly into the application itself. That is, retries and timeouts, monitoring/visibility, tracing, service discovery, and so on, are all hard-coded into the application. However, as application architectures become increasingly segmented into refined, polyglot, and micro-scale services, it is paramount to move the communication logic out of the application and put it into the underlying infrastructure.

In short, a service mesh architecture uses a proxy called a **sidecar container** that's attached to every container orchestration pod or Docker host/node. This proxy can then be attached to centralized control plane software, which is ceaselessly gathering all kinds of operations data such as fine-grained network telemetry data, applying network management policies or proxy configuration changes, and then establishing and enforcing network security policies. The other features are dynamic service discovery, load balancing, timeouts, fall-backs, retries, circuit breaking, distributed tracing, and security policy enforcement between services.

A service mesh solution typically provides several critical features to multi-service applications running at scale. The resiliency patterns such as retry, timeout, circuit breaker, failure, latency awareness, and distributed tracing are being optimally implemented and innately built-in into the service mesh solutions. There are distributed tracing tools such as Zipkin (Zipkin is a distributed tracing system). It helps gather timing data that's needed to troubleshoot latency problems in microservices environment) and OpenTracing. The service mesh solutions also provide top-line service metrics such as success rates, request volumes, and latencies. In addition to that, it performs failure and latency-aware load balancing in order to route around slow or broken service instances.

Kubernetes already has a very basic service mesh solution out-of-the-box. It is the service resource, which provides the service discovery by targeting the necessary pods. The famous round-robin method is leveraged for balancing of service requests. A service works by managing the iptables on each host in the cluster. This does not support the other key features of the typical service mesh solutions. However, by implementing one of the fully featured service mesh systems (Istio, Linkerd, or Conduit) in the cluster, the following capabilities can be obtained easily.

Service Resiliency

Service mesh solutions allow services to talk plain HTTP, and there is nothing to bother HTTPS on the application layer. The service mesh proxies will manage HTTPS encapsulation on the sender side and TLS termination on the receiving side. That is, application components can use plain HTTP, gRPC or any other protocol without bothering about the encryption in transit:

- Service mesh proxy knows which services are to be allowed to be accessed and used.
- It supports the circuit breaker pattern and other resiliency-enablement patterns, such as retries and timeouts.
- It also enables latency-aware load balancing. Traditionally, round-robin load balancing is used and this unfortunately does not take the latency of each target into consideration. The fully furnished service mesh balances the load according to response times of each backend target.
- It has the capability of doing queue-depth load balancing. This can route new requests based on the least busy target by understanding the processing amount of the current request. The service mesh knows the service request history.
- Service mesh can route particular requests marked by selected HTTP header to specific targets behind the load balancer. This makes it easy to do canary deployment testing.
- Service mesh can do health checks and the eviction of misbehaving targets.
- Service mesh can report the requests volume per target, latency metrics, success, and error rates.
- The primary goal of service mesh is to establish service communication resiliency. Service mesh solutions can get integrated with the service registry to identify services dynamically. This integration helps in discovering and involving/invoking appropriate services toward task fulfilment.
- The service security is also substantially enhanced as service meshes can authenticate services so that only the approved services can communicate with one another to implement business tasks.
- Service monitoring is also activated and accomplished through service mesh solutions. If multiple services are chained together to fulfil a service request, then the issue/problem tracking and distributed tracing get greatly simplified through the end-to-end monitoring capability being offered by standardized service meshes.

Considering the growing number of microservices participating and contributing in business workloads and IT applications, the service mesh emerges as a mission-critical infrastructure solution. Service mesh solutions have become an important ingredient in supporting and sustaining microservices-centric applications and their reliability considerably. There are a few open source as well as commercial-grade service mesh solutions on the market. As it is an emerging concept, there will be substantial advancements in the future to strengthen service resiliency and robustness. The ingrained resiliency of services ultimately leads to reliable applications.

The service mesh layer is for efficiently and effectively handling service-to-service communication. Typically, every service mesh is implemented as a series/mesh of interconnected network proxies, and this arrangement is able to manage service traffic better. This service mesh idea has gained a lot of traction with the continued rise of MSA. The communication traffic in the ensuring era of MSA is going to be distinctly different. That is, service-to-service communication becomes the vital factor for application behavior at runtime. Traditionally, application functions occur locally as a part of the same runtime. However, in the case of microservices, application functions occur through **remote procedure calls** (**RPCs**). Thus, the widely articulated and accentuated deficiencies of distributed computing over unreliable **wide area networks** (**WANs**) go up considerably.

Programmers who are dealing with distributed systems understand the fallacies of distributed computing. The key fallacies are as follows:

- The network is reliable
- The latency is zero
- The bandwidth is infinite
- The network is secure
- The topology doesn't change
- There is one administrator
- The transport cost is zero
- The network is homogeneous

The promising and strategic solution approach for enhancing the resiliency in the ubiquitous service era (geographically distributed and disparate microservices communicate with one another) is to embrace the service mesh method. The service mesh relieves application service developers from that burden by pushing that responsibility down into the infrastructure layer.

Service Resiliency

With a service mesh, services running on a container, pod, **virtual machine (VM)**, or **bare-metal (BM)** server are configured to send their messages to a local proxy, which is installed as a sidecar module. That local proxy is designed and destined to do things like timeout, retry, circuit breaking, encryption, application of custom routing rules, and service discovery. All kinds of network monitoring and management activities are being precisely performed by a service mesh. With the unprecedented acceptance of the service mesh concept, there are discussions and discourses between service mesh solutions and other middleware solutions such as **Enterprise Service Bus (ESB)**, **Enterprise Application Integration (EAI)**, hub, and API Gateways.

The service communication is being made resilient through the incorporation of service mesh solution, as portrayed by the following diagram:

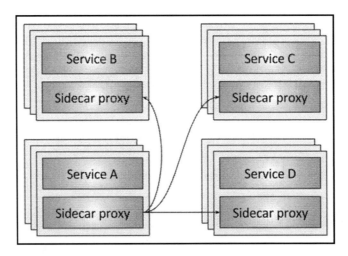

As the preceding diagram shows, there are four service clusters (A-D). That is, the service cluster consists of a service and its instances. Each service instance is empowered with a sidecar network proxy. All network traffic using a variety of communication and data transmission protocols from a service instance flows to other services via its local sidecar proxy. The local proxy takes care of all the needs of service communications, thereby most of the widely reported deficiencies of distributed computing can be fully overcome. We have already indicated the widely agreed and accepted fallacies of distributed computation, and it is being understood that the leverage of service mesh simply and sagaciously eliminates them.

The data plane: In a service mesh, there are two vital modules, that is, the control and the data planes. The sidecar proxy (data plane) performs the following tasks. As described previously, the prominent functionalities of the sidecar proxy are as follows:

- Eventually consistent service discovery
- Health checking
- Routing
- Load balancing
- Authentication and authorization
- Observability

All of these functionalities are the prime responsibility of the data plane of any service mesh solution. Precisely speaking, the sidecar proxy is the data plane. In other words, the data plane is squarely responsible for conditionally translating, forwarding, and observing every network packet that flows to and from services (client, as well as server). That is, the main responsibility of the data plane is to ensure that any service request is delivered from microservice A to microservice B in a reliable and secure manner.

The control plane: The network abstraction that the data plane (sidecar proxy) of service mesh provides is really magical. However, the proxy has to be supplied the right and relevant details to route service request messages to appropriate services and their instances. Also, the service discovery is not being done by proxy. The settings for the load balancing, timeout, circuit breaking, and so on, ought to be specified in an unambiguous manner in the control plane. The actual configuration of the data plane functionalities are done within the control plane. If we correlate the TCP/IP analogy, the control plane is similar to configuring the switches and routers so that TCP/IP will work properly on top of these switches and routers. In the service mesh, the control plane is responsible for configuring the network of sidecar proxies. The control plane functionalities include configuring the following things:

- Routing
- Load balancing
- Circuit breaker/retry/timeout
- Deployments
- Service discovery

The control plane controls a set of distributed and stateless sidecar proxies. The control plane manages and configures the proxies to correctly route traffic. Furthermore, the control plane configures mixers to enforce policies and collect telemetry. The following diagram shows the various components that make up both data and control planes:

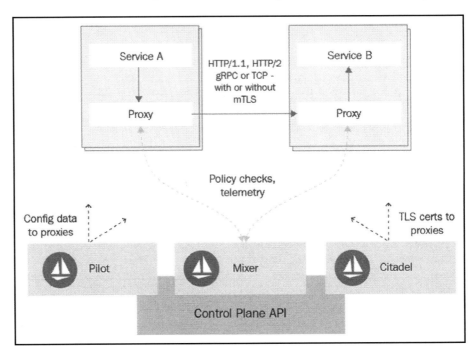

Data plane versus control plane summary

Service mesh data plane: Any standard service mesh solution has to comply to this architecture of having two planes (control and data). The sidecar proxy is the data plane. Every request originating from any application service has to pass through this plane. The data plane is squarely responsible for performing service discovery, health checking, and routing. The data plane also does load balancing and authentication/authorization. Finally, the aspect of observability is indispensable for any service mesh solution. The data plane collects all kinds of performance, scalability, security, availability, and other decision-enabling information.

Service mesh control plane: The control plane monitors, configures, manages, and maintains all the data planes under its jurisdiction. The control plane elegantly provides policies and configuration for all the contributing data planes. The data planes form a kind of distributed system under the centralized monitoring of the control plane. That is the goal of distributed deployment, but the centralized monitoring is getting fulfilled through the leverage of this kind of architecture.

Why is service mesh paramount?

There are a few compelling reasons and causes for the successful introduction and the runaway success of service mesh solutions. Microservices has emerged and evolved as the most appropriate building block for enterprise-grade applications and the optimal unit of application deployment. Furthermore, deploying a number of microservices rather than big monolith applications gives developers the much-needed flexibility to work in different programming languages, application development frameworks, **rapid application development** (RAD) tools, and release cadence across the system. This transition is resulting in higher productivity and agility, especially for larger teams.

There are challenges as well. The problems that had to be solved once for a monolith, such as security, load balancing, monitoring, and rate limiting, need to be tackled for each microservice. Many companies run internal load balancers that take care of routing traffic between microservices. The fact of the matter is that these solutions weren't designed to handle inter-application communication. The Kubernetes platform is certainly contributing for surmounting some of the container life cycle management needs. Still, there are gaps between the supply and the demand.

As microservices are fine-grained, the number of microservices participating and contributing in any IT environment is on the higher side. It becomes very difficult to figure out which services are communicating with one another. Also, if there is any deviation, zeroing down the root and the cause of the problem is a definite challenge for operational teams. The solution is distributed deployment and central management. We need a central monitoring and management solution. Also, we need good visibility into metrics, such as requests per second, response time, number of successes and failures, timeout, and circuit-breaker status, to plan and manage resource capacities for microservices. Finally, we need a competent fault detection and isolation mechanism. It is not advisable to have separate solutions for these shortcomings. We need an integrated and standardized solution to address these issues. For attaining the originally expressed benefits of microservices architecture, service mesh is the way forward.

DNS provides some features, such as service discovery, but it does not provide fast retries, load balancing, distributed tracing, and health monitoring. The old and failed approach is to cobble up several things together to achieve something bigger and better. The new approach is to go for an integrated suite. The service mesh solutions are able to offset the preceding problems sharply by substantially reducing management costs of services, improving observability, and building a better fault identification and isolation mechanism.

Therefore, the focus gets shifted toward the service mesh approach. The service mesh solutions are capable of making Kubernetes more productive for bigger organizations trying to build a large number of microservices using different and distributed teams who own and operate their own microservices.

Forming and empowering service meshes by service mesh-enabling solutions, such as Istio and Conduit, is the way forward. The reliability, security, and stability of microservices are being guaranteed through the formation of service meshes. A network proxy (data plane) is being fit in each container/pod/host. Each proxy serves as a gateway to each interaction that occurs between microservices deployed in different containers. The proxy accepts the connection and spreads the load across the service mesh. A central controller (control plane) astutely orchestrates the connections. While the service traffic flows directly between proxies, the control plane knows about each interaction and transaction. The controller tells the proxies to implement access control and collects various metrics, including performance, security. The controller also integrates with various leading platforms like Kubernetes and Mesos, which are open source systems for facilitating the automated deployment and management of containerized applications.

Service mesh architectures

There are a couple of choices for leveraging the service mesh solutions. A service mesh solution can be presented as a library so that any microservices-centric application can import and use it on demand. We are used to import programming language packages, libraries, and classes in a typical application building and execution. Libraries such as Hystrix and Ribbon are well-known examples of this approach. This works well for applications that are exclusively written in one language.

There is a limited adoption of this library approach as microservicecs-centric applications are being coded using different languages. There are other approaches too, which are explained as follows:

Node agent: In this architecture, there is a separate agent running on every node. This setup can service a heterogeneous mix of workloads. It is just the opposite of the library model. Linkerd's recommended deployment in Kubernetes works like this. F5's **Application Service Proxy (ASP)** and the Kubernetes default kube-proxy work the same. As there is one agent on every node, there is a need for some cooperation from the underlying infrastructure. Most applications can't just choose their own TCP stack, guess an ephemeral port number, and send or receive TCP packets directly. They simply delegate all of these to the OS infrastructure.

This model emphasizes work-resource sharing. If a node agent allocates some memory to buffer data for one microservice, it might use that buffer for data for another service in a few seconds. That is, the resources are shared in an efficient manner. However, managing shared resources is beset with challenges, and hence there is extra coding required for resource management. Another work resource that can be easily shared is configuration information. Instead of sharing configuration details to every pod, the node agent architecture facilitates the sharing per node.

Sidecar is the new model that's widely used by Istio with Envoy. Conduit also uses a sidecar approach. In sidecar deployments, an application proxy in a containerized format gets deployed to every application container. Multiple copies of the proxy may have to be deployed if there are redundant application containers.

The load balancer typically sit a between the client and the server. Advanced service mesh solutions attach a sidecar proxy to a client-side library, and hence every client gets equal access to the load balancer. This means that, the single point of failure of any traditional load balancer gets eliminated. The traditional load balancer is a server-side load balancer, but the sidecar proxy enables client-side load balancing.

The central responsibility of a service mesh solution is to efficiently handle the core networking tasks such as load balancing and service discovery. For ensuring heightened service resiliency, a service mesh solution implements resiliency design patterns, such as circuit breaking, retries, timeouts, and fault-tolerance. When services are resilient, the resulting application is reliable. The underlying infrastructural modules also have to be highly available and stable. IT systems and business workloads have to collectively contribute for business continuity.

Monitoring the service mesh

We need deeper visibility to have a tighter control on any system performing its duties. In the ensuing microservices world, the number of moving parts and pieces is growing steadily, and hence manning each one deeply and decisively is beset with a few challenges and concerns. Automated tools are the way forward to minutely monitor and activate the counter measures in time with less intervention and interpretation from humans. Increasingly, software applications are being presented as microservices-centric containerized applications. The increasingly inspiring and important ingredient in any microservice and containerized environments is service mesh solutions.

Service meshes come with native monitoring capability. They provide a combination of network performance metrics such as latency, bandwidth, and uptime monitoring. They do this for nodes/hosts/physical machines, pods, and containers. They also provide detailed logging for all kinds of events. The monitoring and logging capability ultimately helps to find the root cause of any problem and to troubleshoot.

Distributed tracing turns out to be a key factor for achieving the goal of visibility. The idea here is that it gives each request an ID. As it passes through the network, it shows the path each request has taken. Using this, operators and troubleshooters can easily understand which parts of the network or which microservices instances are slow or unresponsive. These insights simplify and streamline the repair. Thus, monitoring tools are indispensable in microservices environments.

Security is another vital ingredient for achieving the intended success of microservices. Rather than relying on peripheral firewalls for the entire application, the new networking project (Calico) helps create micro-firewalls around each service within a microservices application. This enables the fine-grained management and enforcement of security policies for guaranteeing unbreakable security for microservices. Bringing down one microservice does not have any serious impact on other services. Since the service mesh operates on a data plane, it is possible to apply common security patches and policies across the mesh. A service mesh predominantly secures inter-service communications. A service mesh provides a panoramic view into what is happening when multiple services interact with one another.

Service mesh deployment models

We have discussed service mesh solutions and how they are helping to realize the elusive goal of service resiliency. There are a few different deployment models:

- Involving one proxy instance per hose/node
- Leveraging the popular sidecar deployment of the service mesh proxy

Per-host proxy deployment pattern: In this deployment model, the proxy instance is being used in every host/node. As described previously, one host can be a VM or a BM server. This host is a Kubernetes worker node. Many services can be made to run on a single host. All of these services have to send their various service requests to the destination through the proxy instance. As shown in the following diagram, the proxy instance can be deployed as a DaemonSet in each of the participating hosts:

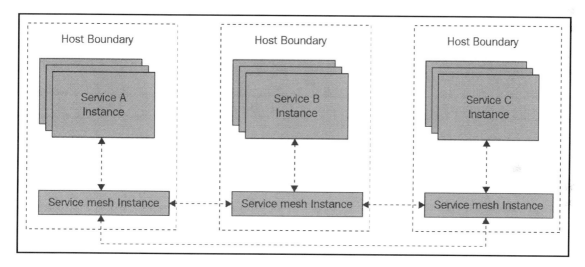

Each host is comprised of one service and its instances. Each service and its instances communicate with other services being deployed in other hosts. The proxy is the intermediary between the distributed services to ensure the resiliency of service communications.

Service Resiliency

Sidecar proxy deployment pattern: In this model, one sidecar proxy is deployed per instance of every service. As mentioned previously, one microservice can have several instances to ensure the aspects of failover and failback. This model is good for deployments that use containers or Kubernetes. As a best practice, every container hosts and runs a microservice. That is, if there are multiple instances for a microservice, then we need that number of containers to uniquely host and manage them in good condition. If, for each container, if we deploy one sidecar proxy, then the number of containers is bound to escalate. Also, it is insisted to have a small footprint for the sidecar proxy. Otherwise, the performance may get degraded. The alternate approach is to deploy a sidecar proxy per a host so that the number of sidecar proxy containers turns out to be less:

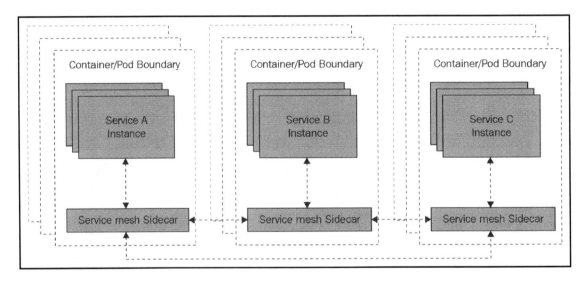

Sidecar pattern for service mesh: Services A, B, and C can communicate with one another via corresponding sidecar proxy instances. By default, proxies handle only intra-service mesh cluster traffic between the source (upstream) and the destination (downstream) services. To a expose a service that is part of a service mesh to the outside word, you have to enable ingress traffic. Similarly, if a service depends on an external service, you may need to enable the egress traffic:

Chapter 9

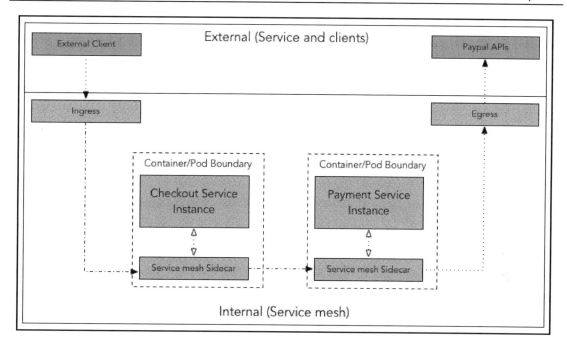

Any service mesh solution has to enable seamless and spontaneous interactions among all the participating microservices. To accomplish any service-to-service communication, a number of vital capabilities are expected out of service mesh solutions. Here is a list of the major competencies of service mesh solutions. The widely used mesh topology in computer networking is being replicated here in the service era to guarantee service stability, availability, and reliability. When services are individually resilient and elastic, then their amalgamation is going to be trustworthy and deterministic. Here is a list of the key characteristics of any standard service mesh solutions.

Dynamic request routing: There are routing rules and tables to empower service mesh solutions to route service requests to a preferred version of the microservice running in different environments, such as development, testing, staging, and production. Dynamic request routing comes in handy for common deployment scenarios such as blue-green, Canary, and A/B testing:

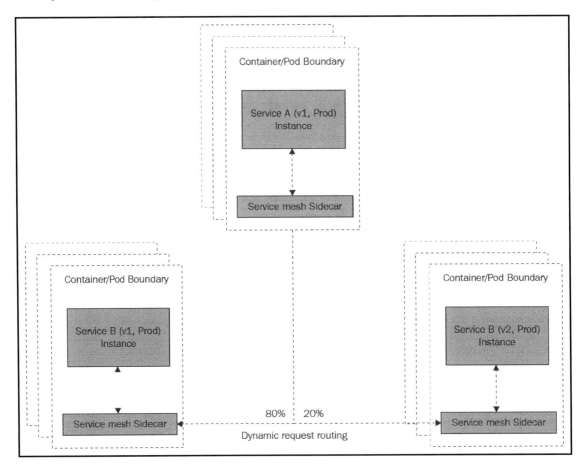

Control plane: The standard architecture of service mesh solutions is to have two separate planes to flexibly do different tasks. Data planes are being attached with every microservice instance. In some cases, a data plane is being embedded with each pod, which typically comprises many containers to accommodate a full-fledged application. If empowering each pod with a data plane instance is unnecessary, every node is stuffed with an instance of a data plane. The control plane is the centralized monitoring and management module. It has the capability of policy establishment and enforcement feature.

Similarly, other details needed for enabling the data plane to work according to the evolving situation is being done at the control plane. We discussed the leading open source service mesh solutions and their various components in detail in next chapter. The routing tasks of the data plane are being activated and accelerated by the control plane. Similarly, service registration and discovery are being performed by the control plane. The important load balancing task is also being managed by the control plane:

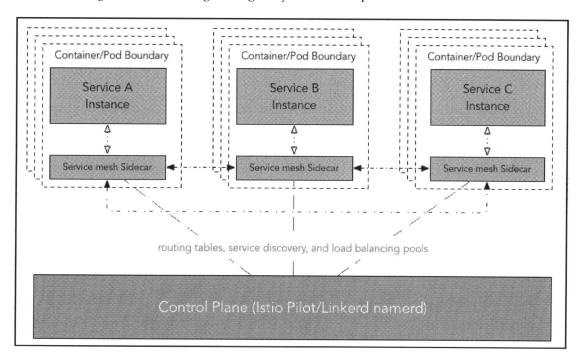

Service discovery: In a microservices environment, each participating service has to register itself in a service registry to enable other services to find and bind dynamically. Service registry is a middleware application, which means that it helps to identify the pool of service instances so that service access and leverage can become smooth and spontaneous.

Load balancing: This is important to balance the load of services. Service requests are being intelligently directed to those services that are not overloaded. The combination of control and data planes of service mesh solutions comes in handy in fulfilling this unique requirement toward ensuring the high availability of services. There are several load balancing algorithms. Some service mesh solutions profess and provide failure and latency-aware load balancing capabilities.

In a sidecar pattern, the functionality of the main container is considerably extended or enhanced by a sidecar container. However, there is no strong coupling between the main and sidecar containers. As we all know, Kubernetes emerges as the key container orchestration platform. Pods are the primary building blocks as per the Kubernetes specification. A sidecar container, which is a kind of utility container, is attached to each pod. The sidecar container is the containerized version of the sidecar proxy, which is the data plane. A pod is comprised of one or more application containers. A sidecar container is predominantly used for supporting and empowering the main application containers in their pursuit. Sidecar containers are not standalone containers, and hence they have to be paired with some business-specific containers to be right and relevant. Sidecar containers are hugely usable and reusable and can be attached with any number of pods and their application containers:

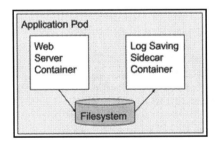

Here is an example of the sidecar pattern. The main container is a web server, and this is being empowered by a log saver container, which is a sidecar container. This sidecar container meticulously and minutely collects the web server's logs from the local disk and streams them to the centralized log collector.

Summary

Containers have definitely simplified how we build, deploy, and manage software applications by abstracting the underlying infrastructure. That is, developers just focus and develop software applications. Then, the developed applications get packaged in a standardized fashion, and shipped and deployed on any system without any hitches and hurdles. They can run on local systems as well as remote systems. With clouds emerging as the one-stop IT infrastructure solution for running and managing all kinds of enterprise, web, cloud, mobile, and IoT applications, applications are being containerized and deployed in cloud environments, through a host of automated tools. However, there is a need for a number of automated tools to automate the end-to-end activities of application development, integration, delivery, and deployment. Furthermore, an application's availability, scalability, adaptivity, stability, maneuverability, and security have to be ensured through technologically inspired solutions. Service mesh solutions have emerged as one of the important ingredients of containerized cloud environments and contribute immensely in elevating service resiliency. In the next chapter, we will be learning about how to use Prometheus and Grafana metrics to create powerful dashboards and alerts.

10
Containers, Kubernetes, and Istio Monitoring

In the cloud world, we need to carry out monitoring to observe the progress and quality of our services and applications over a period of time. Monitoring allows us to keep our applications under systematic review. If something breaks, we want to know what it is and what caused it to malfunction. Monitoring helps us to investigate the failure points in our services. We can make sure that we detect these services early on using anomaly detection. White-box monitoring can help us work out which services are failing and why, and also how to debug them. It can also provide future trends, which means it can detect potential future failures. Here, we will be focusing only on tools that enable us to monitor either our application or our infrastructure:

- **Monitoring the application**: It is very important that the features or services that are being developed are monitored. There should be a proper time-series graph and a dashboard.
- **Monitoring the infrastructure**: If possible, all non-functional services should be monitored, with alerts, such as response times or requests per second. This is useful to catch small issues before they turn into large issues.

We need to monitor our servers and services to fix problems before the end users or customers come across them. Monitoring improves the product quality and makes sure customers are delighted with our services. It also helps us to avoid outage costs. If we have proper monitoring, we can make decisions based on data instead of hunches. In this chapter, we will not only look at how to set up monitoring, we will also enable alerts to notify us when systems are failing. We will then enable alerts to monitor the infrastructure to gather data on errors, performance, and throughput. After that, we will use alerts to measure the user experience of our application and the quality of the services we provide. This will allow us to make good decisions and measure the value we deliver.

In this chapter, we will discuss how we can monitor applications or services running on clusters, pods, and Kubernetes using Prometheus and Grafana. We will cover the following topics:

- Introducing Prometheus and the Prometheus architecture
- Setting up Prometheus
- Configuring alerts from Prometheus
- Introducing Grafana
- Setting up Grafana
- Configuring alerts from Grafana

Prometheus

Prometheus is an open source monitoring tool that was originally built by SoundCloud in 2012, inspired by Google's BrogMon. It is written in GoLang. According to the New Stack Survey of 2017, Prometheus is one of the most widely used tools for monitoring Kubernetes clusters. What makes Prometheus different than other open source monitoring systems is that it has a simple, text-based format, making it easy to get metrics from other systems. It also has a multidimensional data model and a rich and concise query language. Using Prometheus, we can monitor all levels, nodes, container-scheduling systems, and also routers and switches. If we are dealing with large applications and a fast-moving infrastructure, this means that the jobs that we run change rapidly and we have to deploy them around 100 times a day. In this case, Prometheus will be very useful, as it has the ability to discover services. If we have a dynamic infrastructure, we can use Prometheus to detect early failures and determine what's going on in the entire stack. It also helps developers to investigate how and why something went wrong. Prometheus is not, however, very good for producing logs.

Even though BorgMon remains internal to Google, the idea of treating time-series data as a data source for generating alerts is now accessible to everyone through open source tools such as Prometheus. More information about this can be found in the book *Site Reliability Engineering: How Google Runs Production Systems* (http://shop.oreilly.com/product/0636920041528.do).

Let's talk about the positive features of Prometheus:

- It has a multidimensional data model that uses time-series data. It uses a pull model to fetch time-series data over HTTP.

Chapter 10

- It has a powerful and flexible query language. This can be useful when setting up graphs and monitoring dashboards.
- It is easy to integrate with other tools, such as Grafana.
- It is easy to investigate the application failures.

Prometheus, however, does not include the following:

- Raw log/event collection
- Request tracing
- Anomaly detection
- Durable long term storage
- Automatic horizontal scaling
- User authentication management

Prometheus architecture

We can see that Prometheus has many components. The center of the Prometheus architecture is the Prometheus server, which we can run either as one or multiple servers in our infrastructure. This server will actively pull the metrics from our applications. We can directly use the Prometheus metrics in our code base and expose our application on a HTTP endpoint in a specific format where it can pull the parameter. We can then configure it later on our dashboards. In other words, it will scrape and store time-series data:

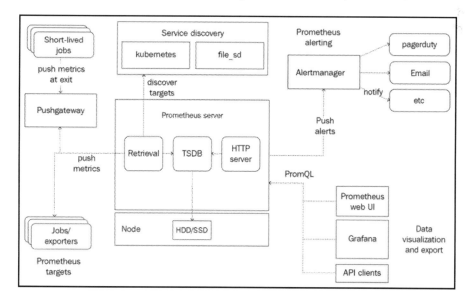

- **Short-lived jobs**: Generally, we have many small jobs running every day, such as clearing a cache or deleting the users. We can push a few important metrics into **Pushgateway**, and then the Prometheus server can pull those metrics.
- **Service discovery**: This is the way in which Prometheus discovers what should be scraped. Service discovery can be carried out by DNS Service, **kubernetes**, or any custom integration.
- **Alertmanager**: As the name suggests, this is used to handle the alerts. We can notify the users or the incident team using **pagerduty**, **Email**, or Slack.
- **Prometheus web UI**: This enables you to view simple graphs and set up the alerts and the state of the monitoring endpoints.

Setting up Prometheus

For this example, we need a few prerequisites. We need both Kubernetes and Istio 0.7 up and running. The reader needs to have basic knowledge of Linux. Take a look at the following steps:

1. First, we will install Prometheus using the `prometheus.yaml` file. You can find this `yaml` file in the `/kubernetes/addons` folder. Run the following command to install Prometheus from the Istio directory:

   ```
   Kubectl apply -f install/kubernetes/addons/prometheus.yaml
   ```

   The output is as follows:

   ```
   Kube@Kubernetes:/opt/istio/istio-0.7.1$ kubectl apply -f install/kubernetes/addons/prometheus.yaml
   configmap/prometheus created
   service/prometheus created
   deployment.extensions/prometheus created
   serviceaccount/prometheus created
   clusterrole.rbac.authorization.k8s.io/prometheus created
   clusterrolebinding.rbac.authorization.k8s.io/prometheus created
   ```

2. Verify that the Prometheus service is running in your cluster as follows:

   ```
   kubectl -n istio-system get svc prometheus
   ```

   The output is as follows:

   ```
   master@Kubemaster:~$ kubectl -n istio-system get svc prometheus
   NAME         TYPE        CLUSTER-IP       EXTERNAL-IP   PORT(S)    AGE
   prometheus   ClusterIP   10.105.135.113   <none>        9090/TCP   4d19h
   master@Kubemaster:~$
   ```

3. Use the following command for port-forwarding. Prometheus will run on port `9090`:

   ```
   kubectl -n istio-system port-forward $(kubectl -n istio-system get
   pod -l app=prometheus -o jsonpath='{.items[0].metadata.name}')
   9090:9090 &
   ```

   The output is as follows:

   ```
   [1] 35637
   master@Kubemaster:~$ Forwarding from 127.0.0.1:9090 -> 9090
   Forwarding from [::1]:9090 -> 9090

   master@Kubemaster:~$
   ```

4. If you are not using Google Cloud, AWS, or Azure, you might not get an external IP. In that case, your service will be running on the IP address of the localhost, `127.0.0.1`, and on port `9090`. We can either use putty or Command Prompt to carry out port mapping using the following command:

   ```
   Ssh -L 9090:127.0.0.1:9090 master@40.76.212.128
   ```

   The output is as follows:

   ```
   C:\Users\       ssh -L 9090:127.0.0.1:9090 master@40.76.212.128
   master@40.76.212.128's password:
   Welcome to Ubuntu 17.10 (GNU/Linux 4.13.0-46-generic x86_64)

    * Documentation:  https://help.ubuntu.com
    * Management:     https://landscape.canonical.com
    * Support:        https://ubuntu.com/advantage

     Get cloud support with Ubuntu Advantage Cloud Guest:
       http://www.ubuntu.com/business/services/cloud

   0 packages can be updated.
   0 updates are security updates.

   Your Ubuntu release is not supported anymore.
   For upgrade information, please visit:
   http://www.ubuntu.com/releaseendoflife

   New release '18.04.1 LTS' available.
   Run 'do-release-upgrade' to upgrade to it.

   Last login: Mon Oct 22 06:39:44 2018 from 167.220.238.138
   master@Kubemaster:~$
   ```

Containers, Kubernetes, and Istio Monitoring

5. Visit `http://localhost:9090` in your browser. You will see the Promethus UI. Good work!
6. We can see that we have tabs called **Alerts**, **Graph**, and **Status**. Click on **Graphs**. Prometheus provides us with an expression browser and built-in graphs.
7. Now click on **Metrics**. This will give us multiple metrics in a drop-down list. We can select any one of these and click on **Execute**:

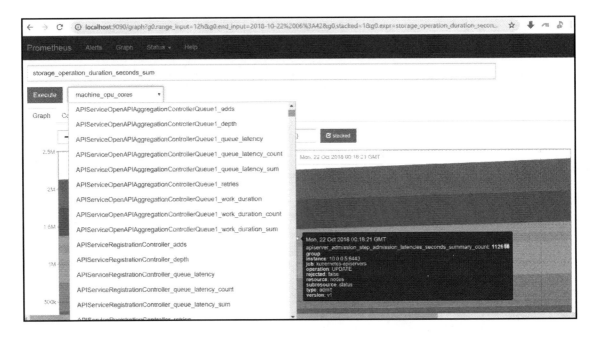

Chapter 10

This will show us graphs based on our metrics and data. We can also see which type of operation, group, instance IP, and job the metrics refer to:

As well as this, we can set up alerts, which we will discuss in more detail in the next section.

Configuring alerts in Prometheus

In this part, we will look at how to design alerts in Prometheus. First, however, we need to understand a few concepts that are used in Prometheus:

- **Metrics**: Metrics are a core concept of Prometheus. We can expose these from our codes, and Prometheus will store them in a time-series format. We can then use them with flexible query language.
- **Labels**: Prometheus indicates the service that a particular metric applies to. Labels in Prometheus are arbitrary, and, as such, they can be much more powerful than just which service/instance exposed a metric.

In the following example, `http_failure_request` is the metric that denotes all the points collected by Prometheus for the product page service, which exposes an HTTP failure request. For example, `service="productpage"` is a label, which denotes that this particular `http_failure_request` metric is for the `productpage` service:

```
# Request counter for the Product Page service( Application created in
ISTIO)
  http_failure_request{service="productpage"}
```

Prometheus can gather metrics from services, VMs, infrastructure, or any other third-party application. To expose and scrape the metrics, it uses the **/metrics** URLs, which return a full list of metrics with label sets and their values without any calculation:

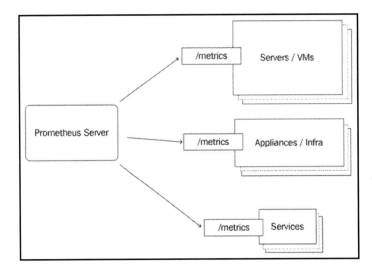

The syntax for how you can create Prometheus alert rules using annotations is as follows:

```
alert: Lots_Of_product_page_Jobs_In_Queue
expr: sum(jobs_in_queue{service="productpage"}) > 100
for: 15m
labels:
   severity: minor
annotations:
   summary: Product page queue appears to be building up (consistently more than 100
jobs waiting)
   dashboard:
https://grafana.monitoring.intra/dashboard/db/productpage-overview
   impact: Product page is experiencing delays, causing orders to be marked as pending
   runbook: https://wiki-internal/runbooks/productpage-queues.html
```

Grafana

Grafana is a widely used open source tool that is used to monitor services and applications by visualizing time-series data. It can tell us how our services or servers are doing by showing us production business metrics. It can carry out both infrastructure monitoring and application monitoring. The official definition of Grafana is as follows:

> "It is the analytics platform for all your metrics. Grafana allows you to query, visualize, alert, on and understand your metrics no matter where they are stored. Create, explore, and share dashboards with your team, and foster a data-driven culture."

One of the main reasons why we would use Grafana over Prometheus is to get perfect visualization and dashboard editing. Using Grafana, it is very easy to create a dashboard and customize it. With Prometheus, on the other hand, we would need to make use of console templates to do this, which makes it a little harder to use. Other features of Grafana include the following:

- Advanced graphing
- Powerful query editors
- Visualization dashboards
- Dynamic queries and dashboards
- Multi-tenant user and organization support
- Client-side and server-side rendering of panels
- Support for many different data sources

Setting up Grafana

Before jumping into how we install Grafana, there are a few prerequisites that we require. We should have both Kubernetes and Istio version 0.7 up and running, and we need to deploy an application for monitoring purposes. We also need to have the Prometheus server running on same box for service discovery. Our sample architecture will look as follows:

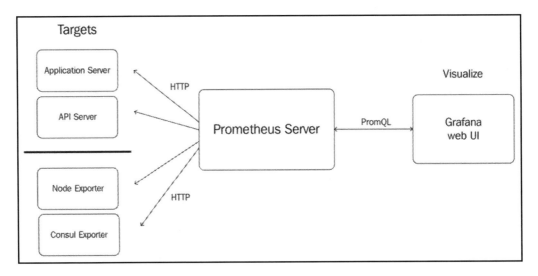

Our target nodes could be anything from application servers, API Servers, databases, or nodes. Prometheus will help us to discover these metrics and pull the data, as we have seen previously. Here, we are going to use the **Grafana Web UI** to visualize a dashboard and graphs:

1. From the Istio base directory, use the following command to install Grafana. In our example, we have already installed Grafana:

   ```
   kubectl create -f install/kubernetes/addons/grafana.yaml
   ```

   The output is as follows:

2. Grafana UI will run on `3000` port. The ports should be opened from the network side, and we need to execute the following command to carry out port forwarding:

   ```
   kubectl -n istio-system port-forward $(kubectl -n istio-system get
   pod -l app=grafana -o jsonpath='{.items[0].metadata.name}')
   3000:3000 &
   ```

   The output is as follows:

   ```
   [1] 90165
   master@Kubemaster:/opt/Istio_prom_grafana/istio-0.7.1$ Forwarding from 127.0.0.1:3000 -> 3000
   Forwarding from [::1]:3000 -> 3000
   ```

3. If you are using Linux VMs, use the following command to carry out port mapping from your Command Prompt:

   ```
   Ssh -L 3000:127.0.0.1:3000 master@40.76.212.128
   ```

   The output is as follows:

   ```
   C:\Users\       ssh -L 9090:127.0.0.1:9090 master@40.76.212.128
   master@40.76.212.128's password:
   Welcome to Ubuntu 17.10 (GNU/Linux 4.13.0-46-generic x86_64)

    * Documentation:  https://help.ubuntu.com
    * Management:     https://landscape.canonical.com
    * Support:        https://ubuntu.com/advantage

     Get cloud support with Ubuntu Advantage Cloud Guest:
       http://www.ubuntu.com/business/services/cloud

   0 packages can be updated.
   0 updates are security updates.

   Your Ubuntu release is not supported anymore.
   For upgrade information, please visit:
   http://www.ubuntu.com/releaseendoflife

   New release '18.04.1 LTS' available.
   Run 'do-release-upgrade' to upgrade to it.

   Last login: Mon Oct 22 06:39:44 2018 from 167.220.238.138
   master@Kubemaster:~$
   ```

4. Visit `http://localhost:3000` to access the Grafana UI. It will look as follows:

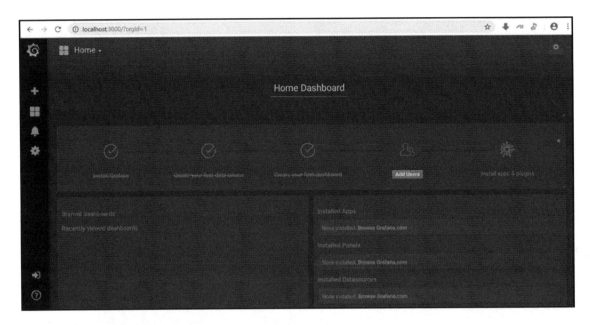

5. After we have installed Isto and the sample application, Grafana will create a few dashboards for us. Click on **Dashboard** to see the default dashboards:

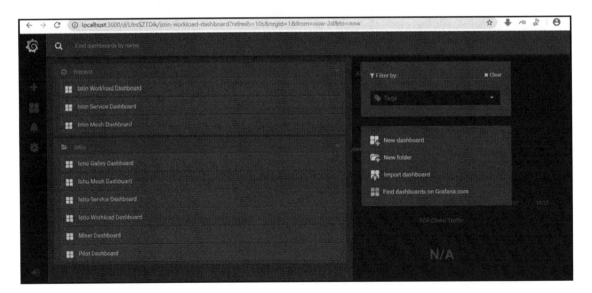

6. We can click on **Istio Mesh Dashboard** to see the global request volume and look at our success and failure rate. It will also show you the **4xx** and **5xx** error codes. To find out more information, we can click on any of the services:

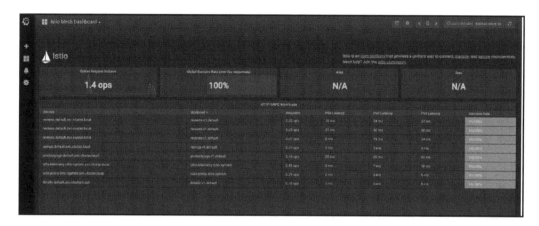

Istio Mesh Dashboard

7. The **Istio Service Dashboard** will look as follows. We can monitor the client request volumes, the server request volumes, the client/server request duration, and the client/server request volumes. We can set up alerts on these metrics easily:

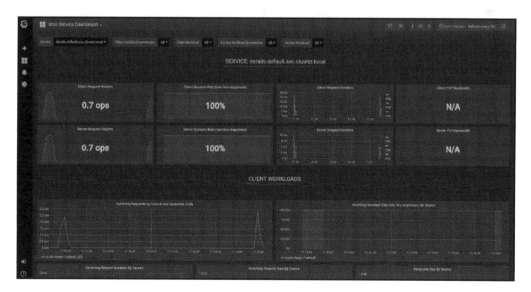

Istio Service Dashboard

The following dashboard will show us the workload on our service or infrastructure by providing us with common metrics such as incoming request volume and request duration. We can also learn about how our network is doing, including the inbound workload and the outbound workload. We can play around with these metrics to create new dashboards:

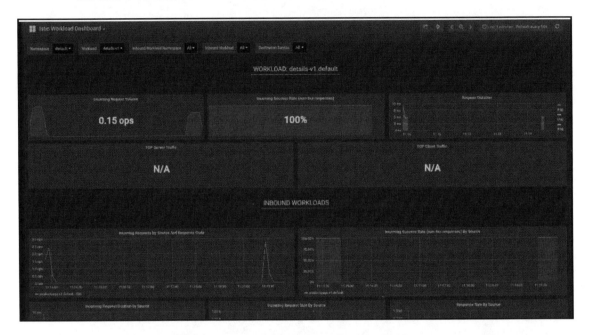

Istio Workload Dashboard

Configuring alerts in Grafana

We can configure alerts in Grafana on dashboards. Grafana provides a query-based alerting system:

1. Run Grafana in your local browser using the `http://localhost:3000/?orgId=1` URL to access the Grafana UI.
2. Click on **Alerting**, then **Notification channels**, and then **New channels**:

Chapter 10

3. Add the data for the new channel. We can select from a wide range of notifications in Grafana, including email, Slack, Microsoft teams, Webhook, or PagerDuty:

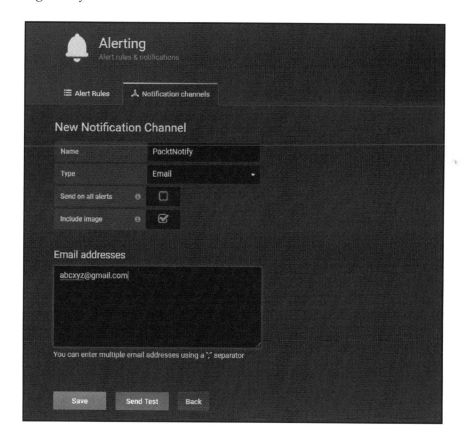

The **New Notification Channel** form will contain the following tags:

- **Name**: This is the name of the notification channel. This value must be unique.
- **Description**: Here, we add additional information that we might want to include for documentation purposes.
- **Type**: Select **Email**, and enter the email address of the recipient. We can enter multiple email addresses, separated by commas.

4. After we create the notification channel, let's define our metrics. To do this, click on the **Dashboard**, go to **New dashboard**, and then click on **Graph**. Under **Panel Title**, click on **Edit**:

Chapter 10

5. We then need to define our metrics. We can use any data source that is supported by Grafana. In our example, as we have already configured Prometheus, we are going to use this as the data source. After we click on **Edit,** Grafana will ask you to select a **Data Source** and **Metrics**. In this case, we have selected storage_operation_duration_seconds_sum as the metric. As you can see, it has created a time-series graph:

6. Click on the **General** tab and define a title for your alert and description:

7. Click on the **Alert** tab to set the definition of the alert. We can set the condition and the threshold value. We also need to define the frequency of the alerts as follows:

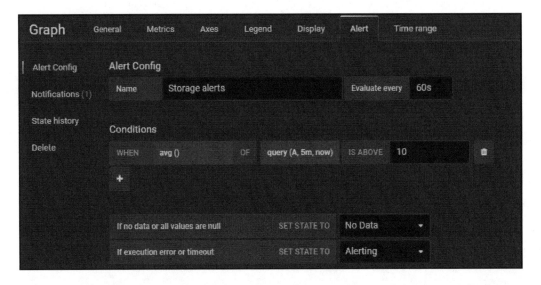

8. After completing the alert definition, save the alert and execute the **Test Rule**. Then, verify whether it is working. For email alerts, we need to configure SMTP:

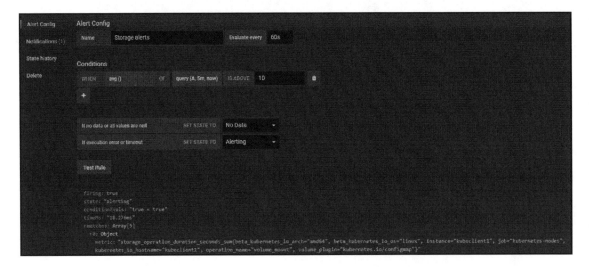

Summary

Monitoring is not a one-time task. We should be regularly measuring what's going on with our Kubernetes pods or our microservices. Monitoring plays a crucial role in the microservice system, as we need to monitor all endpoints in our microservices. To achieve a higher quality product, we should be able to detect failures before our customer does. We should enable anomaly detection and notify our operation team to troubleshoot the problem. We have to set up the necessary monitoring and alerts on both the infrastructure side and the application side. In this chapter, we saw how to use Prometheus and Grafana metrics to create powerful dashboards and alerts.

In the next chapter, we will talk about post-production activities and best practices for ensuring and enhancing the IT reliability.

11
Post-Production Activities for Ensuring and Enhancing IT Reliability

Business automation, augmentation, and acceleration get neatly accomplished through a variety of microservices-based software applications in conjunction with integrated platforms and optimized IT infrastructures. In short, IT is the best and biggest enabler of businesses across the globe. That is, business offerings and outputs are being deftly and decisively enabled by scores of distinct IT advancements. The evolving business expectations are being duly automated through a host of delectable developments in the IT space. These improvements elegantly empower business houses to deliver newer and premium business offerings fast. With intuitive, informative, and inspiring interfaces, software applications are being presented to their customers and consumers to be used in an easy and error-free fashion. Furthermore, this continuous empowerment in the IT space, in turn, facilitates accomplishing more with less, enabling deeper market penetration, attaining fresh customers and retaining the loyalty of current users. Business outputs are seeing a solid and sustainable growth through the smart leverage of pioneering technologies, tools, and tips being unearthed in the IT landscape. Precisely speaking, the role and responsibility of IT in accentuating and accelerating business adaptivity, agility, and affordability is on the climb.

Now, here is a twist. Businesses are insisting on reliable business operations. Here, too, the contributions of IT toward reliable businesses is going to be simply great. IT pundits and professors are therefore striving hard and stretching further to bring forth viable methods and mechanisms toward reliable IT. **Site Reliability Engineering (SRE)** is a promising engineering discipline, and its key goals include significantly enhancing and ensuring the reliability aspects of IT. In this chapter, we are going to focus on the various ways and means of bringing up the reliability assurance factor by embarking on some unique activities in the post-production/deployment phase. Monitoring, measuring, and managing the various operational and behavioral data is the first and foremost step toward reliable IT infrastructures and applications. There are machine learning algorithms besides big and fast data analytics platforms to speed up and simplify the process of extricating actionable insights. There are evaluation metrics aplenty to help out here. This chapter is dedicated to throwing more light on the various log, operational, performance, and security analytics methods.

Thus, we will be covering the following topics:

- Modern IT infrastructure
- Monitoring clouds, clusters, and containers
- Cloud infrastructure and application monitoring
- Monitoring tool capabilities
- Prognostic, predictive, and prescriptive analytics

Modern IT infrastructure

Today, software-defined cloud centers are very popular and profoundly leveraged for business agility, affordability, and productivity. The cloud idea fulfils the infrastructure's automation, optimization, and utilization requirements. The faster maturity and stability of the virtualization movement makes the hardware programming a grand reality. Therefore, infrastructure as code is the buzzword in the IT industry these days. IT infrastructure monitoring, measurement, and management are seeing a lot of delectable advancements with the rise of the cloud paradigm. A variety of IT infrastructure operations are being automated and accelerated through a host of advanced and standardized tools. The simultaneous rise of the DevOps concept, along with a flurry of powerful cloud technologies and tools, has brought in scores of strategic automation and optimization in the IT space. IT self-service, pay-per-usage, and elasticity have become the core IT capabilities.

Cloud service providers invest their talents, time, and treasures in grandiosely automating several tasks of cloud centers, such as load balancing, workload consolidation, continuous integration, deployment and delivery, task and resource scheduling, workflow automation through integration and orchestration, information security, auto-scaling, replication, and VM placement. There is little to no involvement, interpretation, and instruction from humans in successfully running cloud centers that are increasingly hosting a growing array of web, mobile, enterprise, embedded, transactional, operational, and analytical applications. The cloud journey is definitely on the right track, gaining more mind and market shares as days pass by.

In the recent past, containerization is fast penetrating and immensely participating in cloud-inspired IT automation. Some of the persistent drawbacks of virtualization are being surmounted through containerization. The rise of containers, container orchestration, and management tools, such as Kubernetes, microservices-centric cloud applications (native, as well as enabled), and multi-container applications, is leading to the emergence of containerized clouds. Container images are being projected and positioned as the best in class format for application packaging, distributing, shipping, and running any software applications in a highly portable fashion. The convergence of containers and microservices is laying a stimulating and sparkling foundation for next-generation IT environments.

The continued addition of pioneering automation in the IT space is leading to sophisticated and smart infrastructure. The rise of containers, container orchestration, microservices, cloud-native architectures, container-defined-storage, and container-defined-networking lead us to the next phase of infrastructure. Today, we have data centers and server farms blessed by cloud technologies. Also, we have containerized and virtualized cloud environments for meeting different use and business cases. We have public, private, and hybrid clouds leveraging the proven virtualization and potential containerization paradigms.

The cloud journey, starting with bare metal servers, virtual machines, and containers is now tending toward functions. That is, functions emerge as the new deployment and delivery unit. The flourishing model of serverless computing is to automate the various backend services to run functions comfortably. That is, the days of **Function as a Service (FaaS)**, a new business model, is to see reality. That is, developers just focus on creating functions and upload their functions to the cloud. The function deployment, resource provisioning, and infrastructure elasticity for function scalability are being automatically performed by cloud service providers. Thus, the modern infrastructure is to handle the intricacies of serverless computing.

The power of the **Internet of Things** (**IoT**) technologies and tools establishes a deeper and extreme connectivity among the various physical, mechanical, electrical, and electronic devices. Thus, the world is to comprise trillions of digitized entities, billions of connected devices, and millions of software services in the years to unfold. With connected and embedded devices joining in the mainstream computing, there are needs being expressed widely for formulating and firming up edge or fog cloud environments to fulfil real-time data capture, storage, processing and analytics, decision-enablement, and actuation requirements. Thus, the modern infrastructure has to fulfil the nuances of edge or fog computing.

Another paradigm shift is being associated with the faster spread of **graphical process units** (**GPUs**), which act as a complement to the pervasive CPUs. A number of cores can be accommodated in GPUs, and hence GPUs are more popular with cluster and parallel computing models. Big data analytics and data science experiments can be accomplished through the leverage of GPU clusters. As containers do well as the optimized runtime environment for applications and microservices, the future beckons for containerization-inspired data analytics. We have written about the role of Kubernetes in creating and running multi-container applications in detail.

Apart from containerized clouds, **hyper-converged infrastructure** (**HCI**) solutions are also emerging for different business cases. An HCI typically comes with a software-enabled horizontal scaling capability while tightly integrating compute, storage, and networking resources in a commodity hardware box. A **converged infrastructure** (**CI**) or appliance is another highly expensive but robust and turn-key infrastructure solution for application hosting and delivery. Thus, there are lean, dynamic, and adaptive IT infrastructure modules emerging and evolving fast for optimally running business workloads and cloud applications. The challenge is to make the modern infrastructure reliable to fulfil the long standing goals of reliable businesses. There are various ways being recommended. This chapter is going to convey how diagnostic and prognostic analytics on infrastructure log and operational data gives the insights to work upon the reliability goals.

Elaborating the modern data analytics methods

It is very true that competent software solutions can drive business innovation, disruption, and ultimately transformation. So, the number of software engineers grows consistently ahead of the number of IT professionals. Hence, IT automation gains prominence. That is, once an application deployment is over, the application has to be continuously monitored, measured, and managed to ensure the application/workload is meeting the expressed needs (functional as well as non-functional requirements).

The performance, scalability, availability, security, and resiliency parameters ought to be minutely monitored, and if there is any deviation or deficiency, then the necessary countermeasures have to be considered in time, with clarity and confidence. Not only the application but also the underlying runtime/execution environment, the associated middleware solutions and databases, and the various IT infrastructure modules have to be continuously monitored to gain a better grip of their state and behavior. The application delivery depends on a collection of software and hardware modules. Every software and hardware module continuously emits a lot of operational, log, performance, security, and other useful data, and it becomes important to carefully capture, cleanse, and crunch them to extricate useful and usable insights in time.

Data science is the new buzzword in the IT marketplace these days. Data collection, pre-processing, ingestion, filtering, massaging, processing, knowledge discovery and dissemination, decision-making, and actuation are the prominent steps in the end-to-end data science life cycle. The operational and log data being generated by all kinds of software and hardware systems are in a way massive and multi-structured. With a series of mesmerizing advancements in the real-time analytics of big and time-series data, the various analytical capabilities of software and hardware systems' data are to help with designing, developing, and deploying smart and sophisticated systems.

That is, there are two things to be taken into consideration. Firstly, the amount of multi-structured data getting generated and captured is growing exponentially. Secondly, there is a realization by business executives and IT professionals that data hides and carries a lot of useful and usable information and insights. Also, the technologies and tools for capturing, storing, and mining poly-structured data are maturing and stabilizing fast. That is, the process of quickly transitioning data into information and into knowledge is being accelerated through the leverage of pioneering platforms, well-laid processes, enabling patterns, and a dazzling array of tools, adapters, drivers, engines, and connectors. Definitely, it is going to be the data-driven insights and the insights-driven world.

In this chapter, we are going to focus on how various types of data are being exposed to a variety of purpose-specific investigations to extract important insights in time and we will also discuss how the emitted insights come in handy in engineering and establishing multifaceted and state-of-the-art software, as well as hardware systems. Specifically, for IT environments, there are some specific data-analysis procedures, processes, and platforms, which will be explained in the following sections.

Monitoring clouds, clusters, and containers

The cloud centers are being increasingly containerized and managed. That is, there are going to be well-entrenched containerized clouds soon. The formation and managing of containerized clouds gets simplified through a host of container orchestration and management tools. There are both open source and commercial-grade container-monitoring tools. Kubernetes is emerging as the leading container orchestration and management platform. Thus, by leveraging the aforementioned toolsets, the process of setting up and sustaining containerized clouds is accelerated, risk-free, and rewarding.

The tool-assisted monitoring of cloud resources (both coarse-grained as well as fine-grained) and applications in production environments is crucial to scaling the applications and providing resilient services. In a Kubernetes cluster, application performance can be examined at many different levels: containers, pods, services, and clusters. Through a single pane of glass, the operational team can provide the running applications and their resource utilization details to their users. These will give users the right insights into how the applications are performing, where application bottlenecks may be found, if any, and how to surmount any deviations and deficiencies of the applications. In short, application performance, security, scalability constraints, and other pertinent information can be captured and acted upon.

The emergence of Kubernetes

A Kubernetes cluster is readied with Docker images for various applications or microservices. The cluster starts to function. Then, the next prominent step to be considered and performed is to incorporate a proper monitoring and alerting system to gain deeper knowledge about various limitations and issues with any of the constituents, such as worker nodes, pods, and services. Let's start with the basic knowledge of Kubernetes.

Kubernetes is the popular platform that acts as the brain for any distributed container deployment. It is designed to compose multi-container applications and manage microservices-centric applications using containers, which are typically distributed across multiple clusters of container hosts. Kubernetes brings forth doable mechanisms for application deployment, service discovery, scheduling, and scaling. There are automated tools for monitoring Kubernetes environments. The relevance of a container orchestration and management platform goes up with the fast proliferation of multi-container applications, which are typically composite, business-aware, and process-centric.

As a best practice, each container hosts a microservice, and there can be multiple instances of any microservice. That is, microservices and their instances are being hosted in separate containers to guarantee service availability. The other requirements for hosting and running multi-container applications include managing application performance, enhanced service visibility, notification, and troubleshooting. The other noteworthy aspects include dynamic and appropriate infrastructure provisioning and the automated configuration of applications using configuration management tools. Service composition through container orchestration is the most critical aspect of the Kubernetes platform, apart from managing containers and clusters. When clouds are being containerized, the role of Kubernetes for next-generation cloud environments is to escalate considerably.

A Kubernetes cluster is typically made up of a set of nodes under the supervision of a master node. The master's tasks include orchestrating containers that are spread across nodes and keeping track of their state. The cluster is enabled and exposed through a REST API and a UI. The API is a kind of cluster control. The important ingredients of Kubernetes deployment are shown in the following diagram:

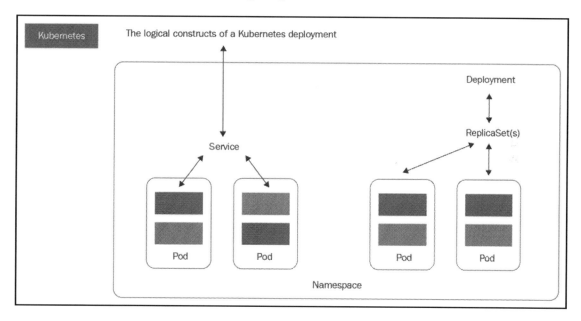

A pod comprises one or more containers. All containers have to run inside pods. Containers are always co-located and co-scheduled. They are run in a shared context with shared storage (https://kubernetes.io/):

- Pods typically sit behind services. Services take care of balancing the traffic and also expose the set of pods as a single and publicly discoverable IP address/port.
- Services can be scaled horizontally, by replica sets, which are there to create/destroy pods for each service as needed.
- ReplicaSet is the next-generation replication controller. ReplicaSet is used for ensuring that a specified number of pod replicas are running at all times.
- A deployment—a higher-level concept—manages ReplicaSets, and provides declarative updates to pods.
- Namespaces are the virtual clusters that comprise one or more services.
- Metadata allows the use of labels and tags to mark up containers based on their deployment characteristics.

Multiple services and even multiple namespaces can be spread inside a physical machine. As indicated previously, each of those services is made up of pods. Due to multiple components, the complexity of monitoring even a modest Kubernetes deployment is on the high side. Kubernetes probes, which is another key module, performs the central function of regularly monitoring the health of a container. If there is any unhealthy container, then it takes the action.

In summary, Kubernetes makes it easy to run distributed computing workloads. Workloads typically run across multiple server instances, and most of the real-world deployments involve hosting and operating multiple workloads simultaneously across the Kubernetes cluster. It is all about distributed deployment and centralized management. Thus, visualizing, sensing, and perceiving containerized environments is crucial for the success of microservices-centric applications and containerized environments. We have written extensively about monitoring containerized environments and about subjecting container data toward container intelligence and operational excellence in the next chapter.

… Chapter 11

Cloud infrastructure and application monitoring

The cloud idea has disrupted, innovated, and transformed the IT world. Yet, the various cloud infrastructures, resources, and applications ought to be minutely monitored and measured through automated tools. The aspect of automation is gathering momentum in the cloud era. Every activity is getting automated through pioneering algorithms and technologically powerful tools. A slew of flexibilities in the form of customization, configuration, and composition are being enacted through cloud automation tools. A bevy of manual and semi-automated tasks are being fully automated through a series of advancements in the IT space. In this section, we are going to discuss the infrastructure monitoring toward infrastructure optimization and automation. There are processes, platforms, procedures, and products to enable cloud monitoring.

Enterprise-scale and mission-critical applications are being cloud-enabled to be deployed in various cloud environments (private, public, community, and hybrid). Furthermore, applications are being meticulously developed and deployed directly on cloud platforms using **microservices architecture** (**MSA**). Thus, besides cloud infrastructures, there are cloud-based IT platforms and middleware, business applications, and database management systems. The total IT is accordingly modernized to be cloud-ready. It is very important to precisely and perfectly monitor and measure every asset and aspect of cloud environments. There is a growing array of approaches for simplifying and speeding up infrastructure monitoring. The operational and logging data of various infrastructural modules and applications throw a lot of insights about their performance, health condition, throughput, scalability, and security. In the ensuing sections, we are going to write about the various technological disciplines that are enabling the monitoring aspect, which is occupying a crucial spot in infrastructure automation.

Embracing the mesmerizing cloud idea is a strategically sound decision for any corporate. A number of business, technical, and user advantages are being easily derived through this cloud enablement process. The cloud conundrum brings the much-needed flexibility in using available capacity of servers, storages, and network solutions. Cloud resources are being made available on demand, and this unique property ultimately results in the optimal utilization of IT resources.

Organizations need to have the capability for precisely monitoring the usage of the participating cloud resources. If there is any deviation, then the monitoring feature triggers an alert to the concerned to ponder about the next course of action. The monitoring capability includes viable tools for monitoring CPU usage per computing resource, the varying ratios between systems activity and user activity, and the CPU usage from specific job tasks. Also, organizations have to have the intrinsic capability for predictive analytics that allows them to capture trending data on memory utilization and filesystem growth. These details help the operational team to proactively plan the needed changes to computing/storage/network resources before they encounter service availability issues. Timely action is essential for ensuring business continuity.

Not only infrastructures but also applications' performance levels have to be closely monitored in order to embark on fine-tuning application code, as well as the infrastructure architectural considerations. Typically, organizations find it easier to monitor the performance of applications that are hosted at a single server, as opposed to the performance of composite applications that are leveraging several server resources. This becomes more tedious and tough when the underlying computer resources are spread across multiple and are distributed. The major worry here is that the team loses its visibility and controllability of third-party data center resources. Enterprises, for different valid reasons, prefer multi-cloud strategy for hosting their applications and data. There are several IT infrastructure management tools, practices, and principles. These traditional toolsets become obsolete for the cloud era. There are a number of distinct characteristics being associated with software-defined cloud environments. It is expected that any cloud application has to innately fulfil the **non-functional requirements** (**NFRs**) such as scalability, availability, performance, flexibility, and reliability.

Research reports say that organizations across the globe enjoy significant cost savings and increased flexibility of management by modernizing and moving their applications into cloud environments. There are options galore for choosing various cloud service and deployment models. There are public, private, and hybrid cloud environments. Enterprises increasingly lean toward the proven multi-cloud strategy. Whatever it is, the management and operational complexities of cloud environments are growing steadily. Cloud monitoring and measurement become a difficult affair. The toolsets that are overwhelmingly used for traditional IT infrastructure are found to be insufficient for the modern IT infrastructure. The automated maneuverability of cloud resources and applications through policy awareness is being insisted upon, and hence the IT service management tools have to be equally empowered to tackle the freshly incorporated IT requirements with ease.

The monitoring tool capabilities

The cloud paradigm brings the much-needed flexibility of assigning resources needed to support demand from cloud users. Establishing and enforcing appropriate policies and rules are important for assigning cloud resources to business applications and IT services. However, the effectiveness of policy management depends on the visibility that organizations have about their cloud resources. Organizations need to have the capability to create, modify, monitor, and update the policies. In short, cloud monitoring tools need to have the previously mentioned cloud-specific features, functionalities, and facilities to realize all the cloud-sponsored benefits.

As organizations deploying cloud computing services trust third-party providers to fulfil the **quality of service** (**QoS**) attributes and performance, as quoted previously, is the key QoS parameter. The monitoring tool has to monitor not only the actual levels of performance, as experienced by business users, but also enable it to help the users to do the **root-cause analysis** (**RCA**) for all those performance degradation problems. The monitoring tool has to have the capability for monitoring application response times, service availability, and page-load times. Peak time traffic monitoring is also required. In addition, the monitoring tools need to be able to handle hybrid and multi-cloud environments that include traditional IT infrastructures.

In conclusion, it is paramount to deploy monitoring and management tools to effectively and efficiency run cloud environments, wherein thousands of computing, storage, and network solutions are running. The logs, operations, scalability, performance, availability, stability, and reliability data showcased through a 360-degree view empowers administrators and manages counter measures immediately to ensure business continuity. The manage engine applications manager (https://www.manageengine.com) allows organizations to monitor levels of SLA achievements for cloud services. This tool also provides troubleshooting and resolution capabilities across cloud environments (private, public, and hybrid).

The key characteristics of this tool are vividly illustrated through the following diagram:

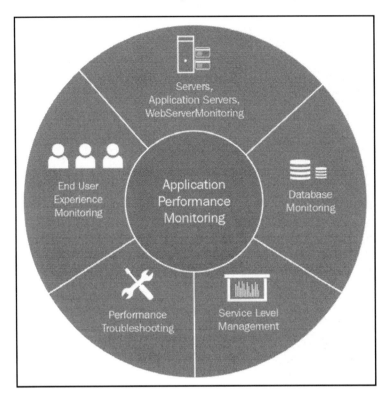

Here are some of the key features and capabilities we need to properly monitor for modern cloud-based applications and infrastructures (https://newrelic.com/):

- Firstly, the ability to capture and query events and traces in addition to data aggregation is essential. When a customer buys something online, the buying process generates a lot of HTTP requests. For proper end-to-end cloud monitoring, we need to see the exact set of HTTP requests the customer makes while completing the purchase: each of the individual product detail pages, the add-to-cart POST requests, the cart view page, the billing and shipping POST requests, and the final submit order page. The ability to capture the raw transaction data is important in cloud deployments, where each request often goes through a number of dynamic components from a web or mobile browser to a CDN, followed by a load balancer, before reaching the application and the microservices.

There are message brokers/queues involved in-between in completing the transaction. Thus, any monitoring system has to have the capability to quickly identify bottlenecks and understand the relationships among different components. The solution has to give the exact response time of each component for each transaction. Critical metadata such as error traces and custom attributes ought to be made available to enhance trace and event data. By segmenting the data via the user and business-specific attributes, it is possible to prioritize improvements and sprint plans to optimize for those customers.

- Secondly, the monitoring system has to be blessed with the ability to monitor a wide variety of cloud environments (private, public, and hybrid). There are a number of public cloud service providers (AWS, Azure, IBM, Google, and so on). The solution has to have all the integration brokers/plug-ins in one place to simplify and speed up the cloud connectivity and integration. The plug-ins need to be there for most of the leading services, such as Elastic Load Balancer, EC2, Lambda, DynamoDB, RDS, and CloudFront.
- Thirdly, the monitoring solution has to scale for any emergency. Cloud environments are extremely and enviously dynamic. The users and data loads are changing rapidly. The number of infrastructural components being used on special occasions is growing exponentially, and hence the availability, stability, and scalability of monitoring systems have to be equally ensured. Increasingly, monitoring solutions are being provided as multi-tenant software. The SaaS model is easy, as it is being updated, patched, monitored, and managed by the provider.

The benefits

Organizations that are using the right mix of technology solutions for IT infrastructure and business application monitoring in the cloud are to gain the following benefits:

- **Performance engineering and enhancement**: Pinpointing any performance issues at all levels and layers, prediction, and prescription of performance-resolution schemes, performance enhancement mechanisms, and so on, can be fulfilled through the automated monitoring of infrastructural modules and applications. Problem anticipation and elimination proactively is the need of the hour for cloud service providers. The resource identification and allocation in an appropriate way goes a long way in solving performance degradation.

- **On-demand computing**: Business requirements, sentiments, and policies change very frequently. IT has to emphatically respond to all kinds of changes happening in the business landscape. Therefore, there is a need for a full visibility into every aspect of cloud resources and applications. The IT flexibility can be implemented through powerful monitoring solutions. The deeper visibility leads to extreme controllability. Then, varying business scopes and any sort of emergencies can be accordingly tackled, resulting in higher business performance and continuity.
- **Affordability**: Achieving cost efficiency through cloudification is one of the key deciders. Through enhanced utilization, automation, sharing, and operating infrastructures at greater scale, cloud providers are able to provide various IT services to their subscribers at a lesser cost. This monitoring capability gives all the data and details in time to monitor cloud application performance, to understand about the resource utilization in real-time and any tricky issue with any infrastructure components.

With the emergence of containers and serverless functions, the role and responsibility of monitoring solutions are bound to escalate in the days ahead. Migrating business applications and services to the cloud brings forth a number of benefits and opportunities to distribute workloads, deliver applications, and expand resources for growing databases. Despite the ease of standing up cloud instances manually or through automation, cloud infrastructure can become difficult to map with lost resources or hidden instances in the sprawling environment. The knowledge discovery and dissemination capabilities of state-of-the-art tools for monitoring business applications and IT services help the concerned to initiate appropriate activities immediately for any kind of problems. The decision-making task gets simplified and streamlined through the dashboard component of the monitoring solutions. Also, all the data that's collected, cleansed, and crunched is carefully stocked in one or more storage environments. The final crucial act is nonetheless the data analytics. We are going to explain every bit about the next-generation data analytics to do diagnostic and cognitive analytics in the ensuing sections for the benefit of our esteemed readers.

Prognostic, predictive, and prescriptive analytics

Any operational environment is in need of data analytics and machine learning capabilities to be intelligent in their everyday actions and reactions. The profoundly impacting environments include IT environments (traditional data centers or recent **cloud-enabled data centers** (**CeDCs**)), manufacturing and assembly floors, plant operations, **maintenance**, **repair**, and **overhaul** (**MRO**) facilities. Increasingly, a variety of important environments are being stuffed with scores of networked, embedded, and resource constrained, as well as intensive devices, toolsets, and microcontrollers. Hospitals have a growing array of medical instruments, and homes are blessed with a number of wares and utensils, such as connected coffee makers, dishwashers, microwave ovens, and consumer electronics. Manufacturing floors have powerful equipment, machinery, and robots. Workshops, mechanical shops, and flight maintenance garages are becoming more sophisticated and smarter with the stuffing of connected devices and instruments.

The concept of **cyber-physical systems** (**CPS**) is seamlessly and securely linking the physical with the virtual/cyber world. The physical assets along with mechanical and electrical systems are being integrated with cloud-enabled and native applications and data sources to exhibit distinct and deft behavior. The self-, surroundings-, and situation-aware capabilities are being realized through this kind of integration and orchestration. These digitized entities and elements generate a lot of data through their interactions, collaborations, correlations, and corroborations. Thus, the discipline of data science gains immense popularity as the data that's generated leads to enviable insights.

As data centers and server farms evolve and embrace new technologies (virtualization and containerization), it becomes more difficult to determine what impacts these changes have on the server, storage, and network performance. By using proper analytics, system administrators and IT managers can easily identify and even predict potential choke points and errors before they create problems.

Various business houses and organizations are methodically using big data analytics to dig down and slice data center operations data. This can uncover hitherto unseen correlations among various IT systems. Furthermore, what sort of impacts new workloads on their underlying resources make are also being understood. With the emergence of streaming and real-time analytics platforms, behavioral and performance insights are being extracted instantaneously, and appropriate countermeasures are being worked and rolled out to sustain the goals of business continuity. That is, through data analytics capability, it becomes possible now to gain a deeper and decisive understanding of the system performance levels. If there is any possibility for any kind of performance degradation, administrators and operational teams can quickly consider various options for overcoming any potential performance-related problems well in advance.

In any cloud center, there are many server systems such as **bare metal (BM)** servers, **virtual machines (VMs)**, and containers. Furthermore, there are many types of networking elements, such as routers, switches, firewalls, load balancers, intrusion detection and prevention systems, and application delivery controllers. In addition to that, there are several kinds of storage appliances and arrays. Every kind of equipment in a cloud environment is to emit a lot of logged data at different junctures. All of this logged data ought to be collected carefully, cleansed, and crunched systematically through automated toolsets for the timely extraction of actionable insights. There are several performance evaluation metrics, and through appropriate data analytics capabilities enshrined in every large-scale enterprise, the preventive and predictive maintenance of every participating and contributing devices and machines can be guaranteed. The emergence of online, off-premise/on-premise, and on-demand cloud infrastructures come handy in speeding up the process of IT data analytics. The infrastructure automation, monitoring, governance, management, rationalization, and utilization are being simplified through the leverage of infrastructure (software as well as hardware) log data.

The data provided by **virtual machine monitor (VMM)** and container platforms can be invaluable in completely and comprehensively analyzing virtual data centers. For example, the hypervisor has a lot of information because it is designed in such a way to use a lot of context-sensitive data to accurately allocate virtual resources. Similarly, in the containerized cloud environments, container-monitoring tools are blessed with a lot of operational data. Extracting hypervisor and container data and submitting them for purpose-specific analysis using analytics engines helps pinpoint a lot of useful information associated with system functioning and performance. The insights generated empower administrators to optimize workloads and identify new systems to host the replicas of the workloads or newer workloads. Not only workloads and virtual machines but also the condition of physical machines and their clusters can be extracted to ponder various advancements.

IT teams need to have complete visibility on their IT infrastructures and business workloads running on them. The enhanced visibility leads to tighter control of their entire stack from the underlying infrastructure up to applications. To ensure high visibility, controllability, and security, the IT team needs intelligent software solutions to monitor the hardware and software stack, manage large-scale compute clusters, and automate the routine but time-consuming and complex operations such as failure handling, OS patching and security updates, and software upgrades.

Machine-learning (**ML**) algorithms are very popular these days. Empowering machines to be smart through a host of self-learning algorithms and models are the central concept behind the enormous success of various ML algorithms. As the data size, structure, speed, and scope vary hugely, it is pertinent to empower machines themselves to capture, stock, and understand all kinds of incoming data without any human involvement, interpretation, and instruction. Handling big data by humans is a time-consuming and tough affair. As personal as well as professional devices are being blessed with the tremendous amount of memory and storage capacities and processing capabilities, the future definitely belongs to cognitive systems and machines.

Machine-learning algorithms for infrastructure automation

The automation level in IT infrastructure management is climbing up consistently with the adoption of cloud technologies and tools. By incorporating and involving the proven machine and deep learning algorithms, the process of acquiring and acting upon the machine intelligence is being meticulously simplified and streamlined. That is, IT machines are being empowered to be intelligent in their actions and reactions to fulfil the different targets of infrastructure optimization. IT systems have to self-learn and understand their operational states and patterns; self-defend against any malicious attacks (internal as well as external); predict the problems through data correlation and corroboration; anticipate varying system capacity and capability needs and act on them instantaneously; raise alerts in time about any kind of anomalies; self-diagnose and self-heal in case of any performance degradation, faults, and failures; be aware of business and operational policies; and automatically upgrade hardware and software systems without any downtime. This vision of infrastructure automation is being driven by swarms of advances in machine and deep learning domains, which are the key portions of **artificial intelligence** (**AI**). The other areas of research interested in AI include computer vision, neural networks, and natural-language processing, and so on.

The intensive focus on automation will help to bring down the number of IT administrators in managing cloud centers. Not only basic cloud operations but also a number of complex operations, such as resource usage monitoring and management, demand forecasting, workload consolidation, resource (VM and container) placement, and capacity planning are also being automated. There are powerful ML algorithms to forecast and predict problems. There are pioneering tools being incorporated in cloud environments to cleverly and cleanly actuate different things.

ML algorithms come in handy in zeroing in on useful anomalies, patterns, deviations, deficiencies, associations, and other knowledge. These insights can be automatically learned and leveraged by machines to continually function in the midst of any attacks (internal as well as external) and load spikes. Thus, the real-time analytics of big data is one such competency being acquired by enterprises to be ahead of their competitors in delivering premium services to their customers, partners, and users.

Log analytics

Every software and hardware system generates a lot of log data (big data), and it is essential to do real-time log analytics to quickly understand whether there is any deviation or deficiency. This extracted knowledge helps administrators to consider countermeasures in time. Log analytics, if done systematically, facilitates preventive, predictive, and prescriptive maintenance. Workloads, IT platforms, middleware, databases, and hardware solutions all create a lot of log data when they are working together to complete business functionalities. There are several log analytics tools on the market.

Everyone knows that logs play an important role in the IT industry. Logs are used for various purposes such as IT operations, system, and application monitoring, security and compliance, and much more. Having a centralized and standardized logging system makes life easy for software developers. They are often being requested to troubleshoot the application, detect issues, enhance the application security, or review the application performance. Thus, application logs are vital to the intended success of software packages. A centralized logging system is a shared service famous for its low-cost maintenance, easy logs searching, and graphical interface. Thus, log collection, retention, ingestion, and processing goes a long way in shepherding and strengthening mission-critical and large-scale applications.

Open source log analytics platforms

If there is a need to handle all log data in one place, then ELK is being touted as the best-in-class open source log analytics solution. There are an application as well as system logs. Logs are typically errors, warnings, and exceptions. ELK is a combination of three different products, namely **Elasticsearch**, **Logstash**, and **Kibana** (ELK). The macro-level ELK architecture is given as follows:

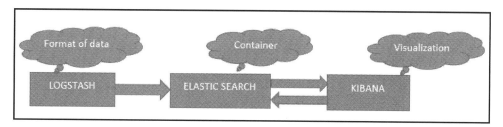

- Elasticsearch is a search mechanism that is based on the Lucene search to store and retrieve its data. Elasticsearch is, in a way, a NoSQL database. That is, it stores multi-structured data and does not support SQL as the query language. Elasticsearch has a REST API, which uses either PUT or POST to fetch the data. Precisely speaking, Elasticsearch is a distributed RESTful search and analytics engine, and there are many use cases emerging for this excellent and elegant search tool. It can discover the expected as well as uncover the unexpected. Elasticsearch lets you perform and combine many types of searches (structured, unstructured, geo, and metrics). Elasticsearch is really fast and can run on your laptop or on hundreds of servers for searching petabytes of data.
  Elasticsearch uses standard RESTful APIs and JSON. The clients can be coded using many programming languages including Java, Python, .NET, and Groovy. As we all know, Hadoop is the most visible and viable mechanism for big data analytics. But Hadoop does batch processing only. If you want real-time processing of big data, then Elasticsearch is the way forward. It is all about leveraging the real-time search and analytics features of Elasticsearch to work on your big data by using the **Elasticsearch-Hadoop** (**ES-Hadoop**) connector. Increasingly, Elasticsearch is being primed for real-time and affordable log analytics.

- Logstash is an open source and server-side data processing pipeline that ingests data from a variety of data sources simultaneously and transforms and sends them to a preferred database. Logstash also handles unstructured data with ease. Logstash has more than 200 plugins built in, and it is easy to come out on our own. Because of its tight integration with Elasticsearch, Logstash is a popular choice for loading data from a multitude of data sources (system and application logs, web and application server logs) into the Elasticsearch database. Logstash offers a number of pre-built filters to readily and rewardingly transform common data types and index them in Elasticsearch.

  Logstash provides plugins for ingesting unstructured and semi-structured logs that are generated by IT servers, business applications, and mobile devices into the Elasticsearch cluster. Elasticsearch indexes the data and readies it for real-time analysis. The prominent use cases include application monitoring and anomaly and fraud detection. Depending on brewing needs, there are a number of alternative solutions to speedily ingest data into the Elasticsearch database. For example, the Amazon Elasticsearch service offers built-in integration with a number of its other services, such as Amazon Kinesis Firehose, Amazon CloudWatch Logs, and AWS IoT to get data seamlessly and to perform the analytics. There are open source solutions such as Apache Kaka and Apache FluentD to build our own data pipeline.

- Kibana is the last module of the famous ELK toolset and is an open source data visualization and exploration tool mainly used for performing log and time-series analytics, application monitoring, and **IT operational analytics (ITOA)**. Kibana is gaining a lot of market and mind shares, as it makes it easy to make histograms, line graphs, pie charts, and heat maps. We can use Kibana to search, view, and interact with data stored in Elasticsearch indices. Furthermore, advanced data analysis and visualization comprising charts, maps, graphs, and tables can be easily accomplished through this unique tool.

- Logz.io, the commercialized version of the ELK platform, is the world's most popular open source log analysis platform. This is made available as an enterprise-grade service in the cloud. The high availability, unbreakable security, and scalability are innately assured. Logz.io intrinsically applies advanced machine-learning capability to unravel critical and unnoticed errors and exceptions in real-time. Furthermore, it throws actionable and contextual data for faster resolution of hidden issues. Logz.io comes out with a suite of analytics and optimization tools, which helps organizations to sharply reduce the overall logging expenses as the data size grows. Logz.io enables users to start ELK in five minutes, perform and scale with ease. The upgrade and capacity management is being taken care of by the service providers. The enterprise version of the Logz.io platform ensures enterprise-grade security toward data security and privacy. Logz.io goes beyond what ELK achieves to create a comprehensive log analytics platform with a number of powerful features, such as integrated alerts, multiple sub-accounts, and third-party integration. Logz.io inherently applies pre-built and usecase-specific machine-learning across data, and user behavior and community knowledge to precisely identify anomalies. In short, it facilitates the goals of the world of data-driven insights and insights-driven decisions/actions.

Cloud-based log analytics platforms

The log analytics capability is being given as a cloud-based and value-added service by various **cloud service providers** (**CSPs**). The Microsoft Azure cloud provides the log analytics service to its users/subscribers by constantly monitoring both cloud and on-premises environments to take correct decisions that ultimately ensure their availability and performance. This unique service collects all kinds of log data that's generated by a user's cloud servers, workloads, and databases. Similarly, it does the same for various resources at a user's on-premises environments. There are monitoring tools being employed in various users environments to facilitate tactical as well as strategically sound analysis. The Azure cloud has its own monitoring mechanism in place through its Azure monitor, which collects and meticulously analyze log data emitted by various Azure resources. The log analytics feature of the Azure cloud considers the monitoring data and correlates with other relevant data to supply additional insights.

The same capability is also made available for private cloud environments. It can collect all types of log data through various tools from multiple sources and consolidate them into a single and centralized repository. Then, the suite of analysis tools in log analytics, such as log searches and views a collaborate with one another to provide you with centralized insights of your entire environment. The macro-level architecture is given here:

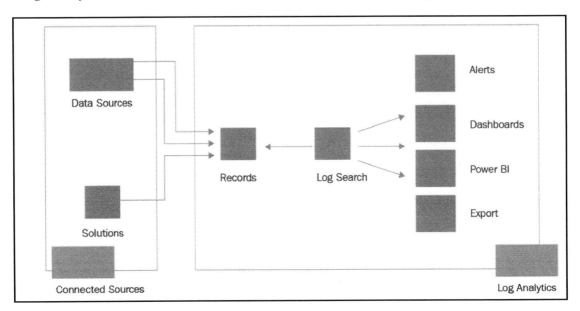

This service is being given by other cloud service providers. AWS is one of the well-known providers. Oracle log analytics monitors, aggregates, indexes, and analyzes all logs from your applications and infrastructures. This enables users to search, explore, and correlate the logs to troubleshoot problems faster, derive operational insights, and make timely and better decisions. IBM empowers DevOps teams by aggregating application and environment logs and extrapolating right insights. The IBM log analytics can retain log data for a longer time and help to quickly detect and troubleshoot persistent issues. The paramount contributions of log analytics tools include the following:

- **Infrastructure monitoring**: Log analytics platforms easily and quickly analyze logs from **bare metal** (**BM**) servers and network solutions, such as firewalls, load balancers, application delivery controllers, CDN appliances, storage systems, virtual machines, and containers.

- **Application performance monitoring**: The analytics platform captures application logs, which are streamed live and takes the assigned performance metrics for doing real-time analysis and debugging.
- **Security and compliance**: The service provides an immutable log storage, centralization, and reporting to meet compliance requirements. It has deeper monitoring and decisive collaboration for extricating useful and usable insights.

AI-enabled log analytics platforms

There are many more common areas such as IT operations and DevOps getting decisively and deftly impacted by AI. One of the core aspects of DevOps is monitoring and logging. It is beneficial for IT administrators and operations managers to collect and aggregate logs in a central place. Typically, these logs are being used for the purposes of audit trail, root-cause analysis, and remediation. This process has been manual. That is, application developers and network specialists frantically hunt for a needle in a haystack to detect whether there is an anomaly or an interesting pattern in the collected and stocked system logs. Today, everything happens in a reactive mode. That is, if there is any downtime, disruption, and deviation, then the system logs are being collected and subjected to a variety of investigations to understand what caused the slowdown and breakdown. By bringing ML to log analysis, the systems become smart by becoming proactive and pre-emptive. The ML algorithms are applied to the logs to automatically detect anomalies and unusual patterns to empower systems to be articulate and adaptive.

As per a Gartner report, AIOps platforms address data collection, storage, analytical engines, and visualization needs. They enable integration with other applications via **application programming interfaces** (**APIs**) for smooth data ingestion. AIOps platforms are being touted as the most efficient and effective for the following use cases.

Post-processing of events streams that come from monitoring tools:

- Bi-directional interaction with IT service management tools
- Possible integration with automation toolsets for implementing the prescriptive information provided by the platform

Algorithmic IT Operations (AIOps) leverages the proven and potential AI algorithms to help organizations to make the path smooth for their digital transformation goals. The adoption of intelligent digital technologies and tools leads to digital innovation, disruption, and transformation. The role and responsibility of IT toward digital transformation is bound to grow and glow. AIOps is being touted as the way forward to substantially reduce IT operational costs. AIOps automates the process of analyzing IT infrastructures and business workloads to give right and relevant details to administrators about their functioning and performance levels. AIOps minutely monitors each of the participating resources and applications and then intelligently formulates the various steps to be considered for their continuous well being. AIOps helps to realize the goals of preventive and predictive maintenance of IT and business systems and also comes out with prescriptive details for resolving issues with all the clarity and confidence. Furthermore, AIOps lets IT teams conduct root-cause analysis by identifying and correlating issues. With the amount of log data grows exponentially, the accuracy of the decisions being taken by AI algorithms tends to be very high, and the subsequent actions are also going to be perfect and precise. The AI algorithms are capable of making appropriate recommendations based on both current and historical data.

Loom

Loom is a leading provider of AIOps solutions. Loom's AIOps platform is consistently leveraging competent machine-learning algorithms to easily and quickly automate the log analysis process. The real-time analytics capability of the ML algorithms enables organizations to arrive at correct resolutions for the issues and to complete the resolution tasks in an accelerated fashion. Loom delivers an AI-powered log analysis platform to predict all kinds of impending issues and prescribe the resolution steps. The overlay or anomaly detection is rapidly found, and the strategically sound solution gets formulated with the assistance of this AI-centric log analytics platform (`https://www.loomsystems.com/`).

Logs are commonly and constantly emitted by IT infrastructures, business workloads, and databases, and all of these ingredients are copiously put up in enterprise and cloud IT environments. With the wider availability of compute clusters and storage arrays, logs are being increasingly gathered and gleaned to produce tips and techniques for application troubleshooting and to achieve the business objectives.

Enterprise-class log analytics platforms

Businesses are working on multiple things to enhance the business efficiency and customer satisfaction. Infrastructure automation is one of the most indispensable activities for any enterprise to be constantly innovative, disruptive, and transformative. Business processes are continuously refined and rationalized to be lean and clean. Competent architectural styles and patterns are being carefully assimilated, while pioneering technologies and tools are being identified and leveraged to bring in scores of perceptible changes to IT and business. As businesses establishments across the world grow fast, the business IT has to equally grow to accommodate the business evolutions and revolutions. Log analytics plays a solid and sustainable role here in shaping up enterprises and their journeys. The point here is that we need enterprise-scale log analytics process and platform. Precisely speaking, any organization, which has the inherent ability to capture and crunch log data in real-time, has the power to grow systematically and sagaciously.

Splunk (https://www.splunk.com/) is an enterprise platform to analyze and monitor a wide variety of data such as application logs, server logs, clickstreams, message brokers, queues, and OS system metrics. Splunk has come out with an easy-to-use yet multifaceted user interface to speed up the process of log analytics. Splunk is equally good at analyzing machine data. We all know that as our everyday devices and machines become integrated with one another, the result through their purposeful interactions is a massive amount of multi-structured data. When the acquired machine data gets methodically processed and mined using self-learning algorithms, knowledge gets discovered instantly, and when the extracted knowledge gets disseminated to actuating machines, there emerge a bunch of smarter machines.

Having understood the significance of log data, companies are showing extra interest in procuring log analytics tools to optimize IT systems, business applications, and connected machines, and to elongate their life. Furthermore, log analytics enables us to optimize business processes. The benefits are really awesome.

The key capabilities of log analytics platforms

Hardware and software infrastructures generate a huge volume of heterogeneous logs. The logs primarily provide rich contextual details, along with the system's description. The logs come handy in the proper prognosis and diagnosis of the system's situation. However, the challenge is that manually preparing and interpreting multi-structured and massive logs is really a difficult thing. The faster maturity and stability of AI (machine and deep learning) algorithms, the greater affordability of IT infrastructure clusters through **cloud-enabled data centers** (CeDCs), and the growing versatility of analytics platforms are good news indeed for the real-time analytics of a huge amount of log data.

The recent log analytics solutions are succulently AI-powered to unearth patterns and predict impending problems. Also, log analytics software solutions are increasingly capable of prescribing the ways and means toward mitigating the predicted problems. In short, log data gets turned into information and tuned for knowledge. They can unravel hitherto-unknown patterns. The decision-makers and operation teams are being told about the hidden issues and limitations. Furthermore, tactical as well as strategically sound solutions for surmounting the articulated and accentuated problems are also being brought forth. The key capabilities of a typical log analytics platform includes the following:

- **Automated log parsing**: The platform streams all logs from any application and will automatically parse and analyze them in real-time to emit usable insights.
- **Problem prediction and correlation**: It predicts problems in our IT environment and detects hidden issues and correlates events among all of our applications.
- **End-to-end root-cause analysi**s: It leverages the amazing developments in the field of AI to get into the root-cause of issues in real-time.
- **Recommended resolutions**: The platform enriches the detected problems with all the contextual information. Then it comes out with the recommended resolutions and action items in real-time, using its ever-growing knowledge base.

Centralized log-management tools

This is an extremely important tool for worldwide enterprise and cloud IT teams. This solution typically connects and manages all the hardware and software from a single dashboard, which gives the much needed 360-degree view. This setup enables system monitoring and maintenance by proactively identifying hiding issues and even correcting them in time. All of this is being made possible just by have a prying eye on application and infrastructure logs. Experts define a log as an official record of events as they happen. Therefore, a log-management tool collects, stocks, and subjects log data, to quickly identify any abnormalities/outliers and take corrective action on them promptly, to prolong a system's life. A futuristic log-management tool not only collects logs but also does a deeper log analysis to come out with actionable and context-sensitive insights, to solve issues irrespective of the log sources and regardless of the logged data format. The key benefits of a log- management solution can be summarized here:

- **Any log and any format**: Logs can originate from any source, and the log data format can be as diverse as possible. The log data usually is big in size due to the faster proliferation of IT systems, software services and machines. Still, the system has to have the wherewithal to handle and make sense out of it.

- **Accommodative and adaptive**: The log-management system can be deployed locally or remotely. It can be centralized or decentralized. Based on the organization's evolving needs, the system has to adapt accordingly in to aggregate and emit insights in an astute fashion.
- **Real-time data analytics**: The speed matters these days. With the availability of technologies and tools for the real-time processing of big data, the futurist log-management software is to be real-time in their decisions and deliveries.
- **Longer raw data retention**: Logs have to be preserved for a longer time so that the current data gets merged with historical data to come out with accurate results.

There are other compliance requirements that are increasingly being fulfilled by the log-management solutions. Thus, log analytics in association with log analytics algorithms and platforms is an important feature for troubleshooting IT systems and business workloads. The performance metrics and data, when analyzed, give the right cues for performance experts and software developers to engineer high-performance systems.

IT operational analytics

We discussed log data and its analytics in the previous section. There are log-management tools and log analytics platforms to gain real-time information about all kinds of software and hardware systems. The insights emitted go a long way in stabilizing and strengthening various systems by proactively attending the systems issues. There is also operational data for all kinds of systems under operation. The data from IT systems contains valuable insights into system usage, the user's experience, and behavior patterns. There are operational analytics platforms and engines, such as Splunk software for monitoring, searching, analyzing, visualizing, and acting on massive streams of real-time and historical machine data, from any source, format, or location. The main advantages of operational analytics are listed here. Operational analytics helps with the following:

- Extricating operational insights
- Reducing IT costs and complexity
- Improving employee productivity
- Identifying and fixing service problems for an enhanced user experience
- Gaining end-to-end insights critical to the business operations, offerings, and outputs

To facilitate operational analytics, there are integrated platforms, and their contributions are given as follows:

- Troubleshoot applications, investigate security incidents, and facilitate compliance requirements in minutes instead of hours or days
- Analyze various performance indicators to enhance system performance
- Use report-generation capabilities to indicate the various trends in preferred formats (maps, charts, and graphs)
- Understand usage patterns, geographical trends, and learn about user and data loads
- Reduce **mean time between failures** (**MTBF**) by proactively addressing issues with real-time notifications
- Get end-to-end visibility of the asset inventory, capacity allocation, and resource consumption

Thus, the operational analytics capability comes handy in capturing operational data (real-time and batch) and crunching them to produce actionable insights to enable autonomic systems. Also, the operational team members, IT experts, and business decision-makers can get useful information on working out correct countermeasures if necessary. The operational insights gained also convey what needs to be done to empower the systems under investigation to attain their optimal performance.

IT performance and scalability analytics

There are typically big gaps between the theoretical and practical performance limits. The challenge is how to enable systems to attain their theoretical performance level under any circumstance. The performance level required can suffer due to various reasons. This includes the poor system design, bugs in software, network bandwidth, third-party dependencies, and I/O access. The middleware solutions such as adapter, connector, and driver also contribute to the unexpected performance degradation of the system. The system's performance has to be maintained under any loads (user, message, and data). There are several metrics such as **request per second** (**RPS**) and **transaction per second** (**TPS**). Performance testing is one way of recognizing the performance bottlenecks and adequately addressing them. The testing is performed in the pre-production phase.

Now, the software is functioning in production servers, and the thing to do here is to continuously and consciously collect all kinds of its operational, usage, and behavioral data, to understand the performance challenges and to ponder about the ways and means of enhancing and sustaining the performance. Also, the application usage data helps in activating auto-scaling engine to provision additional servers to continuously give the ordained services to its subscribers.

Besides the system performance, application scalability and infrastructure elasticity are other prominent requirements. There are two scalability options, indicated as follows:

- Scale up for fully utilizing SMP hardware
- Scale out for fully utilizing distributed processors

It is also possible to have both at the same time. That is, to scale up and out is to combine the two scalability choices. With the faster proliferation of VMs and containers in the increasingly distributed computing era, the aspect of horizontal scalability (scale-out) is prominent and dominant. It takes a couple of minutes for provisioning virtual machines, and many VMs can be created concurrently. It takes a couple of seconds for producing containers, and hence near-time scalability is being readily achieved through the leverage of containers, which are lightweight.

Every company is flooded with a lot of internal as well as external data. Companies are putting the IT capabilities to collect and process the data getting generated to get viable insights out of the data. Due to the massive growth of data, crunching data at a real-time is a challenge for data analytics teams. Cloudification for achieving IT industrialization and other initiatives such as compartmentalization (virtualization and containerization) and consumerization concepts are being lustrously supported through a slew of advanced and automated tools. These advancements not only fulfil the varying expectations of business executives, decision-makers, and other key stakeholders but generate a lot of poly-structured data. The organizations that are in the best position to handle this onslaught of data are those that are able to adjust or scale their IT infrastructures and applications to accommodate any sudden spike in data quantity. Using multiple coarse-grained resources, such as virtual machines and containers, comes in handy for the parallel execution of tasks. The point here is that the underlying IT infrastructure is inherently elastic to guarantee application scalability.

The resource utilization data helps in the real-time and dynamic formulation of the steps to be followed for enabling auto-scaling. The auto-scaling module can be activated if there is a threshold break-in in the usage of memory and processing cores. Thus, scalability analytics is one important ingredient in the post-production stage to sustain and enhance IT systems and business applications. When, and how many additional resources (bare-metal servers, VMs, and containers) with what configurations, and other questions are being precisely answered by scalability analytics so that the resource elasticity can be achieved without many hitches and hurdles. When applications are inherently scalable, then, along with elastic resources, it is possible to have elastic environments for tackling unplanned data and user loads.

IT security analytics

IT infrastructure security, application security, and data (at rest, transit, and usage) security are the top three security challenges, and there are security solutions approaching the issues at different levels and layers. Access-control mechanisms, cryptography, hashing, digest, digital signature, watermarking, and steganography are the well-known and widely used aspects of ensuing impenetrable and unbreakable security. There's also security testing, and ethical hacking for identifying any security risk factors and eliminating them at the budding stage itself. All kinds of security holes, vulnerabilities, and threats are meticulously unearthed in to deploy defect-free, safety-critical, and secure software applications. During the post-production phase, the security-related data is being extracted out of both software and hardware products, to precisely and painstakingly spit out security insights that in turn goes a long way in empowering security experts and architects to bring forth viable solutions to ensure the utmost security and safety for IT infrastructures and software applications.

The importance of root-cause analysis

The cost of service downtime is growing up. There are reliable reports stating that the cost of downtime ranges from $100,000-$72,000 per minute. Identifying the root-cause (**mean-time-to-identification (MTTI)**) generally takes hours. For a complex situation, the process may run into days. The MTTI is lengthy due to various reasons. There are not many tools to speed up the MTTI process. We need competent tools that enrich the value by correlating the data from different IT tools, such as APM, ITSM, SIEM, and ITOM with open API connectors. As microservices and their instances run on containers, IT teams need to manage millions of data points. This transition mandates for highly advanced and automated tools. The pioneering AI algorithms will be commonly used to automate for precisely finding the root-causes.

Root-cause analysis is being touted as an important post-deployment activity for exactly pinpointing bugs and their roots in any software applications. As articulated previously, any standardized APM solution shows you a stack trace for every error and exception that your application throws. At the top of every exception, the APM software tells the class and method where the error gets originated. But the essence of root-cause analysis is to go further down to the root to understand the causes. There are a few software solutions for simplifying the root-cause analyzes.

The continuous adoption of continuous delivery by significantly shortening testing and release cycles from weeks to days is exponentially increasing the likelihood of introducing errors into production.

OverOps (https://www.overops.com/) analyzes code in staging and production to automatically detect and deliver the root-causes for all errors with no dependency on logging. OverOps shows you a stack trace for every error and exception. However, it also shows you the complete source code, objects, variables, and values that caused that error or exception to be thrown. This assists in identifying the root-cause of when your code breaks. OverOps injects a hyperlink into the exception's link, and you'll be able to jump directly into the source code and actual variable state that cause it. OverOps can co-exist in production alongside all the major APM agents and profilers. Using OverOps with your APM allows monitoring server slowdowns and errors, along with the ability to drill down into the real root-cause of each issue.

OverOps enhances log-management

The strongest use case for logs is troubleshooting, which is when your log files include logged errors, warnings, caught, and uncaught exceptions. In most cases, you'll have to dissect the information to understand what went wrong in the execution of your code in the production environment.

The main challenge as far as managing log records is concerned is that they often contain an unmanageable number of entries and require need to manually find the needle in the haystack. OverOps helps in the debugging process by inserting hyperlinks into your existing log files so that operators and developers can instantly see the stack, source, and state behind each event. OverOps also de-duplicates the contents of log files to reduce the operational noise and time associated with analyzing them. Detecting exceptions and logging errors happen in real-time, at the JVM level without relying on parsing logs.

Application Flow Analysis: This capability takes the control and data flow details to hunt down application and transaction errors. Analyzing specific applications, it is possible to measure the performance of individual business transactions. The application map facility visualizes faults, alerts, and tickets in your business application at the individual application flow:

- It automatically discovers the infrastructure topology, as well as the flows that represent the entire business application
- If you select a specific flow, you can visualize the path taken across the supporting infrastructure
- By applying the fault or alert overlay, you can now visualize the specific flows that are impacted by them

Business Transactions Analysis: This is all about deeply analyzing transactions and their performance. The transaction details provide a lot of useful information to work with:

- You can go deeper than this by analyzing the performance of the business transactions
- You can see the number of successful and failed transactions, their response time over time, as well as the latency across each hop in the application services layer
- By clicking on a failed transaction, you can identify the specific Java code in the JVM where the failure occurred
- This information can be passed to your Java developers to fix

There are several approaches and solutions being rolled out to bring reliable and rewarding software applications and IT infrastructures. The refinements, advancements, and enhancements are being etched in all the layers and levels of IT. Researchers are continuously digging down to identify hitherto-unknown limitations, the root-causes for various problems to unveil an ecosystem of tools for enforcing and ensuring IT reliability.

Summary

There are several activities being strategically planned and executed to enhance the resiliency, robustness, and versatility of enterprise, edge, and embedded IT. It is overwhelmingly accepted that the domains of data analytics and machine learning are going to be the key differentiators for corporations in fulfilling the varying expectations of their customers, clients, and consumers. This chapter has described the various post-production data analytics to allow you to gain a deeper understanding of applications, middleware solutions, databases, and IT infrastructures to manage them effectively and efficiently. Machine-learning algorithms enable the formation of self-learning models to predict problems and prescribe the viable solutions to surmount them. Thus, data analytics methods and ML algorithms come in handy in realizing resilient IT. The other important facets include static and dynamic code analyzes to proactively identify bugs in software code to enhance application reliability.

In the next chapter we will be learning about why a multi-cloud approach is gaining unprecedented market and mind shares.

Further Readings

The following are a few references:

- Log Analytics by matomo: `https://piwik.org/log-analytics/`

- Log Analytics by appdynamics: `https://www.appdynamics.com/product/log-analytics/`

- The Fastest Way to Analyze Your Log Data: `https://logentries.com/`

- Log analytics by Dynatrace: `https://www.dynatrace.com/capabilities/log-analytics/`

- Autonomous Digital Intelligence: `https://www.loomsystems.com/`

12
Service Meshes and Container Orchestration Platforms

The future demands that enterprises leverage multi-cloud resources to automate their business operations successfully. The cloud journey thus far is a roller coaster ride. Clouds are typically online, on-demand, and off-premises. There are public, private, and hybrid clouds to comfortably cater to different regions and requirements. There are a number of purpose-centric and agnostic clouds (local and remote) consisting of a growing array of compute resources, such as bare-metal servers, virtual machines, and containers. The other prominent cloud resources include storage, networking, and security solutions. There is another noteworthy development. There are edge/fog device clouds emerging and evolving quickly due to the conscious adoption of the edge/fog computing paradigm. Multi-faceted devices in our everyday environments (personal and professional) are being meticulously clubbed together through middleware solutions to form pioneering fog/device clouds. The edge device clouds are to fulfill the need for real-time data capture, cleansing, and crunching. These produce real-time and actionable insights, which in turn loop back to various actuating devices and applications to adroitly attend people-centric, environment-specific, and time-sensitive tasks. Thus, the cloud journey, without an iota of doubt, is on the right track. It is not an exaggeration to say that the cloud paradigm is being positioned as the one-stop IT solution for all kinds of business evolutions and revolutions.

In the recent past, there has been avid interest by worldwide enterprises in embracing a multi-cloud strategy, which is being termed as the safest and smartest move for business organizations. With the appropriate technologies and tools for crafting hybrid clouds becoming solidified, the move towards employing multiple clouds for hosting and running various business workloads is garnering a more subtle and solid attention. This chapter is therefore dedicated to convey why a multi-cloud approach is gaining unprecedented market and mind shares. Furthermore, to ensure service resilience, we need a couple of infrastructures.

In this chapter, we will be learning about the following:

- Digital transformation
- Cloud-native and enabled applications for the digital era
- Service mesh solutions
- Microservices API Gateway
- The journey toward containerized cloud environments
- The growing solidity of the Kubernetes platform for containerized clouds

About the digital transformation

Digital technologies and tools are becoming pervasive and persuasive. Nations across the globe are competing with one another in observing and absorbing digital processes, platforms, patterns, and practices to build next-generation, smarter systems that are inherently sensitive, perceptive, decision-making, responsive, and active. All kinds of business establishments are eagerly strategizing to be elegantly digitized in their operations, offerings, and outputs. Society is are being made aware of the significant impacts of digitization (edge) and digital technologies. IT organizations are equally keen on bringing forth an arsenal of digitalization-enablement solutions and services. Institutions, innovators, and individuals are overwhelmingly convinced about the tactic as well as the strategic implications of digital disruptions and innovations. The articulation and accentuation of digital transformation is definitely rising with the enhanced understanding of the business, technical, and user benefits of digital technologies, such as data analytics (big, real-time, and streaming), enterprise mobility, the **Internet of Things** (**IoT**), **artificial intelligence** (**AI**), microservices architecture, containerized cloud environments, and so on.

Not only our computers, but also our everyday devices, handhelds, wearables, healthcare instruments, flying drones, industrial robots, consumer electronics, defence equipment, manufacturing machines, and household wares and utensils, are also being systematically connected to one another and also to remote software applications, services, and databases. There are a bevy of connectors, drivers, adapters, and other middleware solutions to enable the smart linkage of digitized artefacts, connected devices, and cloud-based applications. There is a close tie in-between the physical and the cyber worlds. This deeper and decisive connectivity results in highly integrated and insightful systems, networks, applications, and environments. All the anticipated and unanticipated interactions among all the participants and constituents generate a massive amount of multi-structured data. That is, the varying data speed, structure, schema, scope, and size lay a stimulating foundation for bigger and brighter possibilities and opportunities. Connectivity and cognition technologies combine well to speed up the digital transformation. The penetration and participation of microservices, the containerization movement, the availability of container orchestration platforms, service mesh solutions, and API Gateways, have particularly accelerated the realization of the digital transformation and IT reliability.

Cloud-native and enabled applications for the digital era

The projected digital era, therefore, involves and invokes a number of cutting-edge technologies. Assimilating the appropriate technologies is an important factor to construct digital applications . Besides the growing family of technologies, we need more polished and fine-tuned processes. The traditional processes need to be subjected to a variety of enhancements, rationalizations, and optimizations. We also need architectures suitable for building modular applications and for simplifying data management. **Microservice architecture (MSA)** is being projected as the next-generation architectural style for designing modular applications in an agile manner. Massive monolithic applications are being methodically segmented into a dynamic pool of interoperable, publicly discoverable, network accessible, portable, and composable microservices. Distributed and decentralized applications are going to be realized with ease through the smart application of the proven MSA pattern. Furthermore, there are a number of maturing and stabilizing design patterns for developing and deploying microservice-centric applications.

Finally, it is all about the digital applications, platforms, and infrastructures. We need integrated platforms for design, development, integration, delivery, and deployment platforms. As far as the IT infrastructure is concerned for the deployment of platforms and applications, the multi-cloud strategy is being widely preferred due to its various tactic as well as strategic advantages. That is, leveraging multiple cloud resources for hosting and running microservices-centric applications is being considered as a strategically sound move. There are state-of-the-art platform solutions for enabling cloud orchestration, management, governance, security, brokerage, and so on. For the containerized microservices era, there are a number of automated solutions such as container clustering, orchestration, and management platforms, API Gateways and management suite, service composition (orchestration and choreography) tools, service mesh solutions toward resilient microservices, and so on. Thus, not only are massive monolithic applications being meticulously modernized as a collection of interactive microservices to be migrated and run in multiple cloud environments but also microservices-centric applications are being designed, developed, and deployed on cloud environments to reap all the originally expressed benefits of the cloud idea.

Multi-cloud resources are being leveraged to host and run digital applications, and, as mentioned, MSA is the chosen architectural paradigm for modernizing conventional and current legacy applications. New applications are being produced from scratch using MSA patterns, processes, and platforms. Furthermore, on the platform front, we have a variety of development, deployment, delivery, automation, integration, orchestration, governance, and management platforms to speed up the process of realizing and running scores of microservices on **bare-metal (BM)** servers, **virtual machines (VMs)**, and containers. The digital infrastructures typically include commodity servers, high-end enterprise-grade servers, hyper-converged infrastructures, hardware appliances, and hybrid clouds. Advancements and accomplishments in the digital IT space have brought a number of delectable transformations. Digital transformation is accelerating as more and more enterprises work to create and innovate by taking advantage of pioneering digital technologies.

Service mesh solutions

Technically speaking, a service mesh is an additional software layer exclusively added to handle all sorts of service-to-service communications in a reliable manner. Cloud enabled and native applications are being composed out of microservices. For reliable cloud applications, the resiliency of service interactions has to be preserved through technologically advanced solutions.

Service mesh solutions are designed to absorb the service communication responsibility from each of the microservices. The service mesh acts as a proxy that intercepts and implements network communication between microservices. There are several resiliency-enablement design patterns such as retry, timeout, circuit breaking, load balancing, fault-tolerance, distributed tracing, observability metric collection, and all these are optimally implemented and inserted in any service mesh solution. A service mesh is a prime example of the ambassador pattern, which is a helper service that sends network requests on behalf of the application. The principal features of service mesh solutions include the following:

- Ensure that load balancing is provided at the session level based on various parameters such as observed latencies or the number of outstanding requests. This can sharply improve service performance over the traditional layer-4 load balancing.
- Supports layer-7 routing performed based on the URL path, host header, API version, or other application level rules.
- Understands all the HTTP error codes, and can automatically retry failed requests. It is possible to configure the maximum number of retries, along with a timeout period.
- Provides a circuit breaking feature. If a service instance consistently does not respond to client requests, then the circuit breaker in the service mesh will temporarily mark the service instance as unavailable. After a short period, the circuit breaker will try the instance again.
- Leverages service metrics. The service mesh precisely captures all the right and relevant metrics about inter-service calls, such as the request volume, latency, error, and success rates, and the response sizes.
- Enables distributed tracing by adding correlation information for each hop in a request.
- Performs mutual TLS authentication for service-to-service calls.
- Comes with service registry and discovery features.

Service Meshes and Container Orchestration Platforms

The macro-level service communication resiliency is illustrated in the following diagram:

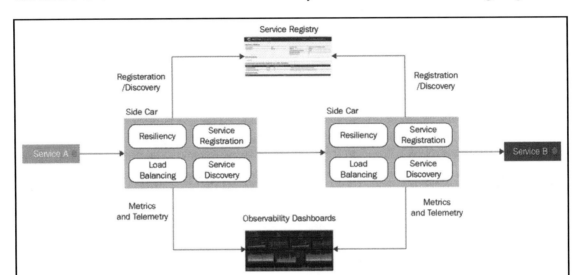

There are a few interesting implementations of service mesh specifications. The most prominent ones among them are Istio, Linkerd, and Conduit. Aspen Mesh is a commercial version.

Linkerd

Linkerd (https://linkerd.io/) is an open source service mesh primarily Finagle and Netty. It can run on Kubernetes, DC/OS, and also on simple set of machines. This is an ultra-light and self-contained service mesh for Kubernetes. It was built with the Rust language and is cloud-native. It rapidly diagnoses runtime issues and gets actionable service metrics. It gets installed in seconds and its design is incremental and composable. Linkerd gives you instant Grafana dashboards and CLI debugging tools for any Kubernetes service with no cluster-wide installation. This offers the following service mesh features:

- Load balancing
- Circuit breaking
- Retries and deadlines
- Request routing

It captures top-line service metrics such as request volume, success rates, and latency distribution. With its dynamic request routing, it enables staging services, canaries, and blue-green deploys with minimal configuration with a powerful language called **delegation tables** (**dtabs**) show as follows:

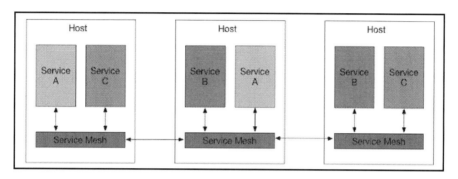

Istio

Istio (https://istio.io/) is an open source platform providing a unique way to connect, secure, manage, and monitor microservices. It supports traffic shaping between microservices, while providing rich telemetry. It ensures fine-grained control of traffic with routing rules, retries, failover, and fault injection. Istio supports access control, rate limiting (throttling), and quota provisioning shown as follows:

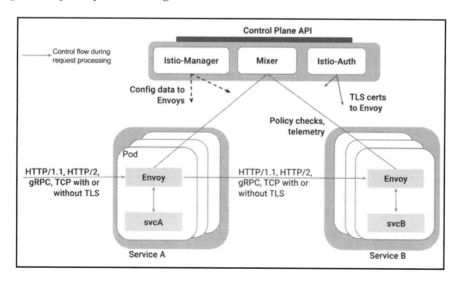

Service Meshes and Container Orchestration Platforms

Istio is built upon a battle tested sidecar (Envoy). Envoy is coded using the C++ language shown as follows:

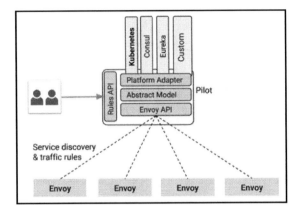

The pilot, **Mixer**, and CA are the key modules in the control plane. These facilitate all the configuration requirement, policy establishment and enforcement, and control flows. The data plane is empowered by **Envoy** proxies. The data plane mediates all service requests and data communications. **Envoy** proxy collects and publishes various metric details to a **Mixer** and there are few popular monitoring tools out of which one is **Prometheus**. The following diagram can help in better understanding:

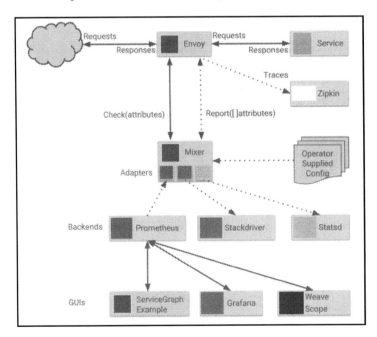

Chapter 12

The Envoy contributes as a layer-4 and layer-7 reverse proxy. It can do complicated traffic management based on rules. This makes the infrastructure extremely nimble for the operations team. For example, the next diagram shows how 1% of the traffic can be routed to an alternate route for A/B testing:

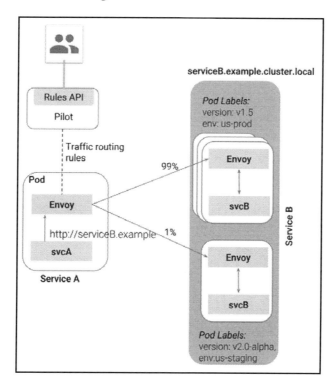

This can be made possible by pushing out the policy change to the Envoy. The Envoy can also perform layer-7 routing for traffic steering based on HTTP headers, as shown in the following diagram:

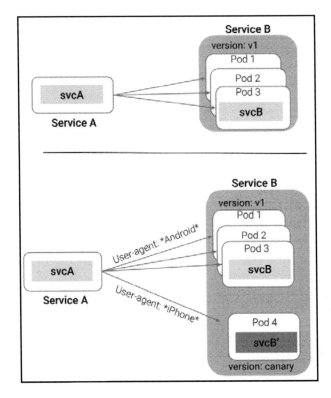

The Envoy also takes care of generating spans and integrating with tools such as Zipkin that provide distributed tracing capabilities, which make observing a complicated distributed interaction and correlating causality a feature of the service mesh.

In these kinds of deployments, there is an adjacent container for every application container as illustrated in the following diagram. The sidecar container handles all the network traffic in and out of the application container:

Chapter 12

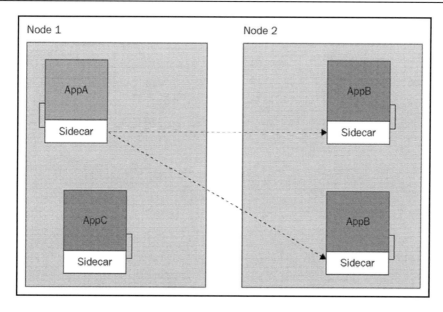

Sidecar is a novel way of providing services to applications. It is especially well adapted for containers and Kubernetes. The sidecar deployment model is bound to the same trust domain as the individual service, and this reduces the attack surface drastically. This type allows services to implement fine-grained policies around inter-service communication that uses cryptographically verifiable identities. For example, **Service A** can be configured to only be allowed to invoke **Service B**, and the interaction will be governed and mandated by the proxy, through the use of **mTLS** certificates with the **Istio CA**:

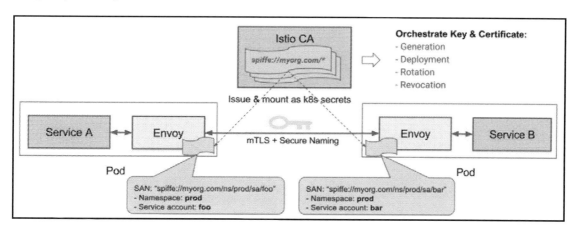

The following table shows the differences between ingress and egress:

Ingress features	Egress features
Authentication	Service authentication
Authorization	Load balancing
Rate limits	Retry and circuit breaker
Load shedding	Fine-grained routing
Telemetry	Telemetry
Request tracing	Request tracing
Fault injection	Fault injection

Apart from these features, ingress also provides annotation, which can be used to redirect the traffic to the service on Kubernetes.

The Istio solution is to address the issues developers and operators face while they move from monolithic applications toward microservice-centric applications. With the surging popularity of the multi-cloud strategy being vociferously adopted by enterprises worldwide, service discovery, load balancing, and failure recovery are becoming more complicated. Istio is also being deployed in multi-cloud environments.

Visualizing an Istio service mesh

Kiali (`https://www.kiali.io/`) is an open source project that works with Istio (`https://istio.io/`) to visualize the service mesh topology. Kiali includes features to map flows, virtual services, circuit breakers, delays, and request rates at a granular level. It provides insight into the behavior/patterns/actions of microservices in an Istio service mesh. Kiali also includes Jaeger tracing to provide distributed tracing, thus providing a unified interface to monitor and manage service communication.

Istio provides a level of indirection around some painful aspects of deployment. Istio, as a service mesh, provides patterns to secure communication between services such as fault tolerance using circuit breaking, retry, timeout, and so on, where routing decisions are done at the mesh level, which eliminates users at a platform level performing all these operations. Also, Istio gives users an opportunity for dependency injection for service-level networking, while Kiali provides a robust web framework to visualize complex service mesh architecture with functional metrics to easily gather information on policies, latency, response times, and requests served and received, which makes it much easier to formulate concrete rule sets.

Kiali can be easily deployed on Kubernetes and all the components should be deployed in the Istio system namespace where the Istio control-plane components are installed. Kiali automatically discovers all the workloads, services, and Istio rules on the cluster, segregated as per the namespace. With the new Istio and Kubernetes the Istio-proxy containers are auto-injected to pods where the namespaces are labeled with `istio-injection=enabled`, eliminating the usage of an explicit `kubectl` inject.

Microservice API Gateway

Microservice architecture (**MSA**), due to its sheer power and distinct competencies continuously strengthens its beneficial footprint as the undisputed unit of agile application design, development, and deployment. MSA is evolving quickly with the continued contributions from scores of third-party tool and platform vendors. Computer scientists, IT professionals, and academic professors across the globe are bringing forth delectable advancements to make MSA groundbreaking and pervasive for the IT world. We have detailed this strategically sound application architecture pattern in other chapters. You can also find other chapters talking about the various contributions of MSA to be penetrative, participative, and pioneering. In the following sections, we want to discuss the need for API gateway solutions and API management suites, and how they fulfill the goals of MSA goals with ease.

Service Meshes and Container Orchestration Platforms

In a nutshell, an API Gateway is a proxy that has information about the main microservice endpoints. It mediates, routes, and invokes a respective endpoint after request verification, content filtering, authentication, and authorization. A functional view of an API Gateway is depicted next:

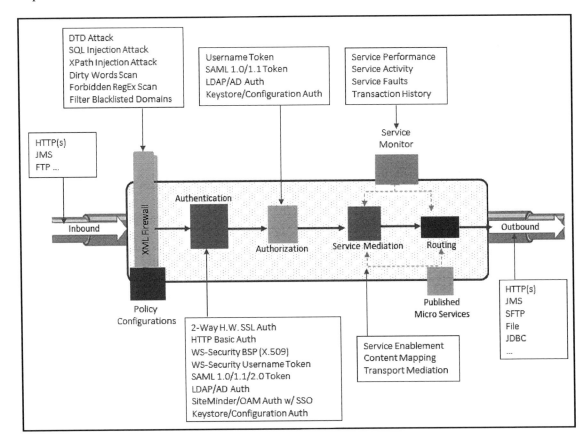

Typically, an enterprise-scale mission-critical application is composed out of hundreds of microservices. An API Gateway can help provide a unified entry point for external consumers, regardless of the number and composition of internal microservices. A typical API Gateway is being stuffed with the following competencies:

- **Content Attack Prevention (CAP)**
- Security policy configuration and enforcement
- API registration and publishing

- Routing and service mediation
- Traffic management and message throttling
- Monitoring of microservices to ensure the QoS attributes are meeting their targets

In short, an API Gateway provides a single and unified API entry point across one or more internal APIs. When a user enters an API Gateway, they may be coming from a variety of devices (web browsers or applications, mobile browsers or applications, and so on). They may expect structurally different responses. The AP gateway aggregates the requests from various client instruments and presents the aggregated one to the target service to facilitate the required processing.

The benefits of an API Gateway for microservices-centric applications

The contributions of API Gateways for microservices are growing as the days go by. The prominent ones are indicated and illustrated next. An API Gateway typically ensures the following:

- **Internal changes get hidden from external clients**: An API Gateway separates external public APIs from internal microservice APIs. This separation provide a flexibilities and number of management capabilities for microservices. Microservices can be replaced, substituted, decommissioned, updated, and so on, without affecting external clients.
- **Tight security for microservices**: API Gateways come in handy for nipping malicious attacks in the bud and propagating stage itself. This acts as an additional security layer for various kinds of security attacks, such as SQL injection, XML Parser exploits, and **denial-of-service** (**DoS**) attacks.
- **Communication protocol translation**: External-facing microservice APIs primarily come with an HTTP or REST-based API. But internal microservices offer different communication protocols, such as MQTT, AMQP, CoAP, and so on. API Gateways are capable of synchronizing between different protocols so that microservices can find, bind to, and leverage one another without a hitch.

- **Reducing microservice complexity**: There are a number of horizontal activities to be done by each participating microservice. They are abstracted out of the microservices and accumulated in an API Gateway. Microservices just focus on the business capabilities. All the plumbing gets accomplished through an API Gateway. The following diagram illustrates how an API Gateway solution links microservices to service clients:

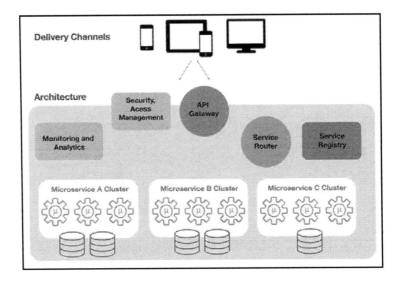

The gateway also helps by recording data for analysis and auditing purposes, load balancing, and caching. The following diagram shows how the gateway typically fits into the overall microservice architecture:

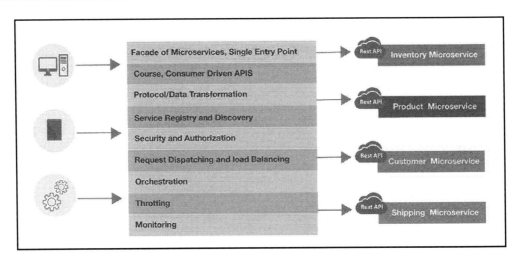

API Gateways have emerged as the most important infrastructure solution for enabling microservices to supply their unique features not only to the other word, but also internal microservices. Enabling security and trust, connectivity, intermediation, enrichment, concierge tasks, policy establishment and enforcement, activation and accomplishment of workflows, are the prime functionalities of API Gateway solutions. A symbolic, sequential request-response workflow between the client and microservice would be as follows:

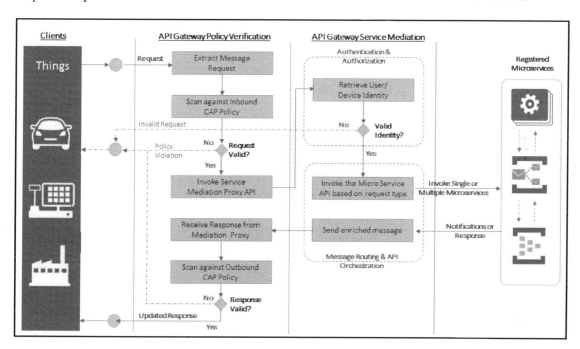

Security features of API Gateways

Security is an important requirement for microservices, which leads to distributed computing. As indicated, the role and responsibility of API Gateways in securing microservices from accidental or deliberate security attacks is on the rise. We are all familiar with the initialism **confidentiality, integrity, and availability (CIA)**. API Gateways ensure unbreakable and impenetrable security for microservices and their data.

The following diagram shows how the much-needed authentication and authorization is done to allow clients to assess and access microservices:

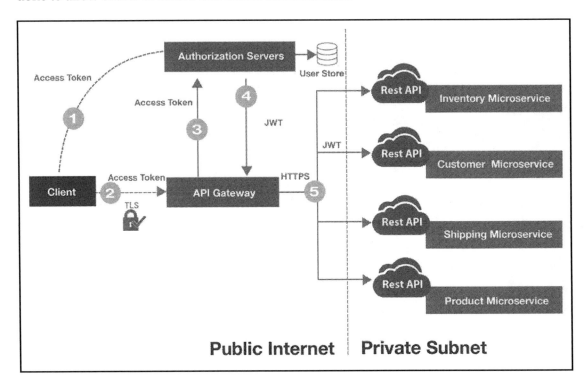

API Gateway and service mesh in action

The following diagram illustrates how an API Gateway and a service mesh can exist. As we discussed, there are also some overlapping features (such as circuit breakers), but it's important to understand that these two concepts are serving fundamentally different requirements, refer to the following image:

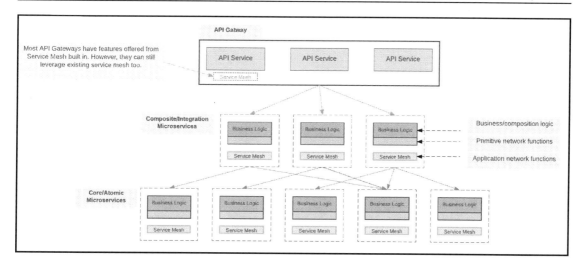

As shown in the preceding diagram, a service mesh is used alongside most of the service implementations as a sidecar, and it's independent of the business functionality of the services. An API Gateway hosts all the API services. An API Gateway may have inbuilt inter-service communication capabilities, but that doesn't prevent an API Gateway using a service mesh to call downstream services (API Gateway | service mesh | microservices).

API management suite

We are heading toward an API world. Everything is API-driven and defined. APIs are transforming the world. Businesses are using APIs to achieve digital transformation. Digital transformation brings with it agility, adaptability, affordability, productivity, and customer delight. We have discussed the nitty-gritty of API Gateway solutions. For the end-to-end life cycle management of APIs, we need a comprehensive management platform, which is termed as the API management suite. This suite of management modules brings additional capabilities such as analytics, monetization, and life cycle management.

The following diagram clearly depicts how the Azure API management solution contributes for the increasingly connected microservice world. The API Gateway is becoming a dominant part of API management solutions:

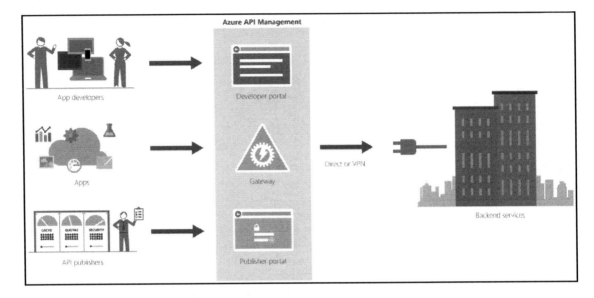

Ensuring the reliability of containerized cloud environments

Managing dependencies and binaries across many applications and customers requires significant efforts. Having realized the need for a comprehensive-yet-compact mechanism for achieving system portability, the Docker people have combined some of the capabilities of Linux cgroups (https://en.wikipedia.org/wiki/Cgroups) and namespaces into a single and easy-to-use package so that applications can consistently run on any IT infrastructure (bare-metal servers and virtual machines) without any tweak and twist of application code. The resulting package is the Docker image (https://docs.docker.com/engine/docker-overview/), and the following benefits accrue from using out of this standardized image. The Docker platform is a collection of capabilities used to take care of the life cycle activities of Docker images and their container instances.

Let's understand more about Docker platform with the help of the following points:

- The Docker image packages the application and the associated libraries into a single package. This helps applications to be consistently deployed across many environments including Raspberry Pi, laptops, enterprise IT servers, cloud servers, and so on.
- The Docker platform provides a variety of Git-like semantics, such as Docker push and Docker commit, to make it easy for application developers to quickly produce Docker images and containers and incorporate them into their existing workflows.
- Docker images are immutable. Committed changes are stored as individual read-only layers. This makes it easy to reuse images and track changes. Layers also save disk space and network traffic by only transporting the updates instead of the entire images.
- Docker containers get realized by instantiating the immutable images instantaneously with a writable layer that can temporarily store runtime changes, making it easy to deploy and scale multiple instances of applications quickly.

Though there were many containerization-enablement technologies and methods, the success of the Docker platform has brought in a real paradigm shift. The huge amount of simplification and standardization brought in through a variety of automation techniques, and tools has made it possible for containers to be pervasive. Containerization is being touted as the next-generation compartmentalization technique for realizing next-generation cloud environments that open up fresh possibilities and opportunities for businesses as well as the technology industry. It is an indisputable statement that the future definitely and decisively belongs to the mesmerizing success of the containerization paradigm. To achieve digital transformation, all the innovations and disruptions provided by the containerization technology are going to be the real game-changer. Containerization is all set to be the fundamental spark for achieving bigger and better things through a host of technological advancements in the days to come.

The journey toward containerized cloud environments

For enabling the real digital transformation, establishing and sustaining containerized clouds are being pronounced as the way forward. With the containerization movement gaining a lot of attention these days due to the Docker containerization platform, cloud servers are being presented as a collection of application and data containers. With the cool convergence of microservices and containers, future cloud environments are going to be heavily containerized. We have written about the MSA pattern and the containerization paradigm. As we all know, the container tool ecosystem is expanding in order to automate most of the tasks associated with running containerized clouds. There are a number of third-party tool and product vendors building a variety of automated tools to simplify and streamline the adoption of containerization technology, especially the surging popularity and widespread us of Kubernetes, which is being recognized as the key container orchestration platform. This has laid the foundation for the realization of containerized clouds. We discussed Kubernetes in detail in previous chapters in this book. Still, there is a gap between demand and supply in comprehensively fulfilling the service resiliency goal. Having realized and understood the need, there came a few service-mesh solutions to guarantee service resiliency. The subsequent sections throw more light on service mesh solutions from the open source community, as well as from commercial-grade vendors. Another software infrastructure solution is microservices API Gateways.

With containers emerging as the standardized packaging format and lightweight runtime environment for hosting and managing microservices, the containerization movement picked up rapidly. Containers ensure real-time horizontal scalability, as they are quicker to boot up. It is easy to create multiple containers quickly with a single command. Container networking and storage are also seeing a kind of stability and maturity with the articulation of powerful technologies and tools. For creating multi-container applications, a few container orchestration platforms have emerged. Furthermore, scores of third-party tool vendors have simplified and streamlined the usage of containers at production environments. Container security is being beefed up with technologically advanced solutions, security standards, and algorithms. There are automated ways of producing Docker images quickly. The container life cycle tasks are getting automated through the Docker platform in association with third-party tools. The Docker tool ecosystem has seen a dramatic increase, and hence container adoption across industry verticals is growing fast. Cloud environments, which thus far are stuffed with BM servers and virtual machines, are being modernized to be filled with hundreds of thousands of containers. Containers are liable for frequent failures, and hence multiple container instances are being used for hosting microservices. The redundant nature of containers ensures their high availability of containers.

For setting up and sustaining containerized cloud environments, the contributions of container orchestration platform solutions are indispensable. The end-to-end life cycle management of containers is taken care of by these special platforms. There are a few such platforms. Among them, Kubernetes occupies the top slot. This chapter is about how Kubernetes can be installed to create container clusters in a systematic manner, by not only clustering containers but also organizing and optimizing them in the formation of complete cloud environments, are being accelerated through the smart leveraging of container orchestration solutions.

The growing solidity of the Kubernetes platform for containerized clouds

Kubernetes is an open source container management system, which is increasingly deployed in enterprise-grade and production-ready cloud environments. Kubernetes is being positioned as the silver bullet for containerized environments. Kubernetes automates several tasks associated with the containerization movement. The well-known contributions of the Kubernetes platform include the following:

- Expertly forming container clusters and managing them
- Being blessed with a number of automated tools for application deployment, scaling, healing, and management
- Provisioning and configuring containers for application deployment
- Simplifying the formation of multi-container applications, which are business-aware, process-centric, and composite
- Optimizing and organizing IT infrastructures to improve resource utilization

The unprecedented growth of the Kubernetes tool ecosystem has come as a solace for developers and administrators to embark on the journey toward containerized clouds. There are also some cloud service providers offering **Kubernetes as a Service (KaaS)**.

Kubernetes architecture – how it works

Take a look at the following diagram:

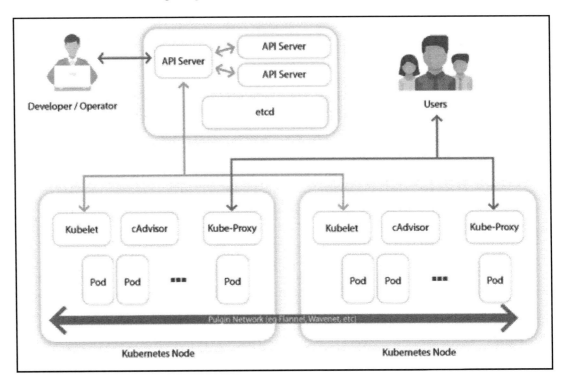

Kubernetes has two key components:

- **Kubernetes master**: This is the primary control unit of Kubernetes. This is for managing workloads and for ensuring smooth communication across all the participating components of the system; it manages workloads and communication across the system. There are several important modules, and each module can run on the master node or can be made to run on multiple master nodes to improve its availability. Its prime modules are as follows:
    - **Storage**: etcd is an open source and popular key value data store, and this is centralized to enable all the nodes in the cluster to access it. Kubernetes uses this database to store all cluster configuration data, and this data collectively represents the overall state of the cluster at any point in time.

- **API server**: This is the most important and RESTful API-attached central management module. This can receive REST requests for bringing forth all kinds of modifications. This serves as a frontend server to control the full cluster and its nodes in a systematic manner. This is the only component that is enabled to communicate with the etcd database and the configuration data.
- **Scheduler**: This is another vital module of the Kubernetes master node, and based on the evolving requirements and resource utilization, the scheduler helps in scheduling the pods on various nodes. This also decides which service is deployed on which pods and nodes.
- **Controller manager**: This runs several controller processes to continuously monitor and manage the shared state of the cluster. If there is any change required in the service, the controller immediately understands the change and starts the necessary activities to attain the new desired state.

- **Worker node**: This is the execution node, and it gets relevant information to adeptly manage container collaboration. Also, this is in constant touch with the master node. It also receives the details from the master node to assign container resources to workloads as per the schedule:
    - **Kubelet**: This module ensures that all containers in the node are running perfectly, without any issues. Kubelet also meticulously monitors whether the pods are in the desired state. If a node fails, then the replication controller is activated to observe this failure and to launch pods in a functional node.
    - **Kube-Proxy**: This doubles up as a network proxy and also as a load balancer. Its main job is to forward requests to the correct pods across nodes in a cluster.
    - **cAdvisor**: This is responsible for monitoring and gathering resource usage and performance metrics on each node.

Further we have following topics which are included in Kubernetes architecture:

- **Pods**: They are the Kubernetes unit of application deployment. Pods, in turn, can comprise one or more containers. Containers can run inside VMs and BM servers. Pods are the single smallest intractable unit in Kubernetes. A pod gets its own IP address, which is shared among its containers.
- **Nodes**: They are the physical machines (in other words, BM servers). Nodes provide the available cluster resources for the Kubernetes platform to keep data, run jobs, optimize workloads, and create network routes. The other prominent component of the Kubernetes platform is Labels, which help Kubernetes and its end users to filter similar resources in the system. They are the glue between participating resources. For example, a service wants to open ports for an application deployment. For monitoring, logging, debugging, and testing purposes, any Kubernetes resource has to be labeled accordingly so that when opening ports, Kubernetes, based on the Labels, does the correct thing. Annotations are used to keep metadata for different objects in the form of freestyle strings. The following is an example for annotation: *Reason for change: Upgrading the application version for security patches.*
- **ReplicaSets**: As previously mentioned, the number of pods to keep applications running comfortably and the addition or deletion of pods is essential. Kubernetes uses ReplicaSets. A replication controller makes sure that a cluster is running the required number of equivalent pods. If there are too many pods, then the replication controller can remove those extra pods. If there are less pods running, then it will add more to maintain the specified number of pods.
- **Kubernetes StatefulSets**: They provide resources such as volumes, stable network IDs, and ordinal indexes from 0 to N to deal with stateful containers. Volume is an important feature to run the stateful application. Two main types of volumes are supported:
    - **Ephermal storage volume**: The volume consists of any number of containers running within a pod. Data is stored across the containers. But if pods are killed, the volume is automatically removed.
    - **Persistent storage**: This is a permanent data-storage mechanism. Even when the pod gets killed or moved to another node, data is stored in a remote location till it gets deleted by the user.
- **DaemonSets**: Certain applications require only one instance of a workload on every node. A good example is a log collector, which collect logs from all the nodes in the cluster. The log collector agent (only one instance) has to be present in all nodes. To create such a workload deployed, Kubernetes uses this feature.

- **Jobs**: As the majority of applications require constant uptime to simultaneously server requests, there is the need for batches of jobs to be spawned and cleaned up once finished. To do this, we can use this feature. A job creates one or more pods and ensures that a specified number of pods gets terminated once the job is over. A good example can be a set of workers reading jobs from a queue of data to be processed and stored. Once the queue is empty, the workers are not required, until the next batch is ready to be processed.
- **ConfigMaps and secrets**: An application has to be completely agnostic to its location. To achieve this, the ConfigMaps capability is used. This is essentially a list of key-value environment variables that are passed to running workloads to determine different runtime behaviors. Secrets are the same, except that they are encrypted to prevent sensitive information, such as keys, passwords, certificates, and so on, getting hacked on the way.
- **Deployments**: In the agile world, we want to build, test, and ship in small chunk, to receive immediate feedback from users. Kubernetes makes it easy to deploy new software or a newer version of existing software, using deployments. These are sets of metadata describing new requirements from a certain running workload. With the assistance of the Kubernetes platform, it is possible to do automated roll outs and rollbacks of applications. Kubernetes also comes in handy in performing canary deployments. A number of promising and potential programming languages are being supported in Kubernetes.
- **Security**: Kubernetes provides a variety of other operational facilities such as DNS management, resource monitoring, logging, and storage orchestration. It is a widely reported that container security is the major barrier for the slow adoption of containers in production environments. While container security drawbacks are simultaneously identified and solved, the Kubernetes platform also addresses security as one of the primary things.

Kubernetes can run not only Docker containers, but also containers from other vendors. Kubernetes supports horizontal infrastructure provisioning and scaling. The automated scaling of newer resources is facilitated through the Kubernetes platform. Kubernetes handles the availability of both applications and infrastructure extremely well. Kubernetes ensures that applications do not fail by consistently checking the health of pods and containers. Another feature for ensuring the high availability of Kubernetes clusters is load balancing. The Kubernetes load balancer distributes the load across multiple pods.

Containerization has gained its mesmerizing popularity because it has the inherent strength and sagacity to accelerate and automate the process of software building, testing, and release.

The growing open source community is consistently adding new features into the Kubernetes platform to present Kubernetes as the highly accomplished and acclaimed platform for smoothening containerized clouds. Kubernetes simplifies the tasks of the DevOps team drastically, ensuring IT agility and adaptivity, which in turn, improve business versatility. Without Kubernetes, software engineering teams have to script their own software deployment, scale it manually, and update workflows. For a large enterprise, these tasks are handled by a large team. Kubernetes by leveraging the various automation being provided by containers, help to develop and deploy cloud enabled and native applications. Precisely speaking, Kubernetes brings in a beneficial abstraction on IT hardware to achieve portability, maneuverability, accessibility, scalability, availability, and so on. In a very short time, Kubernetes has become the most important technology for adroitly running containerized clouds and speeding up application deployment. Here is another macro-level Kubernetes architecture:

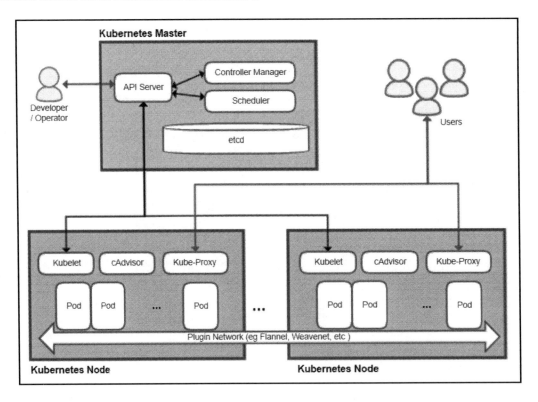

Kubernetes has become an attractive phenomenon for application developers because it takes away the dependency on IT operations team. Kubernetes also speeded up the leverage of the pioneering benefits of the containerization paradigm. Containers are penetrating into production environments because of the power of Kubernetes. Kubernetes not only orchestrates stateless containers, but also works with stateful containers. That means enterprise-level transactional, operational, and analytical applications are also being deployed and managed by Kubernetes. There are several reasons why Kubernetes is sweeping the entire IT world today. Firstly, it can run on any infrastructure and in any environment. There are thousands of open source developers contributing to the Kubernetes community and sustaining the Kubernetes journey. Kubernetes is stuffed with a number of APIs and a full number of modular components, so adding new components and integrating with third-party tools are quite simple.

Installing the Kubernetes platform

Let's create a scenario to create a three-node Kubernetes cluster. In this example, we will create one Kubernetes master and two clients. We are using Ubuntu server 17.10 VMs created using Microsoft Azure. We need to install Kubernetes on the master and both clients.

To install Kubernetes on the master, follow these steps:

1. Upgrade APT using the following command (CentOS users can use `yum update`):

    ```
    apt update && apt upgrade -y
    ```

    ```
    root@Kubemaster:~# apt update && sudo apt upgrade -y
    Hit:1 http://azure.archive.ubuntu.com/ubuntu artful InRelease
    Get:2 http://azure.archive.ubuntu.com/ubuntu artful-updates InRelease [88.7 kB]
    Get:3 http://azure.archive.ubuntu.com/ubuntu artful-backports InRelease [74.6 kB]
    ```

2. Install a few dependencies, `docker.io`, and `apt-transport-https`:

   ```
   sudo apt install docker.io apt-transport-https -qy
   ```

   ```
   root@Kubemaster:~$ sudo apt install docker.io apt-transport-https -qy
   Reading package lists...
   Building dependency tree...
   Reading state information...
   The following additional packages will be installed:
     bridge-utils cgroupfs-mount ubuntu-fan
   Suggested packages:
     ifupdown aufs-tools debootstrap docker-doc rinse zfs-fuse | zfsutils
   The following NEW packages will be installed:
     apt-transport-https bridge-utils cgroupfs-mount docker.io ubuntu-fan
   0 upgraded, 5 newly installed, 0 to remove and 0 not upgraded.
   Need to get 15.3 MB of archives.
   After this operation, 69.3 MB of additional disk space will be used.
   Get:1 http://azure.archive.ubuntu.com/ubuntu artful-updates/main amd64 apt-transport-https amd64 1.5.2 [34.8 kB]
   Get:2 http://azure.archive.ubuntu.com/ubuntu artful/main amd64 bridge-utils amd64 1.5-9ubuntu2 [29.2 kB]
   Get:3 http://azure.archive.ubuntu.com/ubuntu artful/universe amd64 cgroupfs-mount all 1.4 [6320 B]
   Get:4 http://azure.archive.ubuntu.com/ubuntu artful/universe amd64 docker.io amd64 1.13.1-0ubuntu6 [15.2 MB]
   Get:5 http://azure.archive.ubuntu.com/ubuntu artful-updates/main amd64 ubuntu-fan all 0.12.9~17.10.1 [34.5 kB]
   ```

3. Use the following command to install Docker and Kubernetes. Here, we are installing `kubelet`, which is a node agent that runs on each node, and receives an instruction from the master about what to do on the node. `Kube-proxy` is the network load balancer for pods running on the node. `Kubeadm` is the administration tool for setting up and managing Kubernetes clusters, and it runs on the Kubernetes host. `Kubectl` is a command-like interface for interacting with a Kubernetes cluster:

   ```
   apt install docker-ce kubelet kubeadm kubectl kubernetes-cni -y
   ```

   ```
   root@Kubemaster:/etc/apt/sources.list.d# apt install docker-ce kubelet kubeadm kubectl kubernetes-cni -y
   Reading package lists... Done
   Building dependency tree
   Reading state information... Done
   The following packages were automatically installed and are no longer required:
     bridge-utils ubuntu-fan
   Use 'apt autoremove' to remove them.
   The following additional packages will be installed:
     aufs-tools cri-tools libltdl7 pigz socat
   The following packages will be REMOVED:
     docker.io
   The following NEW packages will be installed:
     aufs-tools cri-tools docker-ce kubeadm kubectl kubelet kubernetes-cni libltdl7 pigz socat
   0 upgraded, 10 newly installed, 1 to remove and 0 not upgraded.
   Need to get 95.3 MB of archives.
   After this operation, 493 MB of additional disk space will be used.
   Get:1 https://download.docker.com/linux/ubuntu artful/stable amd64 docker-ce amd64 18.06.1~ce~3-0~ubuntu [40.2 MB]
   Get:3 http://azure.archive.ubuntu.com/ubuntu artful/universe amd64 pigz amd64 2.3.4-1 [55.3 kB]
   Get:4 http://azure.archive.ubuntu.com/ubuntu artful-updates/universe amd64 aufs-tools amd64 1:4.1+20161219-1ubuntu0.1 [102 kB]
   Get:6 http://azure.archive.ubuntu.com/ubuntu artful/main amd64 libltdl7 amd64 2.4.6-2 [38.8 kB]
   Get:7 http://azure.archive.ubuntu.com/ubuntu artful/universe amd64 socat amd64 1.7.3.2-1 [342 kB]
   Get:2 https://packages.cloud.google.com/apt kubernetes-xenial/main amd64 cri-tools amd64 1.12.0-00 [5343 kB]
   Get:5 https://packages.cloud.google.com/apt kubernetes-xenial/main amd64 kubernetes-cni amd64 0.6.0-00 [5910 kB]
   Get:8 https://packages.cloud.google.com/apt kubernetes-xenial/main amd64 kubelet amd64 1.12.1-00 [24.7 MB]
   Get:9 https://packages.cloud.google.com/apt kubernetes-xenial/main amd64 kubectl amd64 1.12.1-00 [8594 kB]
   Get:10 https://packages.cloud.google.com/apt kubernetes-xenial/main amd64 kubeadm amd64 1.12.1-00 [8987 kB]
   ```

4. Use the following command to initialize the Kubernetes master:

   ```
   sudo kubeadm init --kubernetes-version stable
   ```

   ```
   root@Kubemaster:/etc/apt/sources.list.d$ sudo kubeadm init --kubernetes-version stable
   [init] using Kubernetes version: v1.12.1
   [preflight] running pre-flight checks
   [preflight/images] Pulling images required for setting up a Kubernetes cluster
   [preflight/images] This might take a minute or two, depending on the speed of your internet connection
   [preflight/images] You can also perform this action in beforehand using 'kubeadm config images pull'
   [kubelet] Writing kubelet environment file with flags to file "/var/lib/kubelet/kubeadm-flags.env"
   [kubelet] Writing kubelet configuration to file "/var/lib/kubelet/config.yaml"
   [preflight] Activating the kubelet service
   [certificates] Generated front-proxy-ca certificate and key.
   [certificates] Generated front-proxy-client certificate and key.
   [certificates] Generated etcd/ca certificate and key.
   [certificates] Generated etcd/server certificate and key.
   [certificates] etcd/server serving cert is signed for DNS names [kubemaster localhost] and IPs [127.0.0.1 ::1]
   [certificates] Generated etcd/peer certificate and key.
   [certificates] etcd/peer serving cert is signed for DNS names [kubemaster localhost] and IPs [10.0.0.5 127.0.0.1 ::1]
   [certificates] Generated apiserver-etcd-client certificate and key.
   [certificates] Generated etcd/healthcheck-client certificate and key.
   [certificates] Generated ca certificate and key.
   [certificates] Generated apiserver certificate and key.
   [certificates] apiserver serving cert is signed for DNS names [kubemaster kubernetes kubernetes.default kubernetes.default.svc k
   [certificates] Generated apiserver-kubelet-client certificate and key.
   [certificates] valid certificates and keys now exist in "/etc/kubernetes/pki"
   [certificates] Generated sa key and public key.
   ```

   The important thing to note is that after successfully initializing the Kubernetes master, you will see one command that will be required to join any number of machines when it is executed on Kubernetes client node:

   ```
   kubeadm join 10.0.0.5:6443 --token j8pddx.ew4rvqdppx6seclp --discovery-token-ca-cert-hash sha256:00d43aef55fe0fc73041f57e4ebf7676b332bb4c0f53b67a70d2f837a8e30dc8
   ```

   ```
   Your Kubernetes master has initialized successfully!

   To start using your cluster, you need to run the following as a regular user:

     mkdir -p $HOME/.kube
     sudo cp -i /etc/kubernetes/admin.conf $HOME/.kube/config
     sudo chown $(id -u):$(id -g) $HOME/.kube/config

   You should now deploy a pod network to the cluster.
   Run "kubectl apply -f [podnetwork].yaml" with one of the options listed at:
     https://kubernetes.io/docs/concepts/cluster-administration/addons/

   You can now join any number of machines by running the following on each node
   as root:

     kubeadm join 10.0.0.5:6443 --token j8pddx.ew4rvqdppx6seclp --discovery-token-ca-cert-hash sha256:00d43aef55fe0fc73041f57e4ebf7676b332bb4c0f53b67a70d2f837a8e30dc8
   ```

Service Meshes and Container Orchestration Platforms

As you can see, before starting the cluster, we need to run a few commands to and from the non-root user to set up the Kubernetes configuration:

```
mkdir -p $HOME/.kube
sudo cp -i /etc/kubernetes/admin.conf $HOME/.kube/config
sudo chown $(id -u):$(id -g) $HOME/.kube/config
export KUBECONFIG=$HOME/.kube/config
export KUBECONFIG=$HOME/.kube/config | tee -a ~/.bashrc
```

```
master@Kubemaster:/etc/apt/sources.list.d$ mkdir -p $HOME/.kube
master@Kubemaster:/etc/apt/sources.list.d$ sudo cp -i /etc/kubernetes/admin.conf $HOME/.kube/config
master@Kubemaster:/etc/apt/sources.list.d$ sudo chown $(id -u):$(id -g) $HOME/.kube/config
master@Kubemaster:/etc/apt/sources.list.d$ export KUBECONFIG=$HOME/.kube/config
master@Kubemaster:/etc/apt/sources.list.d$ export KUBECONFIG=$HOME/.kube/config | tee -a ~/.bashrc
```

5. Create a pod network for the Kubernetes cluster:

```
kubectl apply -f
http://docs.projectcalico.org/v2.3/gettingstarted/kubernetes/instal
lation/hosted/kubeadm/1.6/calico.yaml
```

```
master@Kubemaster:/etc/apt/sources.list.d$ kubectl apply -f http://docs.projectcalico.org/v2.3/getting-started/kubernetes/installation/hosted/kubeadm/1.6/cal
configmap/calico-config created
daemonset.extensions/calico-etcd created
service/calico-etcd created
daemonset.extensions/calico-node created
deployment.extensions/calico-policy-controller created
clusterrolebinding.rbac.authorization.k8s.io/calico-cni-plugin created
clusterrole.rbac.authorization.k8s.io/calico-cni-plugin created
serviceaccount/calico-cni-plugin created
clusterrolebinding.rbac.authorization.k8s.io/calico-policy-controller created
clusterrole.rbac.authorization.k8s.io/calico-policy-controller created
serviceaccount/calico-policy-controller created
```

6. Start the Kubernetes cluster:

```
systemctl enable kubelet && systemctl start kubelet
```

```
master@Kubemaster:/root$ systemctl enable kubelet && systemctl start kubelet
==== AUTHENTICATING FOR org.freedesktop.systemd1.manage-unit-files ====
Authentication is required to manage system service or unit files.
Authenticating as: Ubuntu (master)
Password:
==== AUTHENTICATION COMPLETE ====
==== AUTHENTICATING FOR org.freedesktop.systemd1.reload-daemon ====
Authentication is required to reload the systemd state.
Authenticating as: Ubuntu (master)
Password:
==== AUTHENTICATION COMPLETE ====
==== AUTHENTICATING FOR org.freedesktop.systemd1.manage-units ====
Authentication is required to start 'kubelet.service'.
Authenticating as: Ubuntu (master)
Password:
==== AUTHENTICATION COMPLETE ====
master@Kubemaster:/root$
```

Installing the Kubernetes client

Perform the following steps:

1. Like Kubernetes master, we need to upgrade APT with the few dependencies `docker.io` and `apt-transport-https`:

    apt update && apt upgrade -y

```
root@KubeClient1:~# apt update && sudo apt upgrade -y
Hit:1 http://azure.archive.ubuntu.com/ubuntu artful InRelease
Get:2 http://azure.archive.ubuntu.com/ubuntu artful-updates InRelease [88.7 kB]
Get:3 http://azure.archive.ubuntu.com/ubuntu artful-backports InRelease [74.6 kB]
Get:4 http://security.ubuntu.com/ubuntu artful-security InRelease [83.2 kB]
```

    sudo apt install docker.io apt-transport-https -qy

```
root@KubeClient1:~# sudo apt install docker.io apt-transport-https -qy
Reading package lists...
Building dependency tree...
Reading state information...
The following additional packages will be installed:
  bridge-utils cgroupfs-mount ubuntu-fan
Suggested packages:
  ifupdown aufs-tools debootstrap docker-doc rinse zfs-fuse | zfsutils
The following NEW packages will be installed:
  apt-transport-https bridge-utils cgroupfs-mount docker.io ubuntu-fan
0 upgraded, 5 newly installed, 0 to remove and 0 not upgraded.
Need to get 15.3 MB of archives.
```

2. Install Docker and Kubernetes using the following command, used to install `kubelet`, `kubeadm`, and `kubectl`:

```
apt install docker-ce kubelet kubeadm kubectl kubernetes-cni -y
```

```
root@KubeClient1:~# apt install docker-ce kubelet kubeadm kubectl kubernetes-cni -y
Reading package lists... Done
Building dependency tree
Reading state information... Done
The following packages were automatically installed and are no longer required:
  bridge-utils ubuntu-fan
Use 'apt autoremove' to remove them.
The following additional packages will be installed:
  aufs-tools cri-tools libltdl7 pigz socat
The following packages will be REMOVED:
  docker.io
The following NEW packages will be installed:
  aufs-tools cri-tools docker-ce kubeadm kubectl kubelet kubernetes-cni libltdl7 pigz socat
0 upgraded, 10 newly installed, 1 to remove and 0 not upgraded.
Need to get 95.3 MB of archives.
```

3. Let's configure Kubernetes from the `Client1` user using the following commands:

```
mkdir -p $HOME/.kube
sudo cp -i /etc/kubernetes/admin.conf $HOME/.kube/config
sudo chown $(id -u):$(id -g) $HOME/.kube/config
export KUBECONFIG=$HOME/.kube/config
export KUBECONFIG=$HOME/.kube/config | tee -a ~/.bashrc
```

```
client1@KubeClient1:/root$ mkdir -p $HOME/.kube
client1@KubeClient1:/root$ sudo cp -i /etc/kubernetes/admin.conf $HOME/.kube/config
cp: cannot stat '/etc/kubernetes/admin.conf': No such file or directory
client1@KubeClient1:/root$ sudo chown $(id -u):$(id -g) $HOME/.kube/config
chown: cannot access '/home/client1/.kube/config': No such file or directory
client1@KubeClient1:/root$ export KUBECONFIG=$HOME/.kube/config
client1@KubeClient1:/root$ export KUBECONFIG=$HOME/.kube/config | tee -a ~/.bashrc
```

Chapter 12

4. To connect the Kubernetes client to the master, use the following command:

   ```
   kubeadm join 10.0.0.5:6443 --token j8pddx.ew4rvqdppx6seclp --
   discovery-token-ca-cert-hash
   sha256:00d43aef55fe0fc73041f57e4ebf7676b332bb4c0f53b67a70d2f837a8e3
   0dc8
   ```

   ```
   [preflight] running pre-flight checks
           [WARNING RequiredIPVSKernelModulesAvailable]: the IPVS proxier will not be used, because the following required kernel modules
           are not loaded: [ip_vs_rr ip_vs_wrr ip_vs_sh ip_vs] or no b
   ipvs support: map[nf_conntrack_ipv4:{} ip_vs:{} ip_vs_rr:{} ip_vs_wrr:{} ip_vs_sh:{}]
   you can solve this problem with following methods:
   1. Run 'modprobe -- ' to load missing kernel modules;
   2. Provide the missing builtin kernel ipvs support

   [discovery] Trying to connect to API Server "10.0.0.5:6443"
   [discovery] Created cluster-info discovery client, requesting info from "https://10.0.0.5:6443"
   [discovery] Requesting info from "https://10.0.0.5:6443" again to validate TLS against the pinned public key
   [discovery] Cluster info signature and contents are valid and TLS certificate validates against pinned roots, will use API Server "10.0.0.5:6443"
   [discovery] Successfully established connection with API Server "10.0.0.5:6443"
   [kubelet] Downloading configuration for the kubelet from the "kubelet-config-1.12" ConfigMap in the kube-system namespace
   [kubelet] Writing kubelet configuration to file "/var/lib/kubelet/config.yaml"
   [kubelet] Writing kubelet environment file with flags to file "/var/lib/kubelet/kubeadm-flags.env"
   [preflight] Activating the kubelet service
   [tlsbootstrap] Waiting for the kubelet to perform the TLS Bootstrap...
   [patchnode] Uploading the CRI Socket information "/var/run/dockershim.sock" to the Node API object "kubeclient1" as an annotation

   This node has joined the cluster:
   * Certificate signing request was sent to apiserver and a response was received.
   * The Kubelet was informed of the new secure connection details.
   Run 'kubectl get nodes' on the master to see this node join the cluster.
   ```

5. Run the following command from the master node, and see the node status:

   kubectl get nodes

   ```
   master@Kubemaster:/root$ kubectl get nodes
   NAME          STATUS    ROLES     AGE    VERSION
   kubeclient1   Ready     <none>    12m    v1.12.1
   kubemaster    Ready     master    89m    v1.12.1
   master@Kubemaster:/root$
   ```

We need to perform similar steps from `Client2`, and rerun the preceding command, and see whether it's successfully connected to the Kubernetes master. We can see that both nodes, `Client1` and `Client2` are successfully connected to the master:

```
master@Kubemaster:/root$ kubectl get nodes
NAME          STATUS    ROLES     AGE    VERSION
kubeclient1   Ready     <none>    22h    v1.12.1
kubeclient2   Ready     <none>    69s    v1.12.1
kubemaster    Ready     master    23h    v1.12.1
master@Kubemaster:/root$
```

[353]

Installing Istio on Kubernetes

A service mesh normally requires an API server, an API client, access control information, a load balancer, authentication and authorization, circuit breaking, and monitoring/tracing.

The service mesh ecosystem includes the following:

- Control plane: Istio, Nelson, SmartStack
- Data plane: Envoy, Linkerd, HAproxy, NGINX
- Open source service mesh control plane

A uniform way to integrate microservices, manage traffic flow across microservices, enforce policies, and aggregate telemetry data was announced in May 2017.

Let's see how to install Istio on Kubernetes:

1. First, we need to download the `Istio tar` file from the following link, depending on your OS:

    ```
    wget
    https://github.com/istio/istio/releases/download/1.1.0.snapshot.1/istio-1.1.0.snapshot.1-linux.tar.gz
    ```

2. Extract the TAR file, move it to the Istio root directory, and install `isto-demo-auth.yml` using this command:

   ```
   kubectl apply -f install/kubernetes/istio-demo-auth.yaml
   ```

   ```
   master@Kubemaster:/opt/istio/istio-1.1.0.snapshot.1$ kubectl apply -f install/kubernetes/istio-demo-auth.yaml
   namespace/istio-system created
   configmap/istio-galley-configuration created
   configmap/istio-grafana-custom-resources created
   configmap/istio-grafana-configuration-dashboards created
   configmap/istio-grafana created
   configmap/prometheus created
   configmap/istio-security-custom-resources created
   configmap/istio created
   configmap/istio-sidecar-injector created
   serviceaccount/istio-galley-service-account created
   serviceaccount/istio-egressgateway-service-account created
   serviceaccount/istio-ingressgateway-service-account created
   serviceaccount/istio-grafana-post-install-account created
   clusterrole.rbac.authorization.k8s.io/istio-grafana-post-install-istio-system created
   clusterrolebinding.rbac.authorization.k8s.io/istio-grafana-post-install-role-binding-istio-system created
   job.batch/istio-grafana-post-install created
   ```

   The preceding command will create the `istio-system` namespace along with RBAC permissions.

3. To verify the Istio installation, use the following command:

   ```
   kubectl get service -n istio-system
   ```

Service Meshes and Container Orchestration Platforms

4. To verify Kubernetes `pods` and container status, use the following command:

   ```
   kubectl get pods -n istio-system
   ```

```
master@Kubemaster:/opt/istio/istio-1.1.0.snapshot.1$ kubectl get pods -n istio-system
NAME                                         READY     STATUS              RESTARTS   AGE
grafana-85689d5548-2rgsg                     1/1       Running             0          107s
istio-citadel-78dc5644c7-4fj5q               1/1       Running             0          106s
istio-cleanup-secrets-zg5rt                  0/1       Completed           0          113s
istio-egressgateway-dbfb4d6f7-758m9          1/1       Running             0          107s
istio-galley-7bf74bfd84-qwhbs                0/1       ContainerCreating   0          107s
istio-grafana-post-install-7p5z9             0/1       Completed           0          113s
istio-ingressgateway-5f87694576-svsqh        1/1       Running             0          107s
istio-pilot-76cc4c68d5-77fn9                 1/2       Running             0          107s
istio-policy-5b8dfffb64-x8pjs                2/2       Running             0          107s
istio-security-post-install-h2hwq            0/1       Completed           0          113s
istio-sidecar-injector-687fc97947-c8vdh      0/1       ContainerCreating   0          106s
istio-telemetry-5b9bc9fdff-s9nqg             2/2       Running             0          107s
istio-tracing-d444f578-r6v9h                 1/1       Running             0          106s
prometheus-6c56b9bf49-6cf9q                  1/1       Running             0          106s
servicegraph-b6959f59d-r8cc8                 1/1       Running             0          106s
master@Kubemaster:/opt/istio/istio-1.1.0.snapshot.1$
```

Let's deploy one application to see how Istio works with Kubernetes. You can use the `bookinfo` sample application, which is already available with the Istio package.

Use this command to deploy the `bookinfo` application, along with all services:

```
kubectl apply -f samples/bookinfo/networking/bookinfo-gateway.yaml
```

In this sample application, we are going to create four microservices:

- `reviews`: Contains book reviews
- `rating`: Contains book ratings
- `details`: Contains book information
- `productpage`: Calls review and details services to get data

```
master@Kubemaster:/opt/istio/istio-1.1.0.snapshot.1$ kubectl apply -f samples/bookinfo/platform/kube/bookinfo.yaml
service/details created
deployment.extensions/details-v1 created
service/ratings created
deployment.extensions/ratings-v1 created
service/reviews created
deployment.extensions/reviews-v1 created
deployment.extensions/reviews-v2 created
deployment.extensions/reviews-v3 created
service/productpage created
deployment.extensions/productpage-v1 created
master@Kubemaster:/opt/istio/istio-1.1.0.snapshot.1$
```

Confirm all services are running using this command:

```
master@Kubemaster:/opt/istio/istio-1.1.0.snapshot.1$ kubectl get services
NAME          TYPE        CLUSTER-IP      EXTERNAL-IP   PORT(S)          AGE
details       ClusterIP   10.109.51.183   <none>        9080/TCP         39s
kubernetes    ClusterIP   10.96.0.1       <none>        443/TCP          47h
nginx         NodePort    10.97.30.24     <none>        80:30355/TCP     20h
productpage   ClusterIP   10.106.145.20   <none>        9080/TCP         39s
ratings       ClusterIP   10.103.87.183   <none>        9080/TCP         39s
reviews       ClusterIP   10.99.199.61    <none>        9080/TCP         39s
master@Kubemaster:/opt/istio/istio-1.1.0.snapshot.1$
```

Confirm the status of all pods using this command:

```
master@Kubemaster:/opt/istio/istio-1.1.0.snapshot.1$ kubectl get pods
NAME                              READY   STATUS              RESTARTS   AGE
details-v1-876bf485f-xcd4b        1/1     Running             0          48s
nginx-55bd7c9fd-5jf9s             1/1     Running             0          20h
productpage-v1-8d69b45c-mzg9d     0/1     ContainerCreating   0          48s
ratings-v1-7c9949d479-k7f7j       1/1     Running             0          48s
reviews-v1-85b7d84c56-25szq       0/1     ContainerCreating   0          48s
reviews-v2-cbd94c99b-qvf2k        0/1     ContainerCreating   0          48s
reviews-v3-748456d47b-2dhv6       0/1     ContainerCreating   0          48s
master@Kubemaster:/opt/istio/istio-1.1.0.snapshot.1$
```

Let's perform the following steps:

1. Use the following command to set up an ingress gateway:

   ```
   kubectl apply -f samples/bookinfo/networking/bookinfo-gateway.yaml
   ```

```
master@Kubemaster:/opt/istio/istio-1.1.0.snapshot.1$ kubectl apply -f samples/bookinfo/networking/bookinfo-gateway.yaml
gateway.networking.istio.io/bookinfo-gateway unchanged
```

2. Then, enter the following command:

   ```
   kubectl get svc istio-ingressgateway -n istio-system
   ```

```
master@Kubemaster:/opt/istio/istio-1.1.0.snapshot.1$ kubectl get svc istio-ingressgateway -n istio-system
NAME                   TYPE           CLUSTER-IP     EXTERNAL-IP   PORT(S)                                                                                                                                      AGE
istio-ingressgateway   LoadBalancer   10.106.88.54   <pending>     80:31380/TCP,443:31390/TCP,31400:31400/TCP,15011:30845/TCP,8060:32578/TCP,853:30848/TCP,15030:32603/TCP,15031:32488/TCP                       21h
```

3. Set `gateway_url` using the following command:

   ```
   export GATEWAY_URL=35.239.7.64:80
   ```

Trying the application

Once you have the address and port, check that the `bookinfo` app is running with `curl`:

```
curl -I http://35.239.7.64:80/productpage
```

If the response shows 200, it means the application is working properly with Istio:

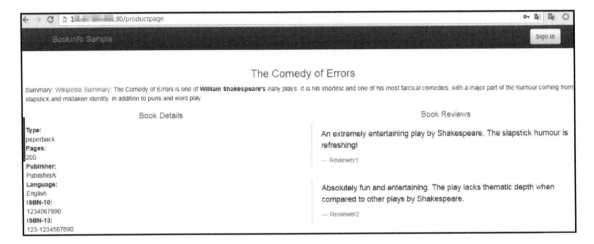

Deploying services to Kubernetes

In this part, we will see how easily we can deploy any services to Kubernetes. In this example, we are going to deploy an NGINX web server into our Kubernetes cluster:

1. Deploy the `nginx` container in the `Kubemaster` node:

   ```
   sudo kubectl create deployment nginx --image=nginx
   ```

   ```
   master@Kubemaster:/opt/kube$ sudo kubectl create deployment nginx --image=nginx
   deployment.apps/nginx created
   ```

2. Configure the network for the `nginx` service:

   ```
   sudo kubectl create service nodeport nginx --tcp=80:80
   ```

   ```
   master@Kubemaster:/opt/kube$ sudo kubectl create service nodeport nginx --tcp=80:80
   service/nginx created
   ```

3. Run the following command to list services:

   ```
   kubectl get svc
   ```

   ```
   master@Kubemaster:/opt/kube$ kubectl get svc
   NAME         TYPE        CLUSTER-IP    EXTERNAL-IP   PORT(S)        AGE
   kubernetes   ClusterIP   10.96.0.1     <none>        443/TCP        26h
   nginx        NodePort    10.97.30.24   <none>        80:30355/TCP   22s
   master@Kubemaster:/opt/kube$
   ```

4. Use the following command to test your deployment:

   ```
   curl kubemaster:30355    // curl servername:port
   ```

   ```
   master@Kubemaster:/opt/kube$ curl Kubemaster:30355
   <!DOCTYPE html>
   <html>
   <head>
   <title>Welcome to nginx!</title>
   <style>
       body {
           width: 35em;
           margin: 0 auto;
           font-family: Tahoma, Verdana, Arial, sans-serif;
       }
   </style>
   </head>
   <body>
   <h1>Welcome to nginx!</h1>
   <p>If you see this page, the nginx web server is successfully installed and
   working. Further configuration is required.</p>

   <p>For online documentation and support please refer to
   <a href="http://nginx.org/">nginx.org</a>.<br/>
   Commercial support is available at
   <a href="http://nginx.com/">nginx.com</a>.</p>

   <p><em>Thank you for using nginx.</em></p>
   </body>
   </html>
   master@Kubemaster:/opt/kube$
   ```

Summary

Microservices are being proclaimed as a groundbreaking architectural style for producing and sustaining business and IT applications. Cloud environments are filled with BM servers, virtual machines, and containers. Microservices can be hosted on these and run to extract and supply their unique functionalities. As the number of microservices is growing rapidly, we need technology-sponsored complexity mitigation solutions and services. API Gateway solutions are being presented as the viable and venerable infrastructure (software or hardware) solutions for bringing in a kind of abstraction to decimate the dependencies-induced problems.

We have also discussed the unique contributions of service mesh solutions and how service mesh and API Gateway solutions fuse together to accomplish bigger and better things for businesses.

Other Books You May Enjoy

If you enjoyed this book, you may be interested in these other books by Packt:

Real-World SRE
Nat Welch

ISBN: 978-1-78862-888-4

- Monitor for approaching catastrophic failure
- Alert your team to an outage emergency
- Dissect your incident response strategies
- Test automation tools and build your own software
- Predict bottlenecks and fight for user experience
- Eliminate the competition in an SRE interview

Practical DevOps - Second Edition
Joakim Verona

ISBN: 978-1-78839-257-0

- Understand how all deployment systems fit together to form a larger system
- Set up and familiarize yourself with all the tools you need to be efficient with DevOps
- Design an application suitable for continuous deployment systems with DevOps in mind
- Store and manage your code effectively using Git, Gerrit, Gitlab, and more
- Configure a job to build a sample CRUD application
- Test your code using automated regression testing with Jenkins Selenium
- Deploy your code using tools such as Puppet, Ansible, Palletops, Chef, and Vagrant

Leave a review - let other readers know what you think

Please share your thoughts on this book with others by leaving a review on the site that you bought it from. If you purchased the book from Amazon, please leave us an honest review on this book's Amazon page. This is vital so that other potential readers can see and use your unbiased opinion to make purchasing decisions, we can understand what our customers think about our products, and our authors can see your feedback on the title that they have worked with Packt to create. It will only take a few minutes of your time, but is valuable to other potential customers, our authors, and Packt. Thank you!

Index

A

AI-enabled log analytics platforms 307
Algorithmic IT Operations (AIOps) 308
ambient intelligence (AmI) 11
Apache Mesos
  about 153, 161
  reference 153
Apex
  about 47
  reference 47
API Gateways 25
API Gateways, design patterns
  about 111
  authentication 111
  authorization 112
  cache 112
  cookies 112
  logging 112
  sessions 112
application 144, 145, 146
application delivery controllers (ADCs) 34
application development and maintenance (ADM) 242
application metrics, microservices
  average application response time 70
  concurrent users 72
  error rate 72
  peak response time 72
  requests per second (RPS) 72
  throughput 72
application monitoring 293, 294
application programming interfaces (APIs) 307
Application Service Proxy (ASP) 255
architectural pattern
  about 167, 168, 169
  Client Server Pattern 168
  Master Slave Pattern 168
  Model-View-Controller Pattern 168
  Peer to Peer Pattern 168
artificial intelligence (AI) 11, 210, 301, 320
asynchronous communication
  need for 214, 216
asynchronous messaging patterns
  asynchronous command calls 222
  event firehose pattern 221
  event sourcing 218
  publisher/subscriber 220
  saga pattern 222
auto scaling groups (ASGs) 151
AWS ECS 151
AWS EKS 159
AWS Lambda deployments, tools
  Apex 47
  AWS Serverless Application Model (SAM) 47
  Chalice 47
  Claudia.js 47
  Serverless 47
  Serverless express 47
  traditional Bash scripts 47
AWS Lambda
  considerations 48

B

backend for frontend (BFF) 25
Ballerina programming
  about 188
  circuit breaker code example 194, 195, 196
  command cheat sheet 201
  control logic expression 197, 198
  data types 196
  deployment 200
  examples 189
  features 188, 189

hello program example 189
Kubernetes deployment code 192, 193
life cycle 200
reference 198
runtime environment 199
Twitter integration, example 190, 191, 192
bare metal (BM) server 38, 80, 212, 250, 300, 306, 322
basically available, soft state and eventually consistent (BASE) 222

C

centralized log management
  about 124
  filters 124
  output 125
  source 124
centralized log-management tools
  about 310
  benefits 310
cgroups
  reference 338
Chalice
  about 47
  reference 47
CI process
  setting up, with GitHub 130
  setting up, with Jenkins 130
Cinder 164
circuit breaker
  about 181
  advantages 181
  closed state 183
  half-open state 184, 185
  open state 184
client resiliency patterns
  about 93
  bulkheads 94
  circuit breaker 94
  client-side load balancing 94
  fall-back processing 94
cloud applications
  about 12
  cloud-enabled 12
  cloud-native 12

cloud enabled applications
  for digital era 321
cloud infrastructure
  about 293, 294
  ubiquity 13
cloud platforms
  ubiquity 13
cloud service providers (CSPs) 305
cloud-based log analytics platforms
  about 305
  contributions 306
cloud-enabled data centers (CeDCs) 299, 309
cloud-native applications
  for digital era 321
clouds
  monitoring 290
  monitoring, with Kubernetes 290, 292
cluster
  about 149, 151
  Apache Mesos 153
  AWS ECS 151
  CoreOS fleet 150
  Docker swarm 149
  ECS service as a cluster manager 151
  monitoring 290
CNCF
  reference 147
code as function deployment example, of microservices
  about 53
  Apex deployment tool 53, 54
  Serverless deployment tool 55
code as function deployment
  about 47
  AWS Lambda, considerations 48
command query responsibility segregation (CQRS)
  about 223, 224, 226, 227
  reference 224
confidentiality, integrity, and availability (CIA) 335
configuration management (CM) tools 212
container management 154
container orchestration
  about 154, 155, 156, 157, 159
  Apache Mesos 161
  AWS EKS 159

    CoreOS Tectonics 162
    Docker compose 163
    Google's Kubernetes 159
    Marathon 161
    OpenStack Magnum 163
    Red Hat's OpenShift 155
container platform-based deployment tools 46
containerization
    advantages 240
    paradigm, delineating 239
containerized cloud environments
    about 340, 341
    challenges 23
    reliability, ensuring 338
    technology drivers 23
containerized clouds
    emergence 212
containerized microservices 22
containers
    benefits 241
    briefing 78, 79
    clustering 147, 148
    containerization paradigm 79, 80
    managing 147, 148
    monitoring 290
    stateful containers 144
    stateless containers 144
Content Attack Prevention (CAP) 332
Continuous Delivery (CD) 15
Continuous Deployment (CD) 15
Continuous Development (CD) 137
Continuous Integration (CI)/Continuous
    Development (CD) tool 115
Continuous Integration (CI)
    about 9, 15, 128
    benefits 128
    code repository 129
    continuous build system 130
    life cycle 129
    tools 129
control groups (cgroups) 22
control logic expression, Ballerina 197, 198
control plane
    about 251
    versus data plane 252

converged infrastructure (CI) 288
CoreOS fleet 150
CoreOS Tectonics
    about 162
    reference 163
cyber physical systems (CPS) 11, 299
Cyber Security Services (CSS) 125

D

data plane
    about 251
    versus control plane 252
data types, Ballerina 196
delegation tables (dtabs) 325
denial-of-service (DoS) attacks 333
deployment models, service mesh
    per-host proxy deployment pattern 257
    sidecar pattern for service mesh 258
    sidecar proxy deployment pattern 258
descriptive scripting language (DSL) 57
design pattern
    about 167, 168, 169, 170, 171
    Algorithm Strategy Pattern 168
    Ambassador 173
    Anti-corruption layer 173
    backends for frontends 173
    bulkhead 173
    cache-aside 173
    circuit breaker 173, 181
    Command and query responsibility segregation
      (CQRS) 173
    compensating transaction 173
    competing consumers 173
    Computational Pattern 168
    compute resource consolidation 173
    event sourcing 173
    Execution Pattern 168
    external configuration store 173
    federated identity 173
    for availability 179
    for performance 178, 179
    for reliability 180
    for scalability 177, 178
    for security 175, 176
    gatekeeper 173

gateway aggregation 173
gateway offloading 174
gateway routing 174
health endpoint monitoring 174
Implementation Strategy Pattern 168
index table 174
leader election 174
Materialized View 174
Pipes and Filters 174
Priority Queue 174
queue-based load leveling 174
reference 175
retry 174
scheduler agent supervisor 174
sharding 174
sidecar 174
static-content hosting 174
strangler 174
Structural Pattern 168
throttling 174
valet key 175
DevOps-as-a-Service (DaaS)
　about 115
　automated alerts, configuring 123
　CD 127, 128, 137
　centralized log management 124
　CI 127, 128
　continuous process development 126, 127
　infrastructure development 126, 127
　infrastructure security 125
　reference 116
　services, types 119, 120
　tool, selecting 116, 117, 119
DevOps
　developers, role 139
　QA team, role 139
　with development team 138
　with QA team 138
digital transformation 320
Docker compose 163
Docker enabled containerization
　about 21
　advantages 21
Docker image
　reference 338

Docker swarm
　about 149
　reference 150
Dynatrace 74

E

ECS service as a cluster manager 151
Elastic Container Service (ECS) 178
Elastic Container Service for Kubernetes (EKS) 178
Elastic Load Balancing (ELB) 179
Elasticsearch, Logstash, and Kibana (ELK) 303
Elasticsearch-Hadoop (ES-Hadoop) 303
Email 268
Enterprise Application Integration (EAI) 217, 250
Enterprise Service Bus (ESB) 86, 217, 243, 250
enterprise-class log analytics platforms 309
error-handling, Rust
　unrecoverable errors 207
event processing engines
　complex event processing 216
　event stream processing 216
　simple event processing 216
event sourcing
　Event Listener 219
　Event Store 219
　Message Receiver 219
event-driven architecture (EDA)
　about 18, 214
　event streaming 215
　for producing reactive applications 223
　publish/subscribe 215
event-driven microservices
　asynchronous messaging patterns 218
　need for 216, 217
　relevance 214

F

Function as a Service (FaaS) 17, 47, 226, 287

G

Git
　installing 136
Glance 164
Google's Cloud Platform (GCP) 46

Google's Kubernetes 159
Grafana
  about 273
  alerts, configuring 278, 280, 281, 282
  features 273
  setting up 274, 275, 276, 277, 278
graphical process units (GPUs) 288
gRPC 28

H

highly reliable IT infrastructures
  about 33, 34, 35
  serverless computing, emergence 35
HTTP1.x/2.x 28
hyper-converged infrastructure (HCI) 81, 288

I

in-memory database (IMDB) 112
information and communication technology (ICT) 10
infrastructure as code (IaC)
  about 15, 212, 231
  back-off algorithms 233
  cascading failures, avoiding 233
  circuit breaking 236
  fall backs 234
  idempotent operations 234
  immutable infrastructure 231
  load balancing 237
  resilience, against intermittent and transient errors 235
  retry 233
  service degradation 234
  stateless applications 232
  timeouts 234
infrastructure security
  about 125
  AWS 125
  Google 125
  Microsoft Azure 125
  reference 125
  Symantec 125
integrated platforms
  autonomous decision making capabilities 90
  bulkhead pattern, issues 89

circuit breaker pattern, issues 90
external monitoring 90
integrated platform approach 91
isolation 90
need for 88
Internet of Things (IoT) 8, 210, 288, 320
Istio
  about 92, 325, 327, 328, 330
  Broker 92
  CA 92
  Envoy 92, 326
  installing, on Kubernetes 354, 355, 356, 357
  Mixer 92, 326
  Node agent 92
  Pilot 92
  reference 325, 330
  visualizing 330
IT as a Service (ITaaS) 12
IT elasticity 16
IT operational analytics (ITOA) 304, 311
IT performance
  analytics 312
IT reliability
  challenges 81, 82, 84, 85
  solution approaches 81, 82, 84, 85
IT resiliency 16
IT scalability
  analytics 312
IT security
  analytics 314

J

Jenkins
  about 47
  CI process, setting up 130
  Git, installing 136
  installing 130, 131
  job, setting up 134, 136
  job, starting 137
  setting up, for GitHub 132, 133
Jersey Framework
  about 59, 60
  reference 59
JFR 74

K

key performance indicators (KPI) 180
Kiali
  about 330
  reference 330
Kubernetes as a Service (KaaS) 341
Kubernetes master
  API server 343
  controller manager 343
  Scheduler 343
  storage 342
Kubernetes
  about 268, 290, 292
  application, checking 358
  architecture 342, 344, 345, 347
  client, installing 351, 352, 353
  ConfigMaps 345
  DaemonSets 344
  deployments 345
  for container orchestration 24, 25, 27, 28
  for containerized cloud environments 341
  growing role, for container era 244, 245
  installing 347, 349, 350
  Istio, installing 354, 355, 356, 357
  jobs 345
  Kubernetes master 342
  Kubernetes StatefulSets 344
  nodes 344
  pods 344
  reference 292
  ReplicaSets 344
  secrets 345
  security 345
  services, deploying 358, 359
  worker node 343

L

Linkerd
  about 324
  features 324
  reference 324
log analytics
  about 302
  AI-enabled log analytics platforms 307
  centralized log-management tools 310
  cloud-based log analytics platforms 305
  enterprise-class log analytics platforms 309
  key capabilities 309
  Loom 308
  open source log analytics platforms 303
Loom
  reference 308

M

machine-learning (ML) algorithms
  about 301
  for infrastructure automation 301
Magnum Client 164
maintenance, repair, and overhaul (MRO) 299
manage engine applications manager
  reference 295
Management design pattern 170
Marathon 161
mean time between failures (MTBF) 179, 312
mean time to failure (MTTF) 37
mean time to resolve (MTTR) 37, 179
message-oriented middleware (MoM) 227
microservice deployment, examples
  code as function deployment 53
  container platform deployment, with Kubernetes 49, 50, 52
  virtual platform-based deployment, with Jnekins or TeamCity 57
microservices API Gateway
  about 331, 332
  API management suite 337
  benefits 333, 334
  security features 335
  service mesh 336
microservices architecture (MSA)
  about 12, 77, 85, 210, 214, 293, 321, 331
  advantages 20
  API services 87
  atomic microservices 87
  composite microservices 87
  containerized clouds, emergence 212
  containers 212
  demystifying 242, 243
  emergence 19

for reliable software 211
microservices layered architecture 86
orchestration platforms 212
microservices design
 asynchronous communication, need for 214, 216
 best practices 213
 event-driven microservices, need for 216, 217
 event-driven microservices, relevancy 214
microservices, monitoring
 about 69
 application metrics 70, 72
 platform metrics 73
 system events 73
 with tools 73, 74
microservices
 about 43
 briefing 78, 79
 code as function deployment 47
 container platform-based deployment tools 46
 deployment 46
 design principles 44, 45
 designing 75
 facts 75
 in current market 75
 RESTful framework, using 57
 Spring Boot, using 57
 teams, dividing 76
 versus SOA 76
 virtualization-based platform deployment 48
modern IT infrastructure
 about 286, 287
 modern data analytics methods, elaborating 288, 289
monitoring tool
 benefits 297, 298
 capabilities 295, 296, 297

N

Network access control systems (NACLs) 34
Neutron 164
node agent 255
Node Package Manager (NPM) 189
non-functional requirements (NFRs) 14, 82, 210, 294

non-functional requirements (NFRs), challenges
 accelerated software programming 15
 agile application design 14
 automated software deployment, through DevOps 15
Nova 164

O

open service broker (OSB) 92
open source log analytics platforms 303
OpenStack Magnum
 about 163
 reference 164
operating system (OS) 240
operational level agreement (OLA) 81
OverOps
 Application Flow Analysis 315
 Business Transactions Analysis 316
 log-management, enhancing 315

P

pagerduty 268
performance engineering and enhancement (PE2) 37
predictive analytics 299
prescriptive analytics 299
prognostic analytics 299
Prometheus, architecture
 alertmanager 268
 Prometheus web UI 268
 service discovery 268
 short-lived jobs 268
Prometheus
 about 266, 326
 alerts, configuring 271, 272
 architecture 267, 268
 features 266
 labels 271
 metrics 271
 setting up 268, 269, 270, 271
Pushgateway 268

Q

QA team
 practices 140

role 139
quality of experience (QoE) 14, 211
quality of service (QoS) 14, 82, 211, 295

R

rapid application development (RAD) tools 253
reactive applications
  command query responsibility segregation
    pattern 223, 224, 226, 227
  with EDA 223
Reactive Manifesto
  reference 19
reactive systems
  about 29, 30, 31
  elasticity 32
  highly reliable 32
  versus reactive programming 31
Red Hat's OpenShift 155, 156, 157, 159
reference architecture (RA) 87
reliability
  of applications 202
reliable IT infrastructures
  about 227
  auto-scaling 230
  fault-tolerance, towards higher availability 229
  high availability 227, 229
  real-time scalability 231
reliable IT systems 211
reliable platforms and infrastructures
  need for 18
reliable software
  containerized microservices 22, 24
  Docker enabled containerization 21
  Kubernetes, for container orchestration 24, 25, 27, 28
  microservices architecture, emergence 19
  need for 19
  reliable applications 28
  resilient microservices 28
remote procedure calls (RPCs) 249
Representational State Transfer (REST)
  about 60, 62, 64, 66, 67, 68
  microservices, monitoring 69
  Spring Boot application, deploying 68
request and response (R and R) model 223

request per second (RPS) 312
resiliency approaches
  enforcing 85
  integrated platforms 88, 89, 91, 92, 93, 94, 96, 97, 98, 100, 102, 103, 104, 105, 106, 107, 109, 110, 111, 112
  MSA 85, 87, 88
resiliency patterns, for microservices
  about 93
  adapter microservices pattern 100
  Ambassador pattern 102
  anti-corruption layer pattern 102
  application decomposition patterns 109
  authorization 112
  backend for frontend (BFF) pattern 98
  bulkhead pattern 97, 103
  circuit breaker pattern 96
  client resiliency patterns 93
  correlation ID pattern 96
  decomposition by resources 109
  decomposition by responsibilities/functions 110
  decomposition by use case 109
  design patterns, in API Gateways 111
  entity and aggregate patterns 100
  gateway 112
  gateway aggregation pattern 104
  gateway offloading pattern 106
  gateway routing pattern 106
  handshaking pattern 97
  log aggregator patterns 96
  microservice design and implementation patterns 101
  microservices deployment patterns 110
  microservices development patterns 97
  operations patterns 96
  serverless/abstracted platform 110
  service registry pattern 96
  services patterns 100
  sidecar pattern 107
  single host and multiple services 110
  single page application (SPA) pattern 98
  single service per host 110
  strangler application pattern 100
resilient microservices 143
Resource as a Service (RaaS) 17

RESTful framework
  with microservices 57
return on investment (RoI) 33
root-cause analysis (RCA)
  about 295
  importance 314
  OverOps 315
Rust
  about 202
  concurrency 207
  error-handling 207
  future 208
  installing 203
  memory management 206
  mutability 206
  programming with 204
  reference 202, 203, 208
  values, borrowing 205
  variables, ownership 205

S

sensitive and responsive (S and R) 216
serverless computing
  emergence 35
Serverless configuration file
  reference 55
Serverless
  about 47
  reference 47
service level agreement (SLA) 82
service mesh solutions, characteristics
  control plane 261
  dynamic request routing 260
  load balancing 262
  service discovery 262
service mesh solutions
  features 323
  for microservice resiliency 26
  Istio 325, 327, 328, 330
  Linkerd 324
service mesh
  about 246, 248, 249, 250, 251, 322
  architecture 254, 255
  data plane, versus control plane 252
  deployment models 257, 258, 259, 261, 262

  importance 253, 254
  monitoring 256
  solutions 213
service oriented architecture (SOA) 78, 243
service-level agreements (SLAs) 38
services, DevOps-as-a-Service (DaaS)
  one-click deployment and rollback, example 121, 122, 123
  types 119, 120
single board computers (SBCs) 8
single point of contact (SPOC) 39
Single Sign On (SSO) 170
Site Reliability Engineering (SRE)
  about 8, 286
  challenges 17, 18
  cloud service paradigm 12
  digital era, envisioning 10, 11
  discipline 16, 17
  distributed computing 9
  growing software participation 14, 15
  growing software penetration 14, 15
  hybrid IT 9
  importance 37, 38, 40
  next-generation hardware systems, characterizing 9
  next-generation software systems, characterizing 8
  toolsets 40
  vitality 36, 37
software requirement specifications (SRS) 126
Splunk
  about 309
  reference 309
Spring Boot
  application, deploying 68
  characteristics 59
  reference 58
  with microservices 57
stateful containers 144
stateless containers 144
subject matter experts (SMEs) 77
system elasticity 29
system resiliency 29

T

TeamCity 47
time-to-live (TTL) 219
total cost of ownership (TCO) 33
transaction per second (TPS) 312
two-phase commit (2PC) pattern 222

V

virtual machine (VM) 38, 79, 210, 240, 250, 300, 322
virtual machine monitor (VMM) 300
virtualization-based platform deployment
  about 48
  Capistrano 48
  CI/CD 48
  Traditional Makefiles 48
  traditional scripts 48
volume containers 144, 145, 146
volume
  ephermal storage volume 344
  persistent storage 344

W

Web Application Archive (WAR) file 68
well-architected framework (WAF) 171
wide area networks (WANs) 249
worker node, Kubernetes
  cAdvisor 343
  Kube-Proxy 343
  Kubelet 343

Made in the USA
Middletown, DE
10 April 2024

52851264R00216